MUSLIM ORGANISATIONS
IN SOUTH AFRICA

Isaac MUTELO

MUSLIM ORGANISATIONS IN SOUTH AFRICA

Political Role Post-1948

Domuni-Press

2023

THIS BOOK IS PUBLISHED BY DOMUNI-PRESS
PHILOSOPHY COLLECTION

ISBN: 978-2-36648-185-3
© DOMUNI-PRESS, January 2023

The intellectual property code prohibits copies or reproductions intended for collective use. Representation or reproduction in whole or in part by any means whatsoever, without the consent of the author or his successors, is unlawful and constitutes an infringement of copyright under articles L.335-2 and following of the Intellectual Property Code.

Foreword

The Glorious Quran describes the people of the book as the children of Abraham – Jews, Christians, and Muslims. While Christianity has remained dominant based on the number of adherents worldwide, Islam is the fastest growing religion today. Many questions about Islam have been asked, especially with regards to its contemporary growth trends, its role in the public sphere and the groups that perpetuate terror in its name. An important issue concerns the relationship between state and religion. Modern democracies are partly built on the centuries-long relationship between religious institutions and political forces. Historically, there has been a relationship between religion and politics in South Africa. In this book, Isaac Mutelo has laboured to comprehensively and thoroughly capture the political involvement of Muslim organisations and individuals in South Africa. He focusses on the way in which Muslim organisations and individuals have been political actors through their contribution to important issues such as nation building, justice and equality, constitutionalism, democracy and economic development.

The reader will be immersed in the entire history of Muslims in South Africa, beginning with how Muslims came to the country, the active role they played during the struggle against apartheid and their ongoing efforts in the public sphere. Thus, this book will help the reader to have a clearer understanding of the political involvement of Islam in South Africa. No comprehensive and critical work which tracks and unpacks the political role Muslims in post-1948 South Africa has been written in recent times. The book is a major contribution in uncovering laudable works that Muslim organisations and individuals in South Africa have done post-1948. Unlike many who ignorantly slander Islam, Isaac Mutelo becomes outstanding by thoroughly seeking knowledge and understanding. He is one among few scholars who have spent their time studying and understanding other religions without prejudice.

I attest that Isaac Mutelo is one of the scholars who view religion as a positive force for unity and peace that must contribute to development, transformation and democratisation processes than degrade and divide people. Just as Islam admonishes humanity to compete in good deeds, I hope more scholars who wish to explore the role of Islam and other religions in the public sphere in divergent contexts will be inspired to follow the example of Isaac Mutelo. This book should serve to inspire Muslim and non-Muslim historians, scholars, lecturers and students of religion and politics, and ordinary readers to explore and understand the issue of Islam and politics in South Africa.

Sheikh Mohammed X Ntshangase
(University of Limpopo, Turfloop Campus)

Acknowledgements

*In the name of the Almighty God,
the Most Gracious and Ever-Merciful*

I express my sincere, humble and selfless gratitude to Dr Heidi Matisonn, Prof Suleman Essop Dangor, Sr Sue Rakoczy IHM, Marion Jordan, Tsitsi Wakatama, members of the Dominican family, my family, friends and colleagues for their support and contribution towards the completion of this book. I am also grateful to students and staff from Arrupe Jesuit University, DOMUNI Universitas, University of KwaZulu Natal and the Catholic University of Zimbabwe.

List of abbreviations

ACDP	African Christian Democratic Party
ANC	African National Congress
ASGISA	Accelerated and Shared Growth Initiative for South Africa
Azapo	Azanian People's Organisation
BCM	Black Consciousness Movement
CDG	Care Dependency Grant
CSG	Child Support Grant
DG	Disability Grant
DP	Democratic Party
DQA	Department of Quranic Affairs
FBO	Faith Based Organisations
FCG	Foster Child Grant
FF-VF	Freedom Front
GOG	Gift of the Givers Organisation
IFP	Inkatha Freedom Party
ICSA	Islamic Council of South Africa
IUC	Islamic Unity Convention
MJC	Muslim Judicial Council
MJCHT	Muslim Judicial Council Halaal Trust
MSA	Muslim Students' Association
MYM	Muslim Youth Movement
NGOs	non-governmental organisation
NIC	Natal Indian Congress
NICSA	National Interfaith Council of South Africa
NILC	National Interfaith Leadership Council
NMC	National Muslim Convention
NP	National Party
NPP	National People's Party
NRASD	National Religious Association for Social Development
NRLF	National Religious Leaders Forum
NW	Neighbourhood Watch
NWA	Neighbourhood Watch Association
OPG	Older Persons Grant

MUSLIM ORGANISATIONS IN SOUTH AFRICA

PAC	Pan African Congress
PAC	Pan Africanist Congress
PAGAD	People Against Gangsterism and Drugs
PEP-IMC	Inter-Ministerial Committee on Public Employment Programmes
RDP	Reconstruction and Development Programme
SACPO	South African Coloured People Organisation
SACRRF	South African Charter of Religious Rights and Freedoms
SAIC	South African Indian Congress
SASSA	South African Social Security Agency
SACBB	South African Catholic Bishop's Conference
SACC	South African Council of Churches
SANDF	South African National Defence Force
SUN	Sizwe Ummah Nation
TIC	Transvaal Indian Congress
UDF	United Democratic Front
UUCSA	United Ulama Council of South Africa
VOC	Voice of the Cape
WKFP	Wes-Kaap Federaliste Party
WVG	War Veteran's Grant

Introduction

The Muslim population in South Africa constitutes a mere 2 per cent of the total population with the majority concentrated in the Western Cape, Gauteng and KwaZulu-Natal. Despite this insignificant percentage, the political influence of Islam, has been significant. The question regarding the extent to which Muslims have played a role in the public sphere by securing an active participation in politics in South Africa, is imperative. It is therefore important to look at the political involvement of major Muslim organisations and associations in terms of their origin, objectives and participation in politics. The political, social and economic engagement of most Muslims in South Africa is influenced by the Islamic faith with which they strongly identify.

Some Muslim organisations and institutions have been actively involved in issues such as religious freedom, promotion of reconciliation, humanitarianism and other social welfare initiatives. In addition, some Muslim organisations seem to hold a 'watchdog stance' – oppose when the state or government officials are wrong and praise when they are right. As part of their efforts to foster political engagement, some Muslims have either joined non-Muslim political parties such as the African National Congress or have formed Muslim political parties and associations. Muslim political parties that have been formed since the early 1990s include *al-Jama-ah*, Islamic Party, Africa Muslim Party (AMP), African Moral Party and Sizwe Ummah Nation (SUN). Post 1994, one of the aspirations of Muslim political parties has been to encourage Muslims to become politically active, represent the interests of Muslims in South Africa and play a political role in society. Apart from Muslim political parties, the People Against Gangsterism and Drugs (PAGAD) was established to fight gangsterism and drug abuse. There have also been Muslim NGOs devoted to humanitarianism such as the Gift of the

Givers Foundation (GOG). As the biggest Muslim NGO in South Africa, the GOG Foundation gives one a different picture on the question of religion and politics in South Africa. Generally, Muslim organisations exhibit different political elements through the notion of political influence; that is, the strategies that have been employed by certain Muslim organisations in the process of sustaining a political role in post-apartheid South Africa.

The political aspirations of Muslims in South Africa are also apparent through various Muslims who held key positions at both local and higher levels of government such as Dullah Omar, Kader Asmal, Aziz Pahad and Hassan Solomons, who have served in various government ministries as Members of Parliament. Several individuals were involved for many years as members of the ANC and Pan African Congress (PAC) before 1994, including Molvi Cachalia, Dr Yusuf Dadoo, Dr Ismail Meer, Ahmed Kathrada and Achmad Cassim. Ebrahim Rasool formerly served as premier of the Western Cape, and later as South African Ambassador to the United States. Since 2017, Muslims such as Ebrahim Patel, Naledi Pandor, Jessie Duarte, Mohamed Enver Surtee and Fatima Chohan have held key government positions. Such examples show that though Islam is a minority religion in South Africa, it has continued to contribute to the political makeup of the new South Africa.

While playing a role on political issues before the inception of apartheid (pre-1948), most Muslim organisations generally focused on "establishing themselves, consolidating their position and taking care of their community needs" (Amra 2001:40), including representing the interests of their community in the public sphere. Their political involvement reached a climax under apartheid (post-1948) when some Muslim organisations joined the liberation chorus by becoming political actors. According to Mutelo (2017:6-7):

> The apartheid political structure was based on a number of well-attested policies and laws which held the system together… However, the strict application of the concept of separate development fostered the birth of separate homelands and policies concerning influx control, pass laws, separate educational institutions, censoring of mixed marriages and so forth.

INTRODUCTION

This period saw the formation of more politically oriented Muslim groups such as the Muslim Youth Movement of South Africa (MYM), the Call of Islam and the Qibla Movement, all of which quite clearly protested apartheid policies by actively participating in the struggle.

There were also larger Muslim organisations such as Jamiatul Ulama South Africa and the Muslim Judicial Council (MJC) that also played a role in politics during apartheid, though they were politically more distanced. Although they were, from a political perspective, somewhat detached, the fact that they claimed to be the most representative bodies of Muslims in South Africa makes it important to recognise their political aspirations.

The major turning point in the political involvement of Islam in South Africa was marked by the end of the apartheid era in 1994. In the democratic South Africa, the Constitution generally defines the role of religion. Therefore, the political role of Islam has been based on the constitutional stipulations on the relationship between religion and politics thereby guaranteeing freedom of religious representation. This understanding is rooted in the Constitution which advocates for the flexible separation between state and religion. South Africa upholds impartiality and the central tenets of liberalism such as tolerance, equality and freedom – all fundamental in fostering liberty of conscience for all. The wording of the South African Constitution on religion gives enough grounding to facilitate the substantial contribution of religions in politics. For example, Sections 15(2), 14(1), 15(3), 19(1) and 30(1) of the South African Constitution make provision for religious freedom and liberty. This grants religious institutions and organisations the ability to participate in political affairs.

In the post-apatheid South Africa, Islam, through some of its organisations, had to adapt to the new political changes and seek renewed ways of political involvement. The constitutional openness to religion continues to be the basis for religious participation in politics, and a reaffirmation of a possible involvement of Islam in politics. As Ebrahim Rasool (2004:98) puts it, "our [South African] constitution was precisely crafted in a way to facilitate the ongoing contribution of religion to and in politics". Since the South African

Constitution grants freedom to every citizen to participate in the political transformation, Muslims have been able to form political parties, support political organisations, contribute to the decision-making processes and involve themselves in the democratic transformation of the country.

This book undertakes a systematic review by examining the contribution of Muslim organisations to South African politics and society. By offering a comprehensive investigation of Muslim organisations, this work unveils the discourse on Islam and politics in South Africa from both historical and contemporary perspectives. This book is divided into seven sections. The first two sections explore three phases of Islamic immigration into South Africa, the early involvement of organisations such as the Natal Indian Congress and the Transvaal Indian Congress. The sections also explore major Muslim organisations during apartheid; namely, the Muslim Youth Movement (MYM), Qibla Mass Movement, Call of Islam and the Muslim Students' Association of South Africa (MSA). The third section explores major Islamic political parties; namely, al-Jama-ah, Islamic Party and the Africa Muslim Party which have been formed over their political participation. While the Islamic Party and Africa Muslim Party are almost non-existent, al-Jama-ah continues to attract some votes, and in the 2019 General Election, it managed to win two seats: one in the National Assembly and one in the Western Cape Provincial Legislature. The fourth and fifth sections explore the political involvement of the Muslim Judicial Council (MJC) and the People Against Gangsterism and Drugs (PAGAD). For example, the sections discuss PAGAD, an Islamic association which became prominent in the late 1990s and continues to maintain a presence in the Western Cape with a mixture of positive and negative political influence during the different phases of its existence. While the MJC has historically employed more conventional and pacifistic strategies in its political involvement, PAGAD has operated from the grassroots and employed unconventional methods some of which have been violent. The sixth section focusses on the public engagement of Muslim Faith Based Organisations (FBOs) in South Africa; namely, the Gift of the Givers, the Islamic Medical Association and Minara Chamber of Commerce. It is important to discuss the partnership which these organisations have historically maintained with the

INTRODUCTION

government and their influence in the public sphere from the perspective of socio-economic empowerment by emphasising their humanitarian activities and the provision of medical and business-oriented facilities and opportunities. The seventh section discusses the major ways through which Muslim organisations have been involved in politics. Apart from individual political involvement by prominent Muslims, Muslim organisations have been involved in South African politics in three ways: namely, overt political involvement, political radicalism, and through social welfare activities. Therefore, the political involvement of Muslim organisations in post-apartheid South Africa has been constitutionally based on the flexible relations between religion and state.

Phases of Immigration and Muslim Identities

Historically, there were three phases of Islamic immigration into South Africa. Dutch colonialists brought the earliest group of Muslims as slaves or political exiles from territories such as Malay, Java and Bengal. Most of these people settled at the Cape of Good Hope in the mid-seventeenth century. The second phase comprised primarily Indian Muslims who were brought to Natal in the mid-nineteenth century as indentured labourers by the British. Another predominantly Muslim group of Indian traders and merchants arrived in Natal towards the end of the nineteenth century. From the dawn of the twentieth century, there has been an influx of Muslim immigrants primarily from Africa and Asia and conversions to Islam have occurred mainly among black communities in South Africa. The question of Islamic identity is important when analysing the political engagement of Islamic organisations. The question of identity has been part of the Muslim history in South Africa and cannot be divorced from its political role. Based on the centrality of religious values, some Islamic organisations and political parties have focused on issues and challenges that affect Muslims. Such an approach is rooted on Islamic identity which emphasises the need for Muslims to work amongst themselves and to promote their aspirations in both the private and public spheres. Though Islamic organisations have been involved in issues affecting the country, they have at the same time emphasised the centrality of representing the needs of Muslims. Such an attempt has to some extent caused some organisations to become politically detached through minimal involvement in the politics of the country.

Phases of Islamic Immigration into South Africa

The earliest history of Muslims in South Africa can be. traced back as early as the twelfth century when the partially Islamised groups, who did not hold purely Islamic beliefs and practices, penetrated or infiltrated the South African region from Mozambique. By the mid- seventeenth century, there were already several Dutch settlers living at the Cape of Good Hope. A central aspect of life at the Cape under the Dutch administration was the use of slaves for cheap labour. The first wave of Muslim immigrants arrived in South Africa and settled at the Cape of Good Hope as early as 1652 and continued until the mid-nineteenth century (Amra 2001:37). This wave of immigrants came primarily from Java, Malaysia and Bengal; having been converted to Islam between the eighth and fourteenth centuries by Arab traders and Sufis. The Dutch colonists who had established their settlements around the Cape brought these immigrants, who were banished as political exiles and slaves, to the Cape. Many of the early arrivals were convicts and they had to work on the harbour and the fortification at the Cape Colony, often under inhumane and harsh conditions.

The first Muslim to come to South Africa in 1654 was an Asiatic from Batavia who was banished to South Africa as a political prisoner. The first free Muslims, known as Mardyckers, arrived at the Cape in 1658 as labourers and protectors of the Dutch colonists at the Cape. From 1676, Muslim political exiles increasingly arrived at the Cape. Since most of the exiled Muslim leaders were men of influence in the Dutch colonies, they were perceived as threats to the economic and political dominance of the Dutch. Among these were Sheikh Mahmood and Sheikh Abdurahman Matabe Shah who had been rulers of Sumatra, an island in present-day western Indonesia. These men were the first to have pioneered the inception and consolidation of the Islamic faith among slaves at the Cape. Although convict imams were considered bandits, "in the eyes of the autochthonous, slave, and free black populations they became leaders of an alternative culture" (Shell 2000:330). In 1681, the Cape of Good Hope was considered the official settlement for political exiles that saw the arrival of more Muslims on South African soil, most of whom had been Muslim religious leaders and who the Dutch East India

Company had banished. At the Cape, they were not allowed to publicly practise their faith and had to gather in private places for worship.

The year 1694 saw the arrival of Sheikh Yusuf from Bantam, a prominent Muslim political exile, an author and revolutionist who was renowned for his great piety. Sheikh Yusuf established the first unified Muslim community at Zandvleit, on the outskirts of Cape Town, which comprised mainly slaves and fugitives. It is estimated that by 1700 there were approximately 1 296 Muslims in South Africa. In 1793, Abdullah Kadi Abu Salaam, also known as Tuan Guru, an exile from Indonesia, spearheaded the foundation of the first Islamic school that became an important centre of learning for slaves and freed black slaves (Bradlow Cairns 1978). This Islamic school was responsible for converting many slaves and Free Blacks to Islam due to its popularity as the earliest centre in the Cape for the teaching of Islam and the Arabic language. The initiative motivated the then cohesive Muslim community to construct a *Masjid* for Muslims at the Cape, which commenced in 1794 under the leadership of Tuan Guru as its first Imam. Around this time, Islam had become common among slaves and the teaching of the Islamic faith encouraged those Dutch masters who had been converted to Islam to start treating their slaves well.

Following the attainment of the freedom of worship at the Cape in 1804, the Muslim population began to increase. The first Muslim cemetery was established in 1805. Although Islam had attained freedom of worship, Muslims continued to suffer political and social inequalities under British rule. By 1834, the number of Muslims was steadily increasing and there was an emancipation of slaves at the Cape. By 1841, there were approximately 7 800 Muslims in South Africa of which 6 492 were based at the Cape, approximately 268 at Stellenbosch and the rest of the Muslim population was scattered across other areas around the Cape (Mahida 1993; Shell 1981).

The second phase of Islamic immigration commenced in 1858 with the arrival of Indian shopkeepers and labourers in Natal, most of whom were Muslim. Ebrahim Mahida (1993:21) notes that "by 1851 the labour situation regarding sugar farming was so serious in Natal that the *Umzinto* Sugar Company brought from Java some

Chinese and Malay labourers". The British brought the first Muslims to Natal to work in the sugar plantations as indentured workers. By the 1860s, 24 Muslims were among the Indian indentured workers who arrived at Port Natal. While the early Muslims who arrived at the Cape were slaves, convicts and political exiles, this was not the case in Natal where Indian Muslims had come as indentured labourers and businesspeople. While some Indians returned to India by the 1870s, most of them became permanent residents of Natal.

Muslims from India continued to arrive in Natal as workers until 1911 when the Indian government put a stop to indentured labour. In 1873, many emancipated slaves from Zanzibar were brought to Natal as apprentice workers in the sugar plantations. Most of these freed 'Zanzibaris' were Muslim. While the introduction of freed Zanzibari slaves ended in 1880, in 1874 Muslim businesspeople from Gujurāt, India arrived in Natal and opened various retail stores in Durban and surrounding areas as well as the interior of Natal for farmers and the local population. As more Indian Muslims commenced trading in larger businesses, more *masjids* and educational facilities were being erected – *masjids* that were being erected by Indian Muslims were also utilised by 'Zanzibaris' Muslims. This resulted in the Muslim identity becoming increasingly visible at Port Natal and surrounding areas.

The distribution of Muslims in the Cape and surrounding areas was steadily increasing, which saw the building of a seventh *masjid*. By 1874 there were 8 948 Muslims at the Cape of whom 6 772 were living in Cape Town, 310 in Wynberg, 775 in Newlands, 292 in Simon's Town and 180 in Rondebosch (Mahida 1993:29). While these Muslims remained concentrated in the Cape area, those in Natal dispersed more quickly and established connections with Muslims from East Africa. The early Cape Muslims remained isolated until at least the 1870s when they initiated a "programme of mosque-building and Islamic revivalism" (Hiskett 1994:174) at the Cape. After 1880, additional traders and merchants from India arrived, settling in Natal, the Cape and parts of the Transvaal. The merchants who were based in Durban were quite successful although the British objected to their conduct of trade and residence. This later led to the establishment of the Natal Indian Congress.

From the 1900s onwards, many Muslim schools, *masjids* and associations were established. For example, in 1903, the South African Muslim Association was founded at the Cape. It was primarily formed to cater for the socio-economic aspects of the Muslim community and to encourage the construction of more Islamic educational facilities. Unfortunately, certain disagreements and internal conflicts caused the South African Muslim Association to be short-lived. Around this time, Muslims in South Africa were generally concerned with safeguarding their faith, religious identity and responding to the needs of the Muslim community. The early Muslim community did not pay much attention to the conversion of the local African communities or play a central role in the political cause of the country. The statistics released by the Department of Statistics (Pretoria) in 1976 stated that there were about 269 915 Muslims in South Africa in 1970 (Mahida 1993:99). Although most of these were predominantly of Malay and Indian descent, there were increasing numbers entering South Africa from other regions and a few local Muslims who had been converted to Islam.

After 1994, the number of Muslim immigrants from other parts of Africa especially North Africa and Malawi increased. This means that in contemporary South Africa, Islam continues to expand. There has also been a rise in conversions to Islam in South Africa. In this regard, Javad Haghnavaz (2014:126) maintains that "there has been an increase in the number of black South Africans converting to Islam particularly among the women and the youth". The rise in conversions, especially in townships, has been partly due to Islam's strong opposition to domestic violence and other social and moral vices. Further, the growth of Islam in South African communities is attributed to the involvement of various Muslim organisations in the social, political and economic transformation of society. Based on the 2002 census, there were 654 064 Muslims in South Africa in 2001, making up 1.46 per cent of the total population. Islam continues to expand in South Africa due to both the ongoing conversions and immigrations. Amra (2001:42) affirms that:

> There are over 500 *masajid* and many more *madaris* throughout SA. There are over 50 Muslim private schools, including some of exceptional quality, producing matric results equal to the best in the country, one Islamic Bank and

a host of organisations throughout the length and breadth of SA.

The number of Muslim mosques, educational facilities and other organisations has been increasing in recent years. The three phases of Islamic inception or settlement showed how Islam came to South Africa and how it generally developed from the arrival of the first wave of Muslims around the mid-seventeenth century to contemporary times.

Muslim Identities in South Africa

The nature and formation of social identity is as complex as the notion of identity itself. The word identity comes from a Latin word *identitas* which roughly refers to a state or quality of being identical. By acquiring a certain identity, one presents oneself as a member of a socially decipherable political, religious, racial or cultural group. Identity, whether personal or social, is an essential part of being human. Identity can promote a high degree of personal and social integration within a community thereby giving one meaning, purpose and goals in life. The social identity theory can be employed to study how individuals classify themselves as members of a certain group – whether religious or secular.

By associating oneself with a specific social group, one becomes aware that one belongs to that category and thus ascribes to its values and ideologies. Social identity refers to "a set of individuals who hold a common social identification or view themselves as members of the same social category" (Stets & Burke 2000:225). In the contemporary South African society, one can have multiple *local* identities which can be referred to as 'intersectionality'. Identities can be compatible thereby promoting wholeness. Multiple identities, or intersectionality refer to the fact that one can be a black South African, a native Xhosa speaker, a Muslim and an ANC supporter. Such multiple *local* identities should not overshadow the more *universal* or *general* form of identity shared by all South Africans through their citizenship and political boundaries – the South African identity. The notion of South African identity which is central to nation building is collective and can be claimed by every citizen.

This is reaffirmed by the preamble of the South African Constitution which clearly states that "we, the people of South Africa... believe that South Africa belongs to all who live in it, united in our diversity" (South African Constitution, preamble). Thus, the broader South African identity is not only about geographical demarcation but also about citizenship, shared aspirations, values and goals. This promotes collective social responsibility and the unification of all multiple *local* identities. As such, the goals and needs of the multiple *local* identities to which the Islamic identity belongs must be envisaged from the perspective of the *broader* South African aspirations. National identity stresses the sense of belonging to a nation or state bound by geopolitical boundaries and distinct cultures, traditions, politics and unifying symbols. Abdul Taliep Baker (2009:27) emphasises various core aspects of national identity:

> This [national identity] usually refers to a group of people belonging to the same nation or country, sharing a common descent, a common language, a common culture and a common religion. However, because of multiracial, multi-cultural and multi-lingual groups in many countries, sharing common traits is not the only distinguishing factor of national identity. It also includes shared values and norms of behaviour, certain duties toward other members, and certain responsibilities for the actions of the members. It is therefore possible for people with difference in personalities, belief systems, geographical locations, time and even spoken language, to regard themselves and be seen by others, as members of the same nation.

Based on the shared elements which are rooted in the historical, cultural, political, social and linguistic aspects of a nation, citizens integrate national identity with their 'other' forms of identities. An individual or social group's attitudes toward national identity has considerable influence on political choices and behaviour. This is because national identity is part of the citizen's definition of self and perception of the world since it limits an individual or group to a specific nation, state or political boundary which has certain common goals and aspirations. National identity promotes cooperation and reconciliation rooted on the sense of common belonging thereby creating public space through openness, tolerance, inclusivity, national loyalty, collective liberty and self-determination. While individuals and groups have certain constitutional rights, they cannot ignore the fact that as citizens they ought to participate in issues that affect the entire South African community. This is because citizen liberties cannot be divorced from the shared commitment to the democratic values, interests and needs of the nation. The South African state upholds the national identity by protecting people's rights and maintaining unity among all citizens through the Constitution and judicial processes. The discussion on national identity brings about important questions concerning the issue of Islamic identity. Some Muslims in South Africa have focussed on the needs of the Muslim community by presenting the political interests of South African Muslims to the government and the public sphere and emphasising the need to safeguard their Islamic identity. The importance of religious identity does not only lie in the centrality of religious beliefs and practices to adherents but also in the fact that Islam is a complete way or code of life. Religious identity is fundamental since Islam embraces all aspects of human life. The Quran itself exhorts Muslims to Follow Allah's guidance in all fields and aspects of human life. For example, the Quran (*Surah Al-Hadid* 57:25-29) says:

> We have already sent Our messengers with clear evidences and sent down with them the Scripture and the balance that the people may maintain [their affairs] in justice. And We sent down iron, wherein is great military might and benefits for the people, and so that Allah may make evident those who support Him and His messenger though unseen. Indeed, Allah is Powerful and Exalted in Might.

Thus, Islamic values are central to the life of Muslims. During apartheid, Muslims in Cape Town began to be referred to as 'Cape Malays' or 'Cape Coloureds', although the classification had been popularised earlier by thinkers such as Izak du Plessis in his book *The Cape Malays* published in 1944. In 1950, this became clear when based on the Population Registration Act 30 of 1950, South Africans were divided into Whites, Indians, Africans and Coloureds. The Coloured category was further sub-divided into other groupings such as 'Cape Malays', 'Cape Coloureds' and 'other Coloureds'. Most Muslims in Western Cape were thus categorised as 'Cape Malay', thereby making terms such as 'Muslim' and 'Malay' almost synonymous. Although in post-apartheid South Africa Muslims in Western Cape are often referred to as 'Cape Muslims', the term 'Cape Malay' continues to be used to refer to Coloured Muslims. While most Malay Muslims continue to be concentrated in places such as Signal Hill and *Bo-Kaap* in the Western Cape, a smaller number can be found in Limpopo, Mpumalanga, North West, Gauteng, Free State and KwaZulu Natal. Spread throughout South Africa, Malay Muslims have remained a dominant Muslim group in the country. The Indian Muslims, who constitute the second largest grouping of Muslims in South Africa have also spread throughout the country, especially in KwaZulu Natal, Free State, Western Cape and Gauteng provinces.

During apartheid, Indian Muslims were generally categorised as 'Indians' due to their Indian descent. Some Indians in Western Cape were classified as part of 'Cape Coloureds'. Since most Indian Muslims during apartheid were concentrated in areas such as Transvaal and Natal, their earliest political influence was through broader Indian associations such as the Natal Muslim Congress and the Transvaal Muslim Congress. The participation of Indian Muslims in these two Indian organisations will be discussed in the next section. Like Muslims in Natal and Transvaal who joined broader Indian associations, Coloured Muslims at the Cape were also actively involved in the political issues and other general concerns of their 'coloured' communities through participating in the broader coloured political organisations. For example, some Cape Muslims were involved in the activities of the Coloured People's Congress (CPC) which was established in 1953 as the South African Coloured People's Organisation (SACPO) with the aim of forming "a militant political movement with mass support among South Africa's 'Coloured' population" (Williams & Hackland 1988:56). The Coloured Persons Representative Council was meant to represent coloureds. It comprised of a group of coloured people who were partially elected. The Coloured Persons Representative Council was first elected in 1969 and then permanently supressed in 1980. Some of the laws that were passed by this council includes the Coloured Persons Social Pensions Law of 1974 and the Rural Coloured Areas Law of 1979.

After its formation, the Coloured People's Congress (CPC) actively participated in the struggle for justice and racial equality and associated itself with other liberation movements through which they sustained substantial political influence. Similarly, some coloured Muslims were involved in the activities of the Coloured Labour Party that was founded in 1969 and led by Sonny Leon, Allan Hendrickse, and David Curry at different stages. In March 1975, the Coloured Labour Party won the majority elective seats in the Coloured Persons' Representative Council. Through its representation in the Council, the Coloured Labour Party attempted to promote racial equality and complete political, social and economic freedom of all racial groups while maintaining its relationship with the apartheid government. While being sympathetic to the government, the Coloured Labour Party made attempts to use the Coloured Persons Representative Council as a means of voicing its opposition to apartheid policies thereby securing the social, political and economic interests of Coloured and black Africans. Nevertheless, unlike the Coloured People's Congress, which was clearly anti-apartheid, the Coloured Labour Party was not generally a challenge to the Apartheid government and thus supported dialogue.

Political Involvement of Muslims During Apartheid

There were several apartheid racial-based policies and laws between 1948 and 1994. The political involvement of Muslim organisations during this period in the struggle for justice, racial equality and democracy is important to the issue of Islam and politics in post-apartheid South Africa. As a result of having been challenged by the apartheid, racially based policies and laws, some Muslim organisations secured substantial political influence in South Africa. In their early political engagement, Muslims joined broader political organisations that were mainly concentrated at the Cape, Transvaal and Natal and dominated by Coloureds and Indians. While there were many Muslim groupings in South Africa namely, Coloured, Indian, White and black African Muslims, the Natal Indian and Transvaal Indian Congresses were among the major ones. It is important to stress the early involvement of Muslims in politics through broader non-Islamic organisations, since a considerable number of members within such organisations were Muslim. The major Muslim organisations that were influential during apartheid include MYM, Qibla Mass Movement and the Call of Islam.

The Apartheid Racial-Based Policies and Laws

Before severe apartheid racially based policies and laws were enforced from 1948 onwards, segregation and inequality already existed. By the nineteenth century at the Cape, social classes had already been introduced – whites were considered as belonging to the upper class, while liberated non-white slaves were a lower class. Gradually, four primary racial classifications; namely, Whites, Indians, Coloureds and black Africans began to emerge. Such social classes were intensified after the formation of the Union of South Africa in 1910 when the Orange Free State, Transvaal, Cape and Natal which had previously existed as separate British colonies came together to form a unified government. In this new government, whites were given voting rights, and coloured men in the Western Cape who met certain property and literacy standards were also given voting rights. This meant some Muslims who fulfilled the requirements would also vote. The new government passed the Native Land Act 27 of 1913 and the British authorities authorised it. Since one of the aims of this Act was to benefit Afrikaner farmers in the former republics by introducing commercial farming, thousands of non-whites were driven out from the concerned areas.

The Act also benefited the British-owned mining companies on the goldfields by causing an enormous influx of black Africans looking for employment. It became increasingly difficult for black Africans to own large amounts of land in certain areas so instead they became wage labourers. Thousands of black Africans, Indians and Coloureds began flocking to towns and cities due to the expansion of industries and goldmining. From 1920, the state began controlling and supressing the number of black Africans especially in urban areas. Although the population of black Africans dominated that of whites in almost all cities, the apartheid policy prevented blacks from infiltrating 'white' locations in cities and most urban areas which made it difficult for black Africans to move to such cities. The Group Areas Act 41 of 1950 made it clear that racial groups classified as White, Indian, Coloureds and black African ought to have their own separate residential areas. People were expected to live in their own racial areas assigned to their group; otherwise, they would be prosecuted for illegally residing in the residential area belonging to another race. Non-whites living in urban areas were required to obtain pass documents, and the employment of non-whites by whites in urban areas was restricted. When the apartheid political dispensation was being enforced and ratified in the years following 1948, strict oppressive and segregationist laws and policies upheld the system.

The introduction of independent homelands gave birth to various policies and laws, including censorship of the freedom of movement, racially segregating residential areas and educational facilities and so forth. The National Party's (NP) "triumph was based on two crucial issues: apartheid and an emotional appeal to Afrikaner nationalism with its implied call to Afrikaner political unity" (Serfontein 1982:7). The apartheid government legalised the segregative policies and laws that had been endorsed but loosely implemented prior to 1948. From 1948 onwards, there were critical racial segregations partly based on the fear of the extinction of the Afrikaner and white supremacy due to the increasingly black majority. Although by 1948 the Afrikaner still considered their identity as separate from that of the English or non-Afrikaner whites, after their triumph of the political battle, the English-Afrikaner political and cultural battle and differences slowly began to disappear. The apartheid government's policy of separate development led to the creation of independent homelands and Bantustans which fostered ethnic groupings as partly enforced by the 1950 Group Areas Act 41, Bantu Authorities Act 68 of 1951 and the Bantu Self-Government Act 46 of 1959.

The enforcement of homelands and Bantustans under the apartheid government resulted in the stricter classification of races into different racial and ethnic groupings. The policy highly affected Muslim and non-Muslim black Africans, Indians and coloureds whose social, civil and political rights had been restricted. Interracial political movements and collaborations among non-whites were equally constrained. Thousands of black Africans, Indians and coloureds were forcibly removed from their residential areas and relocated to new areas. Writing in 1963, Horrell noted that "hundreds of thousands of Coloured people and a small number of Whites are being forced to move their homes. Under allied legislation many thousands of Africans are being removed" (11). The resettlements had vast negative impacts on the economic, political and social aspects of life especially for the marginalised black Africans since their Bantustans were often underdeveloped and highly impoverished. Similarly, the resettlement camps themselves had numerous problems such as poor medical services, housing, water, sanitation, and education standards.

Several anti-apartheid opponents, some of whom were Muslim, experienced detention without trial, whilst others were imprisoned without being charged. Furthermore, the Public Safety Act 3 of 1953, Criminal Law Amendment Act 8 of 1953 and Riotous Assemblies Act 17 of 1956 prohibited all public meetings without the approval of the state by taking strict measures against trade union leaders of the resistance movements. Pass laws and influx control policies were enacted to prevent non-whites from residing in 'white' areas; for example, section 10 of the Urban Areas Act denied black Africans the rights to have permanent residential rights in urban areas. The pass law system demanded that certain races carry an identity document known as 'pass'. If they failed to do so, they would be fined, sentenced or prosecuted immediately. The influx control system prevented an overflow of black Africans, Indians and coloureds who were moving away from their poor and economically underdeveloped homelands to white locations and urban cities.

Furthermore, the apartheid policy demanded that education systems be racially separated. The multi-racial education and mixed universities were banned under the Bantu Education Act of 1953 and the Extension of University Education Act 45 of 1959. Whites, coloureds, Indians and black Africans had their own separate universities and other educational facilities. Most apartheid black African universities slowly became centres of political mobilisation and confrontation due to the politicisation of most black African educational institutions as is clear from the 1976 Soweto uprising and the 1980 school boycotts. Whites, coloureds, Indians and black Africans had their own separate universities and other educational facilities. Most apartheid black African universities slowly became sources of political mobilisation and confrontation due to the politicisation of most black African educational institutions as is clear from the 1976 Soweto uprising and the 1980 school boycotts. Although the government funded non-white schools and universities, the quality of education remained generally poor. For example, black African schools and universities had poor infrastructure, inadequate books and teaching materials, including poorly trained teachers and lecturers. Apart of the segregationist education system, mixed or interracial marriages and sexual relationships were discouraged under the Prohibition of Mixed Marriages Act 55 of 1949 and the

Immorality Amendment Act 21 of 1950. These Acts reflected the key aspects of the 1927 Mixed Marriage Act.

Moreover, South Africans were being actively prosecuted, driven to suicide or into exile for the mere crime of having had sexual relationships or having the desire to marry a person classified as belonging to a different race. In the 1970s and 1980s, most political originations and movements such as the ANC, PAC and the Black Consciousness Movement (BCM) were banned; several anti-apartheid activists fled South Africa for political reasons and most leaders of liberation movements and religious organisations were restrained, tortured and imprisoned. Changes in the apartheid political structure due to both internal and external pressure was gradual, since restructuring was faced with suppression.

Towards the end of 1970, positive changes in the apartheid political structure began to be apparent (Borer 1998). Many reasons are accountable for such changes. Demographically, the independent homelands and Bantustans proved to be impractical due to overpopulation especially in black African areas, whereas the number of whites who owned large pieces of land was gradually decreasing. Similarly, organised strikes and uprisings by black African students such as the 1976 Soweto revolt also created more pressure for political change. In the 1980s, there was strong pressure from freedom fighters, anti-apartheid activists, religious organisations, liberation movements and South Africans who had gone into exile began returning with new political ideas. As numerous laws and restrictions which promoted extreme racial segregation and inequality were being relaxed, the government also tried to introduce an inclusive and tolerant political dispensation which would partly tolerate black African political organisations. By 1978, the apartheid policy still favoured the dominance of whites in terms of land allocation and the share in national income. For example, although by 1978 the number of black Africans was about 19 million and that of whites was only 4.5 million, the white population occupied 87% of the land and about 75% share of the national income. During the 1980s, most Muslim organisations became directly involved in the struggle against most apartheid segregative polices thereby securing a political influence in the public sphere.

Further positive changes to the apartheid policies and laws came from the escalating international pressure and opposition against the apartheid system. Under the 1983 Constitution, coloureds and Indians were permitted to elect a few representatives to the House of Delegates and Representatives, while black Africans remained totally excluded from any political rights. Nevertheless, the promulgation of the Black Local Authorities Act 102 of 1982 continued to foster the formation of Township Councils responsible for controlling the affairs of black African townships by blacks themselves. The state also introduced several strategies and reforms geared towards relaxing certain apartheid policies. This involved the unbanning of the Immorality and Mixed Marriage Acts and elimination of 'petty apartheid' by making public social places open to all races. The phase 'petty apartheid' was used to describe most unnecessary apartheid policies and measures. For example, black Africans were not allowed to use public facilities such as hotels parks, beaches, clubs and road sitting or resting places. Moreover, social events and sports were segregated also following the Group Area Act especially before 1970. The government was "not so quick to dismantle racist laws when they were deemed necessary for the maintenance of the political, economic, and social position of whites" (Borer 1998:47). Such a political approach balanced positive change and repression – although it aimed at fostering collaboration with non-whites, it nevertheless, maintained core principles of the apartheid structure.

The system triggered defiance attempts and campaigns especially from black Africans leading to political unrest and the refusal to accept new reforms upheld by the 1983 Constitution. The early 1980s saw the development of black civic associations such as trade unions and liberation movements that became more organised. The politically marginalised black Africans, Indians and coloureds secured political cooperation through "alliance politics" which led to the formation of the United Democratic Front (UDF) in 1983 which was supported by some Muslim organisations. By 1985, successful mass action campaigns began to be organised by anti-apartheid political and religious movements and organisations. This triggered nationwide campaigns and brought various education institutions, workers unions, public associations and religious organisations to openly strike and protest apartheid laws and policies. Although many people could attend banned public political gatherings and boycott certain government initiatives, Kane-Berman (1993:44) asserts that "political violence as measured by monthly fatalities had been in double digits for most of 1987 and 1988 and for all but one month in the first half of 1989."

The political situation in South Africa between 1990 and 1994 was marked by a mixture of violence and negotiations. The early 1990's saw the enactment of major changes and reforms resulting from the dismantling of the apartheid system and the birth of a democratic state under the ANC. In 1990, the apartheid government unbanned liberation movements and released various political leaders such as Nelson Mandela who had been imprisoned, thereby fostering a cooperative political framework. The period between 1990 and 1991 involved the laying of the foundation for political dialogue, discussions and strategies in which some Muslim organisations and individuals had a substantial political influence. After 1990, political movements had to organise themselves into properly structured political parties with the freedom to campaign and mobilise masses. Towards the end of 1992, political unrests which resulted in the massacre of ANC members led to the deferment of political negotiations and the withdrawal of the ANC from the Convention for a Democratic South Africa. This was followed by various protests and demonstrations organised by political organisations and liberation movements to foster an urgent response and reform from the NP government, although this was sometimes met with violence and massacre of protesters.

By the end of 1992, political negotiations intensified between the NP government and the leaders of other political organisations with the aim of negotiating reform and change in government. The strategy towards a negotiated settlement became vital by 1993 when the political talks once again became public and when opposition political parties could organise rallies and mobilise masses, though tensions were unavoidable and sometimes discussions regarding transition led to violence. Such negotiations were hampered by various challenges such as the withdrawal of the IFP and the Afrikaner People's Front. Consequently, an "Interim Constitution [was] finally agreed on at the Multi-Party Negotiating Forum in November 1993. This provided the basis on which the country's first one person; one vote elections were held the following April" (Callinicos 1996). All persons above 18 years would be allowed to vote regardless of their race or ethnic group, that Members of Parliament who would be democratically elected would then elect a President, and that the government which would win the election would govern the country for only five years.

During the General Election which took place between 26 and 29 April 1994, nineteen established political parties contested, and the ANC won the election with an absolute majority. Although the period leading to the April 1994 General Elections was marked by violence and that dialogue often turned bitter, South Africa was ready to hold its first democratic election. This election involved remarkable compromises based on fears and hopes from both the ANC, the NP and other political parties. The years between 1994 and 1995 were marked by extensive negotiations, formulation and enactment of the new Constitution, extreme reform of the political structure and civil service, a total dismantling of the segregationist apartheid policies and the institution of the Truth and Reconciliation Commission. The 1994 General Election and the proclamation of the 1996 Constitutions were major events that led to the establishment of South Africa as a democratic state.

Muslim Participation through Broader Movements: Indian Congresses

Clearly, different groups of Muslims came to South Africa and settled in different parts of the country. The major groupings of Muslim in South Africa are the Malay, Indian, white and black African Muslims. The early Muslim political engagement in South Africa was through broader non-Muslim organisations and movements such as the Coloured Labour Party, South African Coloured People Organisation (SACPO), the Natal and Transvaal

Indian Congresses (which later formed the South African Indian Congress, or SAIC) and the African People's Organisation. This section focusses only on the political activism of Muslims through the Natal and Transvaal Indian Congresses as a way of demonstrating the early involvement of South African Muslims in broader movements before the formation of Islamic organisations during apartheid.

The early significant political influence of Indian Muslims in South Africa started with the formation of the Natal and Transvaal Indian Congresses. Initially, both organisations sought to represent the interests of the Indian Muslims who had immigrated into the country as indentured labourers, shopkeepers and merchants. The anti-Indian laws concerning land and housing acquisition and other segregationist policies that were being ratified and implemented against Indians and black Africans, triggered the early Indian resistance in South Africa. In the Transvaal, Indians were forced to pay a special tax and to carry a special permit when walking outdoors after 9pm. They were also denied land rights except in special areas popularly known as 'ghettos' allocated to them. In 1894, the Franchise Amendment Bill limited the number of Indians who took part in voting and parliamentary franchise in Natal. The Immigration Law Amendment Bill of 1895 was also implemented to reduce the influx of Indians into Natal and the Transvaal.

Having arrived in Durban in 1893, Mohandas Karamchand Gandhi was aware of the "total abhorrence of the Indians by the White Community" (Mahida 1993:42) in the Natal and Transvaal areas. The oppressive measures and laws that were being introduced caused outrage among Natal and Transvaal Indians, some of whom were Muslim. The plans to organise resistance against discriminatory measures encountered by Indians were spearheaded by Gandhi and prominent Muslims such as Sheth Abdulla and Sheth Haji Muhammad. Based on their efforts, in 1894 the NIC was formed, with Gandhi as its key founder and ideologue. Regarding its goals, NIC was "intended to serve as a forum for the protection of rights the Indians believed they enjoyed as subjects of the British crown" (Bhana 1997:1). Through NIC, Indian Muslims based in Natal and

Transvaal participated in organised campaigns against segregationist policies for the first time.

After its launch, the NIC became the first Indian majority political organisation which sought to protect the rights of the oppressed Indian community in South Africa. The NIC's core members had to sign pledges as a symbol of their commitment to the struggle for equality, justice and rights of 'free' Indians in Natal. The leaders of NIC were confident that the organisation would confront the government over some of the segregationist and anti-Indian legislation that affected the political and economic interests of Muslim merchants and indentured workers. Prominent Indian Muslim merchants dominated the central organisation of the NIC. Between 1894 and 1913, all NIC's presidents and other key officials of the NIC were Muslim merchants. Between 1894 and 1913, the presidents of the NIC were: Abdulla Haji Adam, Abdul Karim Hajee Adam, Mohammed Jeewa, Abdul Kadir and Dawad Mahomed. These were all Muslim merchants who held key positions in big companies and business outlets. For example, Abdullah Haji Adam Jhaveri, first president of the NIC, was already a political activist and had been co-director of Dada Abdulla and Company prior to joining the organisation.

After its launch in 1894, the NIC immediately began playing an influential political role by opposing the oppressive laws through newspapers and submitting petitions to the government and its officials. Between 1894 and 1914, NIC "phrased extra-parliamentary protests, petitions and deputations in the context of discrimination against Indians in general" although it "emphasised the protection of the economic position of merchants and property owners" (Singh and Vawda 1988:3). Although the organisation had intended to reach out to all Indians, its restrictive membership fee policy challenged the goal. The fact that each member had to pay a certain affiliation fee meant that only merchants and businesspeople would form the core membership of the organisation. Initially, the NIC did not have much interest in the political struggles of black Africans and other races, in general, partly due to the idea of Indian nationalism. Apart from trade and immigration issues, highlighting the poor living conditions and rights of indentured Indians in Natal was initially a minor objective of the organisation.

In 1904, another Muslim-majority Indian organisation known as Transvaal Indian Congress (TIC) was officially launched to counter anti-Indian laws in the Transvaal and "to protect vested commercial interests" (Swan 1987:192) of wealthy Indian merchants most of whom were Muslim. The TIC's political strategies in the Transvaal were generally like those of the NIC in Natal. Apart from organising passive resistance initiatives, the TIC and NIC actively participated in Gandhi's resistance campaigns by joining the *Satyagraha* campaign between 1907 and 1913, which culminated in the government's positive response in 1913. Through the *Satyagraha* campaign, both the NIC in Natal and the TIC in Transvaal mobilised the Indian community to engage in resistance through boycotts, protests and marches. Apart from other oppressive policies, the *Satyagraha* campaign was a reaction to the Transvaal Asiatic Registration Act 1 of 1906 that demanded that all Indians carry passes after registering. The Transvaal Asiatic Registration Act 1 of 1906 was passed by the British government in 1907 through the Transvaal Asiatic Registration Act 2. The *Satyagraha* campaign directly challenged the decision that Indians should register. Through Gandhi and the activist efforts of the NIC and TIC, most Indians refused to comply but preferred to be arrested for violating the Act. Ashutosh Kumar (2017:206) affirms that the *Satyagraha* campaign focused on specific issues:

> the annual licence tax of three pounds for every 'free' Indian, a restrictive immigration bill which prevented Indians travelling to or settling in other regions and the refusal to recognise traditional Indian marriages...[and] a concern for the fate of indentured Indians.

When the NIC and TIC involved the indentured workers in the campaign in 1913, thousands of Indian workers went on strike and "on 6 November 1913, over 2000 indentured Indians undertook the Great March from Natal into the Transvaal" (Bhana 1997:24). There was violent confrontation between the police and strikers. Indian workers, in sugar plantations, industrial workers in mines and production factories, including domestic workers in homes and restaurants joined the strike despite several arrests and torture. The severity of the campaign forced the British Government to respond through the promulgation of the Indian Relief Act of 1914. Through the 1914 Indian Relief Act the "$3 tax was repealed ... the right of entry of South African-born Indians into the Cape was restored; the racial reference to the immigration law in the Orange Free State was eliminated" (Bhana (1997:1). Even though the 1914 Indian Relief Act did not eliminate all discriminatory measures against Indians in Natal and Transvaal, this was NIC and TIC's first major political success. Most laws that had been negatively affecting Indian merchants and workers were relaxed due to the government's attempt to address the grievances of the strikers in 1914.

In 1919, TIC, NIC and the CIC (Cape Indian Congress) jointly formed the SAIC which immediately became the umbrella organisation for these Congresses. Even after the formation of the SAIC, NIC remained relatively passive until its revival in the 1930s and 1940s. When Gagathura Mohambry Naicker became NIC's president, the organisation began forming alliances with non-Indian activist organisations as opposed to its earlier links with solely Indian organisations. While emphasising the aspirations of the oppressed Indian community in its political activities, NIC began involving other oppressed communities such as black Africans and coloureds in its mass protests, gatherings and petitions to the government. Despite the efforts of the NIC to form alliance with other anti-apartheid organisations and to open its membership to other races, the emphasis on the interests of the Indian community through the quest to represent the challenges that were faced by Indians did not completely disappear.

Similarly, in the 1930s the TIC was also being revived due to the presence of prominent political activists most of whom were Muslim. By mid-1940s, two renowned Muslim political activists; namely, Moulvi Cachalia and Suliman 'Babla' Saloojee were among the key members who had joined TIC. In 1946, Dr Yusuf Mohamed Dadoo who had been an active Muslim political activist before joining the TIC became its president, which strengthened the political influence of the organisation in the society. Dr Yusuf Mohamed Dadoo and Moulvi Cachalia had a huge influence on Ahmed

Mahomed Kathrada who later became a prominent anti-apartheid activist and pioneered the formation of the Transvaal Indian Youth Congress Corps which later became The Transvaal Indian Youth Congress. In reaction to the Asiatic Land Tenure and Indian Representation Act 28 of 1946 and other unjustified policies, the TIC and NIC organised resistance campaigns consecutively between 1946 and 1948:

> The NIC and the TIC jointly led a passive resistance campaign from 1946 to 1948 in which nearly 2,000 men and women went to prison in protest against a law restricting Indian land ownership... Indians referred to this act as the 'Ghetto Act' and they rejected it in its totality even though Smuts had, 'in-part', granted them franchise. They considered the type of representation it gave them to be inferior, with no compensation for the infringement of their right to possess land. In June 1946, the Indians in Durban launched a passive resistance campaign against the Act. Several hundred Indians put up tents on a municipal site which was within the controlled area, in other words, in the area where the Indians were not allowed to occupy land. When they were arrested, other Indians simply took their place. The campaign continued for several months and the Indian government broke off trade relations with South Africa in support of the protest (South African History Online 2011).

Apart from joining forces with Indian organisations, the TIC and NIC created alliances with liberation movements such as the ANC. At the 1947 joint meeting, the NIC, TIC and the ANC agreed to cooperate in the political struggle. Dr Alfred Bitini Xuma, the ANC President-General; Dr Yusuf Mohamed Dadoo, TIC President and Gagathura Mohambry Naicker, the NIC President, signed the agreement. As Chhabra (1997:21) puts it, the "manifestation in the Xuma-Naicker-Dadoo Pact of 1947 (popularly known as Three Doctors Pact) ... signalled the common" grounds for the three political activist organisations. This move endorses the position that the NIC and TIC had great political influence which was partly spearheaded by the Muslims who held key leadership positions within the ranks of these organisations. The passive resistance strategies of the NIC and TIC in the 1940s and 1950s were becoming multi-racial, given the escalating efforts to represent the interests of all oppressed people in South Africa. When the Group Areas Act was enforced in 1950, "both Indians and Black Africans joined their political forces together to oppose the Group Areas Act" (Mulloo 2004:217). During the late 1940s and 1950s, some of the NIC conferences invited members of the ANC to make the ceremonial openings.

In 1952, the NIC and TIC joined the Defiance Campaign, a multi-racial political mobilisation organised by the ANC, SAIC and the Coloured People's Congress (CPC). By becoming part of the Defiance Campaign, these organisations played a recognisable political role within the broader struggle against apartheid. Due to the harsh repressive measures of the apartheid government, both TIC and NIC, like other activist organisations, became passive from the late 1950s through to the early 1970s. During the period of resurgence and revival of the NIC and TIC between 1971 and 1980s, the organisations became involved in alliances which called for the liberation of all oppressed South Africans regardless of race. For instance, Surendra Bhana (1997:118) asserts that at the conference of the revived NIC in 1972, the following broadened objectives were adopted:

> (1) to strive for a united democratic South Africa on the basis of universal suffrage; (2) to promote the cause of all the oppressed people in South Africa and to oppose racial discrimination; (3) to promote peace, understanding, and goodwill among people of all races in South Africa; (4) to cooperate with all organisations irrespective of race that are striving for democracy by non-violent methods.

The NIC leadership through its more active alliance with other liberation movements and anti-apartheid activist organisations achieved the four objectives. Before the formation of the UDF, the NIC and TIC were among the political organisations which were calling for a united opposition against apartheid's segregatory policies. When the UDF was formed, NIC and TIC became active affiliates of the movement and joined most of its campaigns by helping to mobilise the Indian community. Like the NIC, the TIC in the 1980s adopted objectives such as non-racism and justice and equality for all South Africans. From 1983, both the TIC and the NIC secured remarkable political influence by organising and joining widespread campaigns against the Tricameral Parliament of the apartheid government through boycotts, "house visits, mass meetings, pamphleteering and extensive campaigns" (South African History Online 2011). Having been established in 1983, the Tricameral Parliament was the name given to the structure of the South African racial-based parliament from 1984 and 1994. When the TIC and NIC were disbanded while the political negotiations were in progress during the period of transition (1990 – 1994), some of their members joined political movements like ANC as active members and leaders both at local and national levels.

Muslim Organisations and the Apartheid System

Having explored the involvement of Muslims in broader anti-apartheid movements, it is important to look at four major Islamic organisations that secured political influence during apartheid namely; the MYM, Qibla Mass Movement, the Call of Islam and Muslim Students' Association of South Africa (MSA). Apart from these Muslim organisations, there were also others were involved in the political struggle against apartheid such as the Islamic societies of old Natal and Cape Town. The political involvement and influence of the MJC both before and after 1994 will be discussed later in this project. There were also prominent Muslims such as Faried Ahmed Adams, Mosie Moolla, Abdullah Haron, Ahmed Kathrada, Essop Jassat, Rashid Ahmed Mahmood Salojee, Hoosen Haffejee, Ismail Meer, Farouk Meer, Fatima Meer, Cissy Gool, Ahmed Timol, Aziz Goolam Pahad, Abdul Kader Asmal, Rick Turner, Ahmed Dangor, Jessie Duarte, Cassim Amra, Ebrahim 'Cass' Saloojee, Abdul Khalek Mohamed Docrat, Mohammed Abdulhai Ismail, and many others who secured considerable political influence through anti-apartheid activism.

The Muslim Youth Movement

Ebrahim Jadwat, Mahmud Moosa and Abu Bakr Mohammed, the key founding members, founded the MYM on 16 December 1970 in Durban, South Africa. To outline the direction and goals of the MYM, seven National Conventions were held between 1971 and

1977. The MYM's first National Convention was held in 1971 during which it was officially launched. Most participants of the MYM's first National Convention came from Cape Town, Transvaal and Natal. From its inception, members belonging to established Muslim organisations such as the Muslim Assembly of Cape Town and the Durban Arabic Study Circle who attended the first Convention supported the MYM. Abdulkader Tayob (1995:107) states that the early "conventions were the most visible signs of the MYM in the Muslim community, attended by up to five thousand people". During the National Conventions, foreign speakers such as Mawlana Fazlur Rahman Ansari and Dr Ahmad Sakr who were invited to such Conventions would also give talks about various aspects of Islam around South Africa. Before the formation of the MYM, the Muslim community in South Africa lacked a national organisation that would be involved with the Muslim youth and "project Islam as a complete and comprehensive way of life" (Mahida 1993:99). At its inception, the MYM handbook affirmed that the movement had the following five guiding principles:

> (1) To unify South African Muslims and make them appreciate their Islamic heritage. (2) To intensify Islamic education and bring about a clearer understanding of the spirit of the Qur'an. (3) To create the proper environment by making the Mosque the focal centre of all our activities. (4) To re-discover and emulate the personality of our Holy Prophet Muhammad (Peace and blessing upon him). (5) To make Muslim women an integral part of the whole programme. (Tayob 1995:114)

The leaders focused on arousing consciousness about Islam and its teachings to Muslim youth and the entire *ummah* in South Africa. The early Conventions of the MYM made it clear that the movement was not only targeted at the youth but also that it was geared towards the unity of the entire Muslim community in South Africa and Islamic identity based on the Islamisation of different aspects of life. When it was formed, the MYM was generally apolitical and tended to focus on cultural and religious issues. As such, the organisation did not have any political influence in society during its early stages due to its emphasis on the Islamism programme. Instead, the formation of the MYM was the beginning of the programme of conveying and propagating the Islamic ideology in South Africa. Renowned Muslim scholars from abroad were invited by the MYM to give talks on various aspects of the Islamic faith in many parts of South Africa. During the first three Conventions, the need to create networks that would foster unity and broaden the involvement of the youth around the country was emphasised. From 1973 onwards, the MYM engaged in a new program of creating branches throughout the country and, "by the 1970s, the Muslim Youth Movement was perhaps the only truly national organisation with branches in every major centre in South Africa" (Jacobs 2014:30).

The creation of local branches in most parts of the country led to the formation of branch leaderships who had a representation at the regional level which in turn formed the national executive. With actively functioning branches in Natal, Transvaal and other parts of South Africa by 1975, "the MYM became the first truly national Islamic body in South Africa" (Tayob 1995:109). The programmes and activities in networks and branches, tour lectures and motivational talks throughout the country led to the mobilisation of youth and the spreading of the Islamic faith in areas where it had not yet existed. Most branches often organised children's programmes, Arabic lessons, youth camps and mobilised Muslim students in educational institutions. Publications of the MYM such as *al-Qalam*, *Friday khutbah* booklets and *Handbook* helped the movement to spread the teachings of Islam in different parts of the country. While it focused on strengthening the Islamic ideology at this stage, the organisation remained apolitical by being almost silent on political issues affecting the country generally. The MYM employed the motto 'Islam is a way of life' to emphasise that Islam encompasses all dimensions of life. The inclusivity of the MYM made it welcome women and promote their active participation by promoting various activities which responded to the needs of both male and female members of the Muslim community at several mosques and educational centres. Women were encouraged to participate in their own circles such as the Women's Councils. They also participated in lectures and mosque activities, thereby making them part of the entire project. The MYM was one of the earliest Islamic organisations to involve women and incorporate them within the structures of the organisation and creating women's groups within its broader networks.

From mid-1970s, the MYM began increasing its relations with Muslims from outside South Africa as it was transforming into a movement. Farid Esack (1988:479) asserts that "a close affinity developed between the MYM and what has been referred to as the international Islamic Movement" which was explicit in the regular visits by "luminaries of the Jamaati Islami of Pakistan-such as Khurshid Ahmed and Khurram Murad and others with a Muslim Brotherhood background such as Jamal Badawi and Ahmed Sagr" to South Africa. From 1977 onwards, major changes began to occur within the Movement while emphasising the centrality of training and education as central elements. As a response to the changing political situation, there was the intensification of training programmes at higher levels and in branches which focused on various aspects of the Islamic faith.

The MYM's "vaguely defined social and cultural 'commitment to the establishment of Allah's order in South Africa'" was "no longer adequate given the changing political circumstances in South Africa" (Esack 1988:479). The organisation embarked on intensive training programmes that coincided with the developments that followed Islamic resurgence in Iran. The developments of the Iranian Revolution, which led to the establishment of the Islamic Republic in 1979, became an important element within the MYM. Abdulkader Tayob affirms that:

> its newspaper, *al-Qalam*, traced the progress of the Revolution and organised a rally in support of Iran in December 1979. The writings of Shariati and later, Khomeini and other Iranian mullahs, were added to the shelves of the MYM bookshops and the reading lists for the *halaqat*.

Although the MYM did not view the Muslim resurgence in Iran as directly relevant to the South African context, it perceived the method as an important approach in the social and political resurgence of Islam. Although there were differences in approach between the leaders of the Iranian revolution and those of the MYM, the former had much impact on the MYM. Unlike the *mullahs* in Iran who could mobilise masses in political and social causes, this was impossible in South Africa were some of the goals and strategies of the MYM were criticised by the *'ulama*. The Iranian Revolution inspired the MYM "to focus on international issues" and that "International Islamic resurgence literature was translated into English and spread among the youth of the newly emerging movement" (Lehmann 2006:32). The MYM began sending some of its students abroad for studies on Islam and Islamic thought at universities such as the International Islamic University of Islamabad and created links with international youth organisations such as the World Assembly of Muslim Youth.

The Iranian Revolution inspired the MYM in South Africa to include *'ulama* in its leadership which was explicit when it recruited prominent individuals who had left South Africa to study abroad such as Ebrahim Moosa who had returned from India and Farid Esack who had returned from Pakistan. Before 1977, the MYM was not initially critical of the apartheid dispensation in South Africa but rather focused on promoting Islam and did not clearly oppose apartheid racism and oppression. While the MYM continued to emphasise Islamic ideology, some of its members at higher and lower levels felt that the movement ignored the political and social goals of Islam. This led to some of its key individuals such as Achmat Cassiem and Farid Esack to breakaway and spearhead the formation of stronger anti-apartheid Islamic organisations. Although the MYM tried to join the anti-apartheid chorus by the end of the 1970s, this aspect remained generally underemphasised. Rather than stressing the political agenda, "the MYM's major concern was to develop a paradigm for understanding Islam" (Tayob 1995:152) and Islamic ideology.

The MYM saw the intellectual training of individuals and proselytization as central contributions to the political cause. In its document released in 1983 titled *Our Vision for South Africa*, the MYM maintained that part of its vision was the creation of a non-racial and classless society that supports equality. The MYM also expressed its concerns regarding the fragmentation and divisions of the South African society by stressing that all people ought to be granted opportunities to practise their political and social rights. Some members of the Movement began contributing to the mobilisation of active anti-apartheid activist organisations. For example, the "implementation of the Tricameral Parliament in 1983 and the elections in 1984" (Lehmann 2006:32) caused most members of the MYM to actively participate in the campaigns of the UDF in discouraging people to participate in the racial-based elections of 1984. During this time, the MYM began securing some sort of political influence within the broader anti-apartheid campaign.

Apart from publications such as *Our Vision for South Africa* and the involvement of some of its members in stronger anti-apartheid organisations such as UDF, by 1983 the MYM remained politically aloof due to its insistence on Islamic ideology and the attempts to respond to the criticisms of the '*ulama*. The MYM's lack of critical engagement with the political sphere through public forums was partly due to international influence; for example, Farid Esack (1988:481) maintains that "Professor Salman Nadwi, a Pakistani academic, and one-time leading adviser to the MYM, warned in 1983 that any kind of active involvement in politics was going to destroy the MYM". After 1983, there were major changes based on the call to be contextual (the contextualisation programme) based on the need for substantial involvement in South African politics of resistance. Some members of the Movement began calling for a more practical and pragmatic approach to apartheid.

The MYM began engaging in anti-apartheid activism through public platforms by engaging with issues affecting the South African society. The meetings, newsletters and speeches of the MYM began to be characterised by political activism instead of promoting Islamic ideology. In view of the 1984 Tricameral elections, individuals such as Ebrahim Moosa and Abdul Rachid Omar Omar were pillars of the talks which the MYM were giving in many parts of South Africa encouraging people not to participate in the racial-based elections. The leaders of the MYM joined other organisations such as the Call of Islam in the united initiatives such as the Campaign for Muslim Awareness which furthered the political involvement of Islam in politics and engagement with the state. Similarly, the *al-Qalam* newsletter featured various political and social issues concerning the injustice and inequalities of apartheid between 1983 and 1990. The MYM increasingly became an important part of progressive Islam in

South Africa. Nevertheless, such an attempt to engage actively with the political context was hampered partly by the presence of certain members who were "not prepared to commit themselves politically to the concept of a holistic Islam for which the struggle for justice is a fundamental component" (Esack 1988:482).

The MYM's participation in politics was further emphasised at the General Assembly in 1987 when the new President Abdul Rachied Omar made a commitment to full engagement with the public through active anti-apartheid activism. The General Assembly in 1987 affirmed that its focus would no longer be on the Islamic ideology but that the political involvement and engagement with society would be central. The new leadership was convinced "that the MYM would not be able to make a contribution to the unfolding political process if it had within its ranks *arkan* who were uncommitted to the organisation's political programme" (Tayob 1996:167). The leaders of the MYM committed to the political programme of the apartheid political struggle. The MYM had links with labour union organisations through supporting boycotts by labour unions and organising campaigns on their behalf within Muslim communities throughout South Africa.

Despite its active participation in the political sphere at this stage, the MYM did not actively align itself with major anti-apartheid organisations and movements even though there was a general call for solidarity and united alliance against apartheid. Ursula Günther and Inga Niehaus (2002:91) uphold that "a strategy of 'positive neutrality' was developed which enabled the MYM to participate in resistance activities without making a commitment to any particular political organisation or ideology". Although the MYM became visible in the apartheid political struggle, it did not actively associate itself with major anti-apartheid liberation movements. Nevertheless, the MYM continued to restructure and channel its meetings, quarterly gatherings, publications and discussions on issues such as poverty, workers' rights and justice towards its political aspirations.

From 1989, major changes began to occur within the MYM both at ideological and hierarchical level. Due to the openness of membership and call for change in leadership, the 1990 General Assembly elected Tahir Fazile Sitoto as the first black African to be its president and Fatima Noordien as its first female executive member. The openness of the organisation and active involvement of black Africans in its membership indicated changes in structure. At an ideological level, the MYM now formulated its objectives in terms of the entire South African society instead of an Islamic value system. Its leadership encouraged cooperation with both Muslims and non-Muslims against the oppression and injustices of apartheid. In 1990 at the Islamic Training Programme, the new President of the MYM, Tahir Sitolo, clearly affirmed that the goals of the MYM were to be directed to the creation of a just and non-oppressive society for all South Africans rather than only the Muslim community.

Regarding its direct response to the political changes during the period of transition, the MYM generally supported the political negotiations between the NP government and political organisations. Its stance was different from that of Qibla which was more reluctant to mobilise the Muslim community to participate in the 1994 general elections. After 1990, the MYM held various discussions and meetings at national and regional levels regarding the new direction of the Movement and its strategies regarding the political changes. It continued to be actively engaged in the fostering of a just social order and the struggle against oppression and injustices of the South African society. The changes within the MYM were directed towards a reorganisation of its membership and a change in its policies. This is clearly noted by Abdulkader Tayob (1995:176):

> The regional assemblies, together with the annual Islamic training programmes, conducted extensive discussions and debates on the critique of Islamism, and adopted new positions with regard to internal membership structure, the struggle for justice in South Africa, workers' and women's rights, and inter-faith relations. Moreover, the ideologues of the MYM and their seminar-papers gave the Movement confidence in Islamic discourse it has never had since its founding.

The Qibla Mass Movement

The major anti-apartheid Muslim organisation with an explicit political objective was the Qibla Mass Movement (Qibla). Although the idea to form Qibla developed in 1978, it was officially launched in 1980 at the Cape. Two of the prominent anti-apartheid Muslim individuals; namely, Imam Achmad Cassiem and Yusuf Patel organised a group of students in Cape Town to spearhead the establishment of Qibla. Before the formation of Qibla, Imam Achmad Cassiem had been a columnist for *al-Qalam* and *Muslim News* where he expressed critical views regarding the injustices and oppressive policies of the apartheid system. The formation of Qibla was partly due to the dissatisfaction of the political role of major Islamic organisations such as MYM, the Muslim Student's Association and the *'ulama.* After attending the "first Leadership Training Programme" of the MYM in 1977, Imam Achmad Cassiem "was not convinced of the efficacy of MYM's response to racist structures in South Africa" (Tayob 1995:151). Although some members of the MYM and Muslim Student's Association left these organisations to join Qibla, it was not an offshoot of former Islamic organisations or movements. The founding of Qibla with the hope that it would become a mass movement indicates the confidence that its founders had when establishing the organisation. Although the founders of Qibla had hoped that the organisation would instil mass mobilisation, this was never achieved, and its following remained rather limited. Although Cassiem remained a dominant figure of the organisation, Qibla promoted shared leadership to avoid personality cults.

Qibla was formed on the need for a Muslim organisation that would present an Islamic perspective in the South African context. For the founders of Qibla, this required a conceptual or ideological orientation which promoted 'a purely Islamist ideology'. Qibla began publishing and distributing books and pamphlets unravelling the root causes and ills of apartheid and calling on Muslims to resist the system. Qibla also founded various educational and anti-poverty organisations which further helped it to gather support and gain popularity from the wider Muslim community. When establishing Qiblah, Achmad Cassiem was convinced that resisting all forms of oppression was part of the Islamic heritage. For example, writing in 1992 Achmad Cassiem was convinced that "the historical records of the Muslims show that the greatest resistance to colonialism was encountered in those countries inhabited by Muslims" and that "in the contemporary situation it is again the Muslims in Iran, Afghanistan, Palestine and Lebanon who are rising successfully against the super-powers" (14). Qibla's hope of providing the solution to the oppressed masses in South Africa against injustices and inequalities, was explicitly stated in one of its pamphlets:

> Islam declares war on racism and racialism. This is more than a mere battle of words. As proof, we offer Muslims as the only truly consolidated anti-racist force in the country. This has been historically maintained for 300 years because it is an ideological unit and not a nationality, tribe and race or class (Haron 2017:18).

Qibla merged its anti-apartheid slogans with Islamic principles by affirming that certain portions of the Quran and *Hadith* are against exploitation, racial discrimination and inequality. This meant that apartheid, racism and other injustices had to be resisted since they were inconsistent with the Islamic faith. Although it isolated itself from mainstream political movements and organisations in its political activism, Qibla secured loose connections and ideological alignments with the PAC and the Black Consciousness Movement. Its vague links with the PAC was apparent in its pamphlets which, while calling on the people to resist apartheid offered solutions that where consistent with Islamism.

Despite its vague links with the PAC, like the MYM and MSA, Qibla remained critical of the Call of Islam's inter-religious solidarity against apartheid and affiliation to political organisations such as UDF. By the time Qibla associated itself with the PAC, the latter had already begun organising military training in countries such as Sudan, Iran and Libia for some of its members. Although Qibla was not officially affiliated with the PAC, the strategies and ideology of the PAC, especially being part of the armed struggle and opposing affiliation to mainstream anti-apartheid movements, were apparent within Qibla. The political links Qibla secured with PAC partly exposed it to the Iranian revolutionary strategies. As such, the PAC would have been the only major political organisation that implicitly influenced Qibla.

The Iranian Revolution had a significant impact on Qibla, its formation and political involvement during apartheid. Members of

Qibla were inspired by the success of the Iranian Islamists who effectively overthrew the leadership of Shah Mohammad Reza Pahlavi and created an Islamic Republic, having mobilised civil society against the regime. In the process, Qibla espoused "a pragmatic and revolutionary view of Islam inspired by the Iranian Revolution" (Palombo 2014:35). Most Qibla members were attracted to the ideas of prominent Iranian leaders such as Ayatollah Khomeini whom they perceived as a role model. Qibla emphasised the centrality of jihad and mobilised masses to fight against apartheid through radical and militant strategies. While asserting that oppression and inequality are contrary to the dictates of Islam, Qibla asserted the possibility of an Islamic Revolution in the South African context.

Moreover, based on the example of Iran which was "viewed as a guide, spiritually as well as politically, for liberating the Muslim community" (Lehmann 2006:36), Qibla developed the slogan 'One solution, Islamic revolution' which was often inscribed on its stickers. David Africa (2007:229) outlines the six-staged strategy which Qibla members thought would enable them to achieve their objective of an Islamic state in South Africa:

> (1) Creating an *awareness* amongst the Muslim community of a certain social or political issue of concern; (2) *Mobilization* of the community around either domestic or international issues; (3) *Conscientizing* the Muslim community about the relationship between these specific issues and the more general, global struggle for an Islamic State; (4) *Challenging the authority of the state*. This is done by means of mass mobilization, protest actions and the gradual introduction of armed violence; (5) An *armed revolution* against the existing order. QIBLA regards the existing social order in South Africa as inherently and structurally violent and sees its violence against this system as a defensive means. This armed revolution is aimed at overthrowing the current social order and replacing it with an Islamic State; (6) The *armed defence* of the Islamic revolution follows the success of the revolution.

For Qibla, the struggle against oppression was vital even to the extent of martyrdom. Qibla in one of its pamphlets affirmed that

"Jihad ... is the Islamic paradigm of the liberation struggle ... an effort, an exertion to the utmost, a striving for truth and justice" (Esack 1995:107). Having been influenced by the slogans and ideas of the Iranian Revolution, Qibla perceived revolution as a way of eliminating the apartheid dispensation, though it did not outline exactly how such a move would happen. One of the major challenges for Qibla was how the Islamic revolution would happen in a country were most people are non-Muslim. Although Qibla had many supporters and followers in the wider circle, its core membership team remained significantly small. Qibla was never really able to offer a method within the South African, and especially within the apartheid context, to achieve the establishment of an Islamic republic as the ultimate goal. Although such a revolutionary strategy partly inspired the radical approach towards the Qibla's anti-apartheid activism, it did not enable the organisation to achieve much political influence in the country.

Qibla viewed the Islamic resurgence in Iran as archetypal for Muslims in South Africa and other parts of the world to follow. For Qibla, if the ideas of the Iranian Revolution are rightly applied to South Africa, there can be the possibility of transforming the country into an Islamic state. As local defenders of the Islamic Revolution, most members of Qibla saw the urgent call for liberation as crucial. Based on a passion for revolution, Qibla was one of the major catalysts behind the political mobilisation of the Muslim community. Farid Esack (1988:486) clarifies this as follows:

> It is, however, precisely this indomitable belief in the Qadr (Power) of Allah that has bewildered the armed forces and the police when they confronted the Muslims on the streets of Cape Town. Whilst the Call of Islam may have been the main organising body for many of these events, it was Qibla which provided the revolutionary fervour. It has been the belief in Qadr which has enabled the Muslims to become a force to be reckoned with and feared by the South African regime. The police and the armed forces have correctly perceived that they are encountering a hitherto unknown element in the liberation movement.

When the period of transition, which was marked by political negotiations dawned, Qibla initially rejected such a process. Qibla together with Azanian People's Organisation (AZAPO), PAC and the New Unity Movement instead "called for a Constituent Assembly where the oppressed would chart out their own future" (Esack 1997:213). Having perceived the negotiations as a sell-out, Qibla demanded that the Constituent Assembly should take place before any negotiations with the apartheid government were organised. Unlike the Call of Islam and MYM, Qibla continued to stress the revolutionary language and strategies of the 1980s. According to Farid Esack (1997:213), Achmat Cassiem in *Muslim News* explained why Qibla rejected negotiations in this way:

> Can a thief draw up a legitimate will to let his children inherit his stolen property...? Peaceful co-existence between oppressors and oppressed does not feature on the agenda of the oppressed, and especially not on that of Muslims. We cannot...direct any of our legitimate demands to an illegitimate government. Is this too difficult to understand? ... too difficult to digest? Or is it the sacrifices that follow this understanding, which are too great to bear?

Although Qibla was supportive of the PAC in the period leading to the 1994 general elections, some of its members did not primarily support Muslim participation in the elections. A similar position was held by the Mujlisul Ulama of South Africa which did not only consider the elections as *Kufr* and impermissible, it also condemned Muslims who held government positions and those who would contest for government positions. In the document, *Muslim Participation in Kufr Politics,* the Mujlisul Ulama of South Africa held that the practice of "voting, especially for a non-Muslim government, is un-Islamic. It is *haraam* for Muslims to vote for *kufr* and even Muslims who are *fussaaq* ... voting should therefore not be of any concern to Muslims" (Mujlisul Ulama of South Africa 1994).

Although the debate surrounding the permissibility of Muslim participation in politics on the eve of the first elections touched Qibla, most of its organisation members did not wholly reject Muslim participation in politics but cautiously encouraged people to vote. Qibla used Radio 786 as a way of popularising its message though this was hampered partly by the call to make this Radio Station "conform to the somewhat liberal standards of the Independent Broadcasting Authority" (Esack 1997:226). Such a conservative and non-progressive approach reduced the political influence of the organisation during a period when most anti-apartheid and liberation organisations and movements were participating in the political negotiations and democratisation process. During the period of transition, Qibla inspired the formation of front organisations. A key front organisation that was formed to mobilise support for Qibla to boycott the general elections in 1994 was the Islamic Unity Convention (IUC) established shortly before the 1994 general elections as a front of Muslim religious affairs, political participation, welfare and educational aspects.

Qibla also inspired the formation of the PAGAD which was formed in 1996, Cape Town and absorbed some of its core ideologies. Qibla also began functioning through international solidarity commissions or committees such as "the Bosnia Support Group and Muslim Against Global Oppression (MAGO) as well as more established fronts such as the IQRAA Foundation and the Islamic Unity Convention (IUC)" (Africa 2007:229). Although Qibla continued to secure a 'shadowy' presence post-1994, it has done so by establishing and involving itself in front organisations, especially PAGAD.

The Call of Islam

The Call of Islam was launched in 1984 in the Cape by Shamil Manie, Ebrahim Rasool, Maulana Farid Esack, Adli Jacobs and Imam Hassan Solomon as its key founding members. Maulana Farid Esack had been incorporated into the MYM and the MJC after his return from studies in Pakistan before the creation of the Call of Islam. While pursuing his studies in Karachi, Pakistan, he was also working with Christian organisations that embodied Christian liberation theology. For example, while in Pakistan, Maulana Farid Esack worked with the Breakthrough Christian organisation, which according to Palombo (35) "embodied Christian liberation theology and solidarity with the poor from Latin America". Having felt that the political involvement of the MYM was inadequate, he left it and spearheaded the formation of the Call of Islam. Shamil Manie, Ebrahim Rasool and Adli Jacobs had also been part of the leadership of the MYM and the Muslim Youth Association.

Before the founding of the Call of Islam, Imam Hassan Solomon and Ebrahim Rasool had also been part of the leadership of the UDF. When the MYM approached them to make the choice to either remain as its members or leave them for the UDF, they chose to leave the MYM and became part of the founding members of the Call of Islam. The influence these members exerted on ordinary Muslims and their initial ties with the MJC contributed to the tremendous political success of the organisation. When the Call of Islam was formed, some senior members of the MJC such as Shaikh Abdul Gamied Gabier its chairperson and Shaikh Faiq Gamildin its assistant secretary identified with it. Farid Esack and Imam Hassan Solomon had also served in the leadership of the MJC. The Call of Islam was formed at a time when the MJC had withdrawn its alliance from UDF. When the MJC withdrew its affiliation from UDF, the founders of the Call of Islam felt the need for a Muslim organisation that would form alliances with secular liberation movements such as UDF in order to respond effectively to the prevailing situation. The ideas of the founders of the Call of Islam had been influenced by both the MYM of which they had been a part and the social, political and economic realities of the early 1980s.

Imam Hassan Solomon and Ebrahim Rasool broke away and formed the Call of Islam due to the inadequate strategies and approach of the MYM in their political activism. Having felt that the political direction of the MYM was ineffective, they founded the Call of Islam which would develop a clear political programme in the struggle, based on a "commitment to the creation of a non-racial, non-sexist, democratic and just South Africa" (Solomon 1987:10). As such, they had to create a Muslim organisation which would actively engage with the political developments of apartheid and align itself practically and ideologically with other liberation movements and organisations such as the UDF. The beginning of the Call of Islam was partly based on the introduction of certain political reforms of the apartheid state such as the decisions of the 1983 Tricameral Parliament which was to be followed by the elections in 1984. The Tricameral Parliament instituted many Constitutional proposals. For example, only whites were allowed to vote while Indians had a House of Delegates, Coloureds had a House of Representatives within the white House of Assembly created by the racially segregated parliament. From its inception, the Call of Islam emphasised the need for the eradication of racial segregation, exploitation and inequality.

As soon as it was formed, the Call of Islam mobilised masses to protest the Tricameral Parliament. The leaders and members of the Call of Islam viewed the new Constitutional proposals with suspicion. This was because although it offered Coloureds and Indians a Representation in Parliament, black Africans remained excluded from Parliamentary roles. The Call of Islam was formed during "that time that the apartheid state started introducing 'reforms' with the aim to strengthen the state's control in the face of a mounting social and economic crisis" (Hassan 2011:61). The Call of Islam merged religious conviction and political activism in its private and public forums. Maulana Farid Esack explicitly elucidated the religious basis for the organisation's struggle against apartheid:

> There is a verse of the Quran where Allah says: and fight them on until there is no more tumult and oppression...' we say then that at this stage our essential task is to break down racist capitalism; this is how Islam is operating at public level...In the call of Islam, we remain committed to Islam, and believe that our Islam at this time means to struggle side by side with other (non-Islamic) democratic forces (Nkrumah 1989:523).

Clearly, Farid Esack presents Islam and its sacred texts as being one of the motivational factors for political engagement. Reading the Quran and interpreting it within the political happenings of apartheid became a central part of the Call of Islam. This was based on the efforts to search for an interpretation of the Quran that would be applicable and relevant to the situation of the people and their daily experiences. Through one of its pillars, such as Maulana Farid Esack, the Call of Islam sought to find a Quranic approach that would be suitable to the South African context. For example, based on his Quranic theology of liberation, Farid Esack (1997:83) affirms that "speaking about liberation during the apartheid years in South Africa has made the meaning of liberation obvious enough: liberation from all forms of racism and economic exploitation". Such an idea emphasised the direct involvement of Islam as a religion in the social and political struggle of apartheid through action and theological reflection.

The commitment to the political situation was apparent in the Call of Islam's mass mobilisations, the distribution of newsletters and creation of study groups through which it actively participated in anti-apartheid activism. This was reflected in texts such as *The Review of Faith*- a manual that was produced in 1984 and instantly became a source for critical conscientisation, reflection and study. The Call of Islam often distributed pamphlets, which reflected anti-apartheid sentiments at educational institutions, religious gatherings and at the rallies of other liberation organisations and movements. The pamphlets and manuals stressed the need to boycott elections, urged masses to avoid collaborating with the government and to avoid taking up leadership positions in the apartheid government. Matthew Palombo (2014:36) explicitly expresses this:

> The Call distributed anti -apartheid pamphlets at mosques, UDF rallies, schools, and churches, and rallied tens of thousands of Muslims to the struggle, often presenting arguments from the Quran and Sunna (the precedent of the Prophet Muhammad) for jihad against apartheid, non - collaboration, and boycotts of elections and government positions.

The Call of Islam created local chapters in Durban and Transvaal of highly dedicated individuals who were also active members of other political activist organisations; this increased the popularity and support of the organisation from the Muslim community. The Call of Islam also gathered support in Transvaal between 1984 and 1985 when Maulana Farid Esack gave various lecture tours in the province. Moreover, the Call of Islam fostered the active participation of ordinary Muslims and women as part of its ideology. The Call of Islam immersed itself within the "culture of its community using its symbols (such as its spiritual days), cultural expressions (such as its spiritual tradition), and even its often-conservative leaders to reinforce the struggle against apartheid" (Jacobs 2014:9). Rather than emphasising professionalism in its activist initiatives, the Call of Islam incorporated the wider Muslim community as a way of drawing support.

Central to the Call of Islam's political involvement was its interaction and alliance with the other liberation movements and anti-apartheid organisations especially UDF. The Call of Islam created links with the World Conference on Religion and Peace through the South African Chapter of World Conference on Religion and Peace. For example, Shamil Jeppie (1991:13) assert that "when the first State of Emergency was declared in July 1985, the Call of Islam had activists in Cape Town with close ties to the United Democratic Front, and ultimately affiliated to the United Democratic Front". By affiliating to the UDF, which was one of the major anti-apartheid activism movements in the 1980s, the Call of Islam was exposed to various opportunities such as access to funds, professional skills and the ability to have some of its views discussed at national meetings of the UDF through the presence of its representatives within UDF. Its role was recognised by Oliver Tambo in 1988 alongside other larger anti-apartheid movements and organisations due to its activities, association with the UDF and its active political involvement in the struggle. This reaffirms the assertion of Mahida (1993:130) that the "UDF and the African National Congress [ANC] … identified the Call of Islam as their allies in the Muslim community". Through some of its publications, it was apparent that the ANC had high regard for the Call of Islam.

Therefore, while other Muslim organisations were embarking on the solidarity against apartheid through allying with secular liberation movements, the Call of Islam prioritised such an initiative. Because the Call of Islam regarded solidarity or alliance as a crucial element in its struggle against apartheid, it did not resist working with other liberation movements and non-Muslims. By being part of the wider struggle rather than isolating themselves, members of the Call of Islam attempted to cooperate and create alliances with other liberation movements without necessarily compromising their Islamic faith. The Call of Islam realised that belonging to liberation movements was very important in the united efforts against apartheid, which partly meant "burying of ideological differences in the course of confronting the common enemy" (Esack 1988:493). The Call of Islam introduced what was known as the '*Campus Call*' which encouraged Muslims to unite with others against the apartheid system. The Call of Islam also collaborated with other religious organisations through its emphasis on interreligious solidarity against the unjust and oppressive apartheid system. Imam Gassan Solomon, as quoted by Adli Jacobs (2014:12), aptly expresses this as follows:

the unity of the oppressed which is vital can only be achieved by engaging the enemy in all possible ways – where true Muslims, true Christians and all progressive organisations stand shoulder to shoulder to break down the granite wall of Apartheid and open the doors of freedom to each and every soul in this country.

However, the Call of Islam saw other liberation movements such as BCM as having been limited in their goals. By emphasising on an exclusively black nationalism, the BCM also excluded whites who were active anti-apartheid activists. Regarding the impact of international influence on the Call of Islam, its leadership did not generally consider the political ideas and thoughts of the Pakistani Jama'at and Egyptian Muslim Brotherhood as directly applicable to the South African context. According to Rania Hassan (2011:64), Adli Jacobs said that:

> The MYM, the MSA experience and the *ekhwan* (Muslim Brotherhood) experience has not suited our conditions…what we needed in fact was to find our own tools; we cannot adopt other people's tools. They are grown up in their social conditions. We needed tools of analysis, tools of understanding, tools of slogans and understanding that are grown from our own experience in our community experience.

Following Adli Jacobs, the Call of Islam stressed the importance of a contextual approach to the political situation and the uniqueness of the South African experience. Although the Call of Islam was not directly influenced by the outside world such as Pakistani Muslim thinkers, Iranian and Libyan Revolutions, such international developments of Islamic resurgence had an impact on the organisation. Following Farid Esack, Uta Lehmann (2006:34) argues that "the writings of the Iranian scholar Ali Shariati circulated among its ideologues and even literature of the Mujahedin i Khalq of Iran was read and discussed". Nevertheless, international influence such as from the Iranian Revolution and foreign personalities such as Sayyid 'Ibrāhīm Ḥusayn Quṭb who was popularly known as Sayyid Qutb did not have a huge impact on the Call of Islam in the way that they had on Qibla and the MYM, the two-other major anti-apartheid Muslim Organisations.

During the period of transition, the negotiations which were often done between leaders of major political organisations and the NP meant that the political engagement of activist organisations such as the Call of Islam were marginalised. While aligning itself with ANC, the Call of Islam perceived the political negotiations as a process in which the entire Muslim community would participate. In 1990, the Call of Islam convened the National Muslim Convention (NMC) that was attended by various Muslim representatives in South Africa. The Convention discussed issues such as the permissibility of Muslims to form solidarity with non-Muslims, "attitudes to negotiations with the apartheid regime … the right of all to shelter, a living wage, and a decent health system" (Esack 1997:213) and Muslim-state relations.

Despite the activism done by the Call of Islam, the end of the apartheid regime crippled its active political role. The Call of Islam had been formed based on the injustices and oppression of apartheid, and when the political situation began to change, between 1990 and 1994, leading to the creation of a democratic state, the goals and objectives of the organisation became unclear and redundant. Some members of the Call of Islam have attributed the disappearance of the organisation to the end of apartheid, a political force that inspired the creation of the organisation in the first place. Hassan (2011:66) gives reference to Suraya Bibi Khan who affirmed that:

> Because our purpose at that time was to get rid of oppression, any form of oppression. We felt from an Islamic point of view it was our duty to fight for the country. If the country does not have oppressive laws against us as Muslims, then there is no reason for us to fight.

The Call of Islam had been formed to mobilise people against apartheid which was perceived as a common enemy; without it, the direction of the organisation became uncertain. In post-1990, the Call of Islam became more supportive of the ANC. For example, between 1990 and 1994 the Call of Islam continued to participate in the political process through mass mobilisation and a wider distribution of newsletters and other publications. Esack (1997:218) cites the *Muslim Views* which in December 1993 affirmed that "the Call has decided to campaign for people to vote ANC. [This is] the only real way for this country to build justice, democracy, nonracialism and peace". Furthermore, many members of the Call of Islam acquired positions within the government, and the ANC. Such a loss of key leaders created a leadership vacuum within the organisation. For instance, Ebrahim Rasool who had been a key founding member of the Call of Islam, became Premier of the Western Cape and its provincial leader consecutively.

The Muslim Students' Association of South Africa

The MSA was launched at an inaugural conference in January 1974 as a national representative body for Muslim students from academic institutions. The inaugural conference, which was hosted by the University of Cape Town's MSA, was attended by already existing Muslim students' organisations such as Hewat Islamic Association, Cape Muslim Students Association, Cape MSA, University of the Witwatersrand Islamic Association and the University of Durban-Westville Islamic Association. When the MSA was established, it became a national forum for Muslim students with offices throughout the country. The Cape Muslim Students Association was founded in September 1969 in District Six, Cape Town. Mahida (1993:103) points out the major reason for the formation of the MSA and the names of the first office bearers:

> The Muslim Students' Association of South Africa [MSA] became a symbol of the Muslim students bold and creative to the challenges of our times. As there was no single organised body to motivate the Muslim students and to cater for his/her needs and to co-ordinate Muslim thought and action, the MSA was launched in 1974. The following were the first office bearers: M G E Hendricks, G Abader, S E Dangor, I Essop, S Nordien, M A Dhansay, M G Jassiem, A Mukuuddem and others.

The establishment of the MSA was met with positive response from Muslim students which led to the subsequent creation of MSA's chapters at different higher institutions of learning and secondary schools throughout South Africa. As a result, the MSA became a national student wing whose major goal was "to practically establish the comprehensive, dynamic and revolutionary value system of

Islam" at campuses and secondary schools (*Al-Mizaan* 1983:8). The MSA outlined four short-term objectives through which it sought to materialise its primary goal. The objectives aimed at fostering the Islamic character within the organisation, promoting the values and message of Islam at educational institutions, mobilising and organising Muslim students to participate fully in MSA's activities. MSA pledged to:

> Deliver the message of Islam to the students and to evoke in them a desire to study Islam and to fulfil its moral obligations; to organise all those students who are prepared to work for the establishment of Islamic ideology under the banner of the MSA; to remind the student of his/her responsibility to the community and to form closer links between the two; and to struggle for the establishment of an Islamic society free from economic, social and political exploitation" (Mahida 1993:103-104).

Through its objectives, the MSA in the 1970s and 1980s devised various programmes and activities as a way of offering guidance and direction to Muslim students throughout South Africa. The national leadership and administration organised national executive meetings to coordinate MSA's activities and visits between campuses. The MSA organised various come-together activities such as youth camps, weekly *halaqaat* (scholarly circles for study), seminars and local and national conferences to strengthen unity, enforce the practice of Islam and encourage research on issues relating to Islam. At campus level, MSA maintained prayer rooms, organised orientation weeks for recruiting new Muslim students, including Islamic weeks geared towards the promotion of the Islamic faith to non-Muslims. The MSA also ensured that libraries had material about Islam such as books and magazines which would be easily accessed by Muslim students. By June 1984, the MSA had three properly functioning regional offices; namely, Natal Region based in Durban, Transvaal Region based in Johannesburg and the Cape Region based in Cape Town.

The MSA had various publications such as the *Worldview* published in Cape Town, *Al-Talmiz* published in Johannesburg, *Al-Mizaan* and *Iqra* published in Durban, *Hisaf* Newsletter for secondary school students and *Inqilaab*, an annual magazine for the

Muslim community generally. Through its National Secretariat in Durban, the MSA also published and distributed several newsletters, bulletins and brochures throughout the 1970s and 1980s. The Muslim Student Newsletter was the official newsletter of the Muslim Students Association. The *Muslim Student Newsletter* contained current news updates concerning local and international news on Islam, other issues concerning the country and reports from National Executive Meetings. The *Muslim Students' Association of South Africa Information Brochure* contained various updates and information regarding the MSA and its activities. The MSA also had the Bulletin of the Muslim Students' Association of South Africa. Apart from the promotion of the Islamic faith and its values, the MSA was involved in political activism in South Africa through apartheid resistance. The political involvement of the MSA was centred on the zeal of the organisation's leadership to establish an Islamic community that is free from any political exploitation, inequality and injustice. The MSA used its publications to oppose various apartheid policies and appeal to Muslim students throughout the country to reject all forms of injustices and inequalities. As Mahida (1993:104) affirms, "since 1976 the MSA has been very articulate against the apartheid government and its policies. A number of their publications were banned by the state authorities".

From its formation, MSA was critical of the apartheid injustices in the race-based education system. Even when the Education and Training Act repealed the Bantu Education Act of 1953 in 1979, the fact that the latter still upheld a racially segregative education system raised criticism and opposition from the MSA leadership. For example, *Al-Mizaan* in February 1983 criticised the inferior education system which it perceived as having been crippled by racial divisions. The MSA maintained that genuine freedom of thought and expression was "influenced by the single most important factor i.e. an inferior educational system. With the creation of "tribal" colleges, inferior education, primarily aiming at stifling freedom of thought" (*Al-Mizaan* 1983:2). The MSA was convinced that the inferior education system granted to black Africans, Coloureds and Indians was meant to hinder independent thinking and meaningful freedom of expression concerning political, economic and social issues. In the 1980s and early-1990s, MSA harnessed the Arab-Israel conflict to serve the local anti-apartheid struggle. For example, a pamphlet of the MSA in 1987 stated that "the oppressed in South Africa can never be liberated if we collaborate with Zionism and imperialist in any of its guises" (Shimoni 2003:176).

The MSA considered the anti-apartheid activism of South Africans who maintained relations with what they considered to be "the Zionist and racist State of Israel in occupied Palestine" as "suspect and hypocritical" (Shimoni 2003:176). When the South Africa's National Peace Accord (NPA) was established to prevent violence, provide safety for political negotiations and promote public accountability between 1990 and 1994, the MSA criticised the limitations of this forum. In a feature article published by *Al-Mizaan* in November 1991, MSA's Mohsin Jeenah (1991:1) affirmed:

> Despite the new structures and mechanisms spawned by the National Peace Accord in its bid to halt the violence, at the end of the day those responsible for investigating incidents and allegations of police misconduct will still be the police themselves...we need the capacity to bring about a new style of policing, a mechanism for encouraging commitment to change on the part of the police.

The MSA maintained that police officers who caused some of the violence which resulted in the creation of structures such as the National Peace Accord, which would be investigated by police themselves, was a mistake on the part of the government. Although the MSA maintained some political influence in society through publications and releasing statements against certain apartheid policies, its major emphasis was on the promotion of Islamic values and the Islamic faith on campuses. For example, the report and summary of proceedings from the MSA's Second National Executive Meeting held from the 13th to the 16th of December 1980 in Durban shows that this gathering did not discuss any issues relating to the South African political situation but focused solely on the study, safeguarding and promotion of the Islamic faith and value system on campuses.

Therefore, while the MSA played an important role in uniting Muslim students and promoting Islamic values in universities, its influence in the political situation was less hegemonic. Nevertheless, its political influence both as an organisation and through individual members such as Ganief Hendricks, Rashied Omar, Na'eem Jeenah and Ebrahim Rasool was recognisable and led to the banning of some of its publications by the apartheid regime. The MSA underwent transformation post-1994. Its website claims that:

> It [The Muslim Students' Association] has grown to be one of the largest student representative bodies in South Africa. The MSA aims to assist in developing students and creating an active citizenship. This is done by developing structures to create a national and influential student representative body, leadership development programs, advocating for social, political and economic justice through campaigns, social projects and humanitarian initiatives that are all student based. MSA has a constituency across eighteen campuses in eight cities across South Africa. The MSA continues to be an active role player within society by striving for student development (Muslim Students' Association 2022).

Islamic Identity and the Anti-Apartheid Political Struggle

Some Muslim organisations which have been involved in politics have emphasised the need to maintain their Muslim identity. For example, by the time MYM was formed, Muslims in Natal and the Transvaal had already been stressing their religious identity. In that context, some Islamic organisations stressed the need to safeguard Islamic identity in a context of injustice, oppression and racial inequality. The guiding principles which the MYM adopted at its inception clearly show that although the organisation was somewhat open and inclusive, it was tied to its Islamic identity and project of Islamisation mainly by inspiring Muslims to become more conscious and active. Like the Black Consciousness Movement which advocated for an authentic and exclusive Black identity, the organisation stressed the need for an authentic Islamic identity based on the Islamic way of life. However, the initial and vaguely defined social, cultural and religious commitment of the MYM to establish Allah's order in South Africa had become inadequate in the changing political scene. Hassan (2011:61-62) posits a similar critique of the MYM:

> Regarding the political situation in South Africa, the MYM discussed the political situation in the country but no focus was given to the anti-apartheid struggle, per se, for example, as an integral part of their activities, different MYM branches were expected to undertake relevant research covering different aspects of the injustices of apartheid, in that sense it seems that taking part in the anti-apartheid activity as such was not a central aspect that the Quranic classes discussed nor a focus of any of the organisations' projects...As for the question of how to face apartheid, the MYM advocated the idea of training individuals from an Islamic perspective as a way to fight apartheid, arguing that if the organisation had launched a general liberation movement, 'it would not necessarily have contributed to an Islamic reign'. It is against this backdrop that MYM opted to increase its efforts to proselytise.

Since the MYM was primarily a youth organisation established to make Muslim youth conscious of their Islamic identity and inspire them to become active members of their communities, its emphasis on fostering an Islamic ideology and representing the aspirations of the Muslim community was justifiable. The challenge, however, was based on its political involvement in the public sphere – its emphasis on Islamic identity crippled its contribution to the political situation in its early stages. One might question how the MYM could have possibly secured an influential role in the anti-apartheid struggle while being immersed in the whole project of Islamisation of society and Islamic identity. Although the MYM achieved little success in its political activism due to the emphasis on Islamic identity, in the 1980s the organisation joined the anti-apartheid chorus. The MYM's entry into the political sphere in the late 1980s represents the political aspirations of Muslims in South Africa.

Unlike the MYM, the Call of Islam was not greatly concerned with the question of Islamic identity for many reasons. For example, some of its founders had broken away from the MYM which they perceived as politically inactive and conservative. Further, the Call of Islam was formed at a time when the social, political and economic crisis was becoming severe and the anti-apartheid chorus stronger. While the MYM remained politically reserved, due to its insistence on Muslim interests and identity, the Call of Islam from its inception drew itself to the centre of the political arena by openly challenging the apartheid system and its policies while calling for the liberation of all South Africans, regardless of religion. The Call of Islam went beyond the early calling of the MYM to work among Muslims by emphasising the need to be part of the wider struggle. The Call of Islam emphasised the need for unity against apartheid, oppression, exploitation, and racial-based politics. Thus, while the Call of Islam remained an Islamic organisation, it departed from the MYM's methodology of maintaining an 'authentic religious identity' and created links with liberation movements such as UDF, thereby gaining political influence in society.

Like the Call of Islam, Qibla was partly formed due to the dissatisfaction by its founders with the MYM's approach to the deteriorating political situation in South Africa. When it was formed, Qibla's approach was greatly influenced by factors such as Islamic principles, revolutionary concepts and anti-apartheid struggle slogans. Although it called for unity against injustice, racism and exploration, the organisation adopted the MYM's quest for an Islamic identity which negatively affected its ability to openly cooperate with non-Muslims in the anti-apartheid struggle.

However, although Qibla did not openly cooperate with other liberation movements, its political discourse reflects a clear attempt to promote unity in the anti-apartheid struggle in a way that the MYM failed to do in its early stages. For example, unlike the MYM which was strictly exclusive and unwilling to join pluralistic liberation movements in its early stages, Qibla developed vague links with liberation movements such as the PAC and advocated Christian-Muslim relations during apartheid in its political discourse. While Qibla was relevant before 1994, mainly because of its alliance with the PAC, the failure of the PAC in the elections in 1994 also meant the failure of Qibla.

Muslim Political Parties

The advent of democracy, which was preceded by a period of political transition, brought about various opportunities for the transformation of the South African society. With its openness to all religions, cultures, ethnic groups and traditions, the post-apartheid era has witnessed the participation and active involvement of Muslims in the public life of the country, especially in its political, economic and social revolutions and renewal. It is from this perspective that Muslim political parties have been formed in South Africa from as early as the 1990s, beginning with the establishment of the Islamic Party in 1990 in the Western Cape. Since then, there has been several Muslim parties such as the Africa Moral Party, Al-Jama-ah Political Party and the most recently formed SUN. What is common among these political parties is their emphasis on the centrality of projecting Islamic values and principles in the public sphere. To some extent, this aspect has affected their more inclusive objectives which integrate the needs of the entire society in different ways. It is important to discuss three of these Islamic political parties; namely the Islamic Party, the Africa Moral Party and the Al-Jama-ah Political Party. These three Islamic parties have had a longer historical record and significant political influence in South Africa.

Background to the Emergence of Islamic Political Parties

Between 1990 and 1995 there were fundamental changes in terms of the role of religion in the changing political scene. Since the winds of change began to be felt with the release of key political prisoners such as Nelson Mandela, Muslims felt the need to actively participate in the emerging democratic political order. The period of transition was marked by substantial negotiations between the NP and other parties such as the ANC, the Inkatha Freedom Party (IFP) and the PAC. The position of Islam prior to 1990 had been motivated by the political crisis, which had brought religion to the centre stage of the political arena. The place of Muslims in the political realm during the period of transition was determined by both the reforms within the South African Islamic community and the changing political milieu which "meant responding to a variety of political, social, economic and cultural transformations which, in some instances, required entering previously uncharted territory" (Nadvi 2008:622).

The early 1990s were marked by the emergence of violence and negotiations, a context where some key Muslim leaders played a role of mediation in the political dispensation. They supported the negotiating forums and took up leadership positions in some political parties especially the ANC. Several prominent Muslims also "participated in campaigns regarding the unbanning of various apartheid laws and policies and the call for the return of political expatriates." (Mutelo 2017:15). The negotiations to determine the governing institutions were also geared towards the appointment of joint non-elected institutions to help govern part of the transition period. For example, several Muslims such as Ebrahim Patel, Dullar Omer, Mohamed Ahmed Kathrada, Naledi Pandor and Hassen Ebrahim were vital role players in the drafting of the 1993 Interim or Transitional Constitution. This period spearheaded the formation of a new and transformed political order due to the unbanning of political parties such as the ANC and the PAC. This resulted in various changes and reforms which began to materialise or take form by 1994.

The formation of democratic structures and institutions, the independent judiciary and the relationship of separation with interaction between the state and religious institutions, which began to be felt soon after 1994, have all been vital signs of change. Since the dawn of the democratic era in South Africa, Muslims have been grappling to find ways of defining themselves both ideologically and politically. Various Islamic bodies and organisations that have emerged since the 1990s to represent the needs of Muslims, both in the private and public sphere, substantiate such a view. Lubna Nadvi (2008:3) asserts:

South African Muslims, diverse as they are, are a crucial component of this democracy. However, they are faced with challenges that require radically alternative approaches to those that have up to now defined their responses to these challenges, in order to ensure that they do not become denuded as a community.

The emphasis on Islamic religious practices and identity, especially on the part of Indian and Coloured Muslims, which partly developed during apartheid, found some Muslims unprepared to address the key social, political and economic needs and issues affecting the broader society. Before the 1994 election, several Muslims had already been appointed at national and local levels to serve in the established political parties and other institutions. Some Muslim politicians who contested the 1994 elections under established political parties such as the ANC won at parliamentary and municipal levels. Some people perceived these Muslims as being there partly to represent the interests of the Muslim community. Since 1994, several Muslims such as Ebrahim Rasool, Naledi Pandor Hassan Solomons, Dullah Omar, Farida Muhammad, Fatima Hujjaij, Anver Surtee, Fatima Chohan, Ebrahim Patel, Jessie Duarte, Ismail Mohamed, Ebrahim Ebrahim, Aziz Pahad, Essop Pahad, Ahmed Kathrada and Ismail Vadi have held key government positions both in cabinet and the national assembly.

However, the extent to which such a presence of Muslims in established political parties and government institutions and bureaucracy actually represented the aspirations and interests of Muslims has been questioned. For example, "when Imam Hassan Solomons of the MJC was appointed in 1994 to serve in the Justice and Trade Industry Ministrie" (Matthee 2008:188), some Muslims thought that he would spearhead the Muslim aspirations in the public sphere. As such, a substantial number of Muslims has been voting for non-Muslim political parties. In 2000, the *Muslim Views* newspaper featured a full-page advertisement from the ANC under the subheading 'ANC Call to Muslims'. According to Heinrich Matthee (2008:208), the advertisement read:

> Muslims enjoy constitutional protection of their religion and freedom to worship. At the same time, we call on Muslims in South Africa not to segregate or marginalise themselves. You

must participate together with others in building the new South African nation with new acceptable moral and social values.

Nevertheless, most Muslims in South Africa found themselves in a dilemma in the 1990s. Although Muslims were well represented in the established non-Islamic majority parties, there was a perception that Islamic parties or at least their representatives should be put in parliament to represent Islamic interests and values in the socio-political arena. While some recognised the presence of Muslims in established political parties, they maintained that these are answerable to their respective parties. As Abdulkader Tayob (1998:1) puts it, "these leaders represent a broader cross-section of South Africa than only the Muslim community" and that "they are answerable to their parties and constituencies". The attempts of Muslims to seek direct representation led to the creation of Islamic political parties.

An analysis of the manifestos and goals of Muslim parties that have been formed indicate that party leaders and supporters are convinced that they have the power to represent their religious interests socially and politically. Such prospects led to the mobilisation of some Muslims "along religious lines to create a political party to contest the national elections and have a voice in parliament, to address issues relating to Muslims" (Nadvi 2008:622). Almost all Islamic parties are meant to ensure direct representation of the Islamic standards in parliament and society. Furthermore, the aspirations of Muslims to participate more directly in politics were based on the possibilities opened by the new democratic dispensation. Towards 1994, South Africa began presenting itself as an open and democratic society in which some Muslims were inspired to form Islamic political parties.

While the democratic system upholds the democratic principles and values based on a non-racial, non-ethnical, non-sectarian ethos, some Muslims as minorities wanted to exercise their democratic rights by voicing their unique identity. This is vital in a democratic context as it promotes nation-building and essential elements such as diversity and equality. The openness and impartiality of the emerging political system was reassured by the fact that in the 1994 Provincial and National assembly elections, over 18 political parties registered to contest. For example, regarding part of the reason why Al-Jama-ah political party was established, the website of the party itself attests:

> The Constitution of South Africa supports the system of a multi-party democracy, as opposed to a single party state. According to The African Peer Review Mechanism (APRM), domination of one political party in South Africa will be detrimental to freedom in South Africa. What is best for South Africa is a diversity of political parties with competing policies" (Al-Jama-ah 2018).

Clearly, one of the reasons for the formation of Muslim political parties was based on the desire by some Muslims to create a common political platform for all Muslims which would then ensure Muslim input in national and provincial legislation and policy. Some Muslims felt that in the new South Africa they had the power to play a positive role in the public sphere by both presenting the interests of their religious community and contributing to the democratic transformation of society as a whole. According to Heinrich Matthee, the formation of Muslim political parties can also be accredited to the fluidity and disillusionment of some Coloured and Indian communities in the Western Cape regarding some of the established political parties. By 1994, there were recognised and well-established black-majority parties such as the ANC (founded in 1912) and the IFP (founded in 1975), and white-majority parties such as the NP (founded in 1914). By contrast, the Coloured communities in the Western Cape were politically fragmented and disjointed which prevented any Coloured-majority party from being formed.

Towards the 1994 election, some Indian and Coloured Muslims in the Western Cape, particularly in Cape Town were uncertain whether they should vote for a non-Muslim political party or not. Some prominent Muslims such as Achmad Cassiem, founding member of Qibla encouraged Muslims not to participate in the election. The IUC, based in the Western Cape shortly before the 1994 election, "adopted this rejectionist political stance … and called on Muslims to boycott the election" (Salih 2009:198). Similarly, some leaders of the MJC made a public statement ahead of the 1994 election declaring its intention not to be aligned to any specific party.

The MJC also provided certain guidelines Muslims should consider before choosing a party to campaign for, support or vote for. Although most Muslims ignored such calls by taking up leadership positions in the already established political parties and actively participating in the elections, the rejectionist political stance persisted largely among Coloured and Indian Muslims in the Western Cape. Thus, within the broader Indian and Coloured communities in Cape Town, the early Muslim political parties emerged. The founders of the early Islamic political parties such as the Islamic Party and the AMP were skilled, middle-class businesspersons and professionals.

The Islamic Party

The Islamic Party was formed as a regional or provincial party based in the Western Cape. The Islamic Party was formed in 1990 by Naushad Omar, the principal of Cambidge High School, and launched in Athlone, Cape Town. In 1990, the party distanced itself from apartheid structures but promised to register and participate in the post-apartheid non-racial elections. Although the party emphasised its openness to all South Africans when it was established, it upheld Islamic principles and ideology. Soon after its establishment in 1990, the Islamic Party outlined its core objectives. Regarding its political policy, the party stressed its strong rejection of the apartheid discrimination, and instead supported the negotiation process and the need for non-racial and impartial elections. For the Islamic Party, there should be regular democratic elections, a multi-party democracy that protects all cultures, religions and languages; there should also be a total autonomy of institutions such as educational and financial institutions, the press, judicial system and broadcasting subjected to religious moral policies. In that regard, the Islamic Party stated:

> (1) The party supports a system of multi-party democracy with regular elections and proportional representation, (2) the party does not accept the system of 'the winner takes all'; the new constitution should ensure that laws should be passed in parliament in proportion to a party's support to ensure that each vote carries equal value, (3) the party believes in the deconcentration of political power to prevent any abuse of

power. One method of achieving this is through a geographical federation, and that (4) Bill of Rights determining all human rights, entrenched in the constitution and enforced by the courts, and not violating the *Shariah* (Mahida 1993:143-144).

The party also proposed that all laws and policies be passed in a democratic parliament where all parties have equal value, and that there ought to be a "decentralisation of political power to prevent any abuse of power" (South African History Online 2017) through geographical federation. Furthermore, the political policy of the Islamic Party stressed the centrality of a Bill of Rights stipulating all human rights and respect for the Islamic Shariah law based on the democratic Constitution and enforced by the legal system. Concerning its social policy, the party affirmed its opposition against social disintegration and what they perceived as social decay including abortion, prostitution, promiscuity and illegitimate children that they were convinced ought to be seriously addressed. The leaders of the party were convinced that to eradicate crime, criminals should be severely punished, the socio-economic factors perpetuating crime should be thoroughly addressed, and that employment should be made available to young people who end up being members of gangs and crime syndicates.

Moreover, the supply of alcohol, cigarettes, drugs and other dangerous intoxicants should be stopped since alcoholism and drug abuse lead to immorality, crime, health problems, road accidents and possible death. Thus, the party, in its discourse, opposed immoralities such as gambling, intoxication and drug abuse that damage society. The Islamic Party challenged the government on women's rights by insisting that women should play a greater role in the economic, religious, and political transformation of the country. To eradicate malnutrition, hunger and poverty, the government should either employ more people or device a state-financed unemployment scheme. The party also recommended affordable education and the restructuring of the entire education system:

> Affordable education of a minimum standard should be provided to all people; any discrepancies in spending should be eliminated over a reasonable period, say five years; the foundation of the wealth of this country should rest on

education and work skills; education should be restructured to gear it more productively to the needs of the economy (South African History Online 2017).

The state should provide adequate shelter in the form of 'site and service' schemes to the poor and those who cannot afford formal housing. The Islamic Party held that the government should be tasked with providing housing to the less privileged and poor. Similarly, public hospitals should provide minimum but decent health services and facilities to the poor and those in informal settlements and rural areas. Regarding its economic policy, the Islamic Party proposed the freedom of the market system, private property rights and enterprise based on values such as stability, equality, efficiency and equity without exploitation and monopoly. The government should protect property rights, provide subsidies for the private sector, and materialise inclusive economic planning and administration initiatives that minimise unemployment and inflation but encourage equity and growth.

The party appealed to individuals who accumulated excessive wealth through unjustified apartheid ways 'to pay back the money' in the form of a negotiable general wealth tax which would in turn be used to finance healthcare and education systems, provide jobs, training programs and support entrepreneurship and small businesses. At the same time, the government was supposed to return the land to the people who were relocated due to the Group Areas Act 41 of 1950 and other apartheid policies: "people who were dispossessed because of group areas, homelands, etc should have their land returned where possible, otherwise fair compensation should be paid" (Mahida 1993:145). The Islamic Party believed that the government should be a welfare state which should eliminate inequality and poverty, prohibit extravagant consumption, abolish all laws which impede small businesses and informal economy, and make the labour and capital cooperate.

Finally, the economic policy of the Islamic Party upheld the necessary right of every citizen to join trade unions, the rights of workers to go on strike, and that an independent consumer-affairs department be instituted to protect consumers from opportunism and exploitation. The Islamic Party also included the need to protect the environment in its social policy by stating that "the protection of the environment should be balanced with development needs" (South African History Online 2017). Despite having appealing and broad objectives, the Islamic Party did not make many substantial achievements between 1990 and 1993. Although the party challenged the apartheid government on few occasions, its main success was the involvement of some of its leaders in the negotiation process with the NP government.

In 1994 under Abdullah Gamieldien as party leader and Sherif Mohamed as general chairperson, the Islamic party campaigned for the provincial elections in the Western Cape. The party continued to uphold its foundational objectives through its social, political and economic policies together with certain moral principles and Islamic values. In its 1994 campaigns, the party stressed Islamic values, concerns and ethos which were clear in its vision. For example, in 1994, the *Muslim Views* newspaper reported that the Islamic Party sought to promote the unity of the Muslim community in South Africa, establish the Islamic legal system and court, and expand its political influence in the country. As such, they thought of the Islamic Party as a forum which would give Muslims power as a religious community. The party leaders regarded their party as a way to "lobby on issues of concern to Muslims, and a means of projecting a strong Islamic code in the political, social and economic spheres" (Matthee (2008:193).

The leaders of the Islamic Party also thought of their party as being there to monitor legislation and how it affected people at the local level in the Western Cape. The moral aspect was so important to the party to the extent that it made its opposition against abortion, homosexuality and pornography apparent. Although it was meant to be a regional party, some of the issues that the Islamic Party addressed in its campaigns were national and broad. For example, the party leaders clearly stated that the Islamic Party sought to promote economic development in Western Cape and beyond. The party was ready to collaborate with other political parties in its promotion of an impartial and morally upright economic scheme, even as a coalition partner. In the 1994 General Election which took place between 26th and 29th April, the Islamic Party contested at a provincial level in

Western Cape. The Islamic Party did not contest in the National Assembly at the national level.

According to the results of the April 1994 Western Cape provincial legislature election, the NP polled 1 138 242 votes or 53.2 per cent of the voters (with 23 seats); the ANC obtained 705 576 votes or 33.0 per cent of the voters and the Democratic Party (DP) obtained 141 970 votes or 6.6 per cent of the voters (with 3 seats) (Election Resources on the Internet 1994). Moreover, the Freedom Front (FF-VF) obtained 44 003 votes or 2.1 per cent of the voters (with 1 seat); the African Christian Democratic Party (ACDP) obtained 25 731 votes or 1.2 per cent of the voters (with 1 seat); the PAC obtained 22,676 votes or 1.1 per cent of the voters and the AMP obtained 20 954 votes or 1.0 per cent of the voters (Election Resources on the Internet 1994). The Islamic Party obtained 16 762 votes or 0.8 per cent of the voters. However, like other parties such as the AMP, the PAC, the IFP and Wes-Kaap Federaliste Party (WKFP), it did not obtain any seat in the provincial legislature (Election Resources on the Internet 1994). The poor performance was partly due to poor organisation, lack of adequate support from Muslims and late registration in the election. Although it performed poorly, the votes it managed to get show that it had achieved substantial political influence, especially in the Western Cape.

The Africa Muslim Party

The AMP was formed in 1994 by Wasfie Hassiem, Gulam Sabdia, Abdullah Osman, Shaikh Rashaad, Shaukat Thokan, Sikander Mohammed and Shaikh Rashaad as founding members from Johannesburg, Pretoria and Cape Town. When the party was formed, Dr Imtiaz Suleman was elected as its national leader, with Abdullah Osman as the leader of the Council of Elders and Mr Gulam Sabdia as the National Chairman. The leaders of provincial executives formed the party's national executive or leadership. After its establishment, the party leadership did not emphasise that they were aiming at forming a government for South Africa, but that they hoped to contribute to the emerging democratic society.

While the central goals of the AMP were broad, the party's primary aim was to represent the interests of the Muslim community by ensuring that they were taken seriously in the decision-making process. From the start, the party leaders engaged in substantial dialogue with the Muslim population to gather support. However, in its publications and discourse, the party maintained its inclusivity by stressing that it catered for the interests of both Muslims and non-Muslim South Africans, especially in the promotion of morality. The party emphasised that it aimed at promoting good moral principles, working towards the eradication of hunger and poverty, and fostering a social setting in which various customs, languages and beliefs are not segregated. The AMP also sought to address the inequalities in the trading conditions, the challenges of corruption and nepotism, and to improve educational, healthcare and housing facilities, including the provision of free services to the disadvantaged and poor.

The AMP also promised that it would promote "adult education to increase literacy in the society and to promote small and medium size business and start up entrepreneurs in businesses that are beneficial to the majority of the people" (Straton 2014). Furthermore, the AMP affirmed that it would promote the understanding and tolerance of all people regardless of their cultural background, religion, race, ethnicity and so forth, and ensure that all traces of racism and bigotry were completely eradicated. Regarding the business sector, the AMP sought to promote new entrepreneurs, small business outlets and medium-sized businesses to the majority of the people. Since the giving of considerable powers to the people at the local level is essential, the party leaders argued for the devolution of powers from the national to the provincial and community levels.

The AMP favoured the decentralisation of power from the central government to the provinces and communities so that the minority Muslim community would maintain its own political space. Subsidiarity through the transference of maximum power to autonomous provinces and communities would make the people at the provincial and constituency level have absolute control over their resources and how their taxes would be used. The goals of the AMP were broad and divergent. Despite the broad party programme, the leaders maintained that the "Africa Muslim Party AMP's main motivation was and is to ensure that the interests of its constituents are well served and are well represented" (South African Promo Magazine 2009). Such a motivation was meant to bring all goals and aims of the party together under the slogan 'serving the people'.

One of the key motivations for the formation of the AMP was based on the conception that the Muslim community had power to influence politics in South Africa's democratic context. Thus, despite the emphasis of the party on being open to all people, it retained its Islamic element both in its discourse and in publications. Although the party intended to function nationwide, it generally confined itself to provinces such as the Western Cape with its considerable Muslim population. The African Muslim Party had more political influence than the Islamic Party both within and beyond the Muslim community. Historically, in its politics of mobilisation, the party has always tended to emphasise the Muslim identity in its attempt to gather support from the Muslim population. Thus, the party leaders often claimed that the AMP is well-established in most Muslim communities in South Africa.

In South Africa's 1994 National and Provincial Assembly elections, 19 parties registered. At this election, the AMP put forward about "60 candidates for the National Assembly and 25 for the Provincial Assembly" election (Straton 2014). In its campaigns, the AMP had a countrywide reach. According to the results of the 1994 election for the National Assembly, the ANC polled 12 237 655 votes or 62.65 per cent of the voters (with 252 seats), the NP obtained 3 983 690 votes or 20.39 per cent of the voters (with 82 seats), the FF-VF acquired 424 555 votes or 2.17 per cent of the voters (with 9 seats), the DP obtained 1.73 per cent of the votes or 338.426 of the voters, the PAC obtained 243 478 votes or 1.25 per cent of the voters (with 5 seats), and the ACDP obtained 88 104 votes or 0.45 per cent of the voters (with 2 seats) (Matthee 2008:195). A temporary electoral commission and not the current Electoral Commission of South Africa ran the 1994 election. While less than ten percent of whites (especially the Afrikaner-speaking whites) voted for black-majority parties, about ninety-four percent of black Africans voted for the ANC.

The AMP with its almost 85 candidates for the National Assembly and Provincial Councils did not obtain any seats at both levels. However, for the National Assembly, it gained 34 446 votes or 0.18 per cent of the voters out of which 15 446 of the votes came from the Western Cape alone (Matthee 2008:195). The AMP also won 1 235 votes from the Eastern Cape, 324 from the Orange Free State, 7 413 from Gauteng (Pretoria-Witwatersrand-Vereeniging), 6 790 from KwaZulu Natal, 437 from Northern Transvaal (Limpopo), 906 from Eastern Transvaal (Mpumalanga), 1 386 from North West Province and 320 from the Northern Cape (Hassan, R 2011:93). By contrast, for the election of the Provincial Councils, the AMP obtained 20 954 from Western Cape, 17 931 from KwaZulu Natal and 12 888 from Gauteng (Pretoria-Witwatersrand-Vereeniging) (Hassan 2011:93). The AMP also gained votes from other provinces; for example, 320 votes from Northern Cape, 1,386 votes from North West Province, 324 votes from the Orange Free State, and 906 votes from Eastern Transvaal or Northern Province (Mpumalanga and Northern Transvaal).

Although most voters who voted for the AMP were Muslim, most of the Muslim population voted for well-established parties especially the ANC in which several Muslim candidates contested and won seats in some cases. The AMP did not get the support it had anticipated from both the Muslim community and non-Muslims. The party leaders blamed the lack of adequate time to prepare, lack of support and unity as the main causes of the poor performance. Despite this, after the 1994 election the AMP did not attempt to strengthen the party by preparing sufficiently for the 1999 Western Cape provincial poll. When the AMP contested in 1999 at the provincial level in Western Cape, it only managed to obtain 4 333 votes or 0.22 per cent of the voters, without winning a single seat.

By contrast, the Democratic Alliance obtained 1 012 568 votes or 51.46 per cent of the voters (with 22 seats), the ANC obtained 620 918 votes or 31.55 per cent of the voters (with 14 seats), the Congress of the People obtained 152 356 votes or 7.74 per cent of the voters (with 3 seats) and the ACDP obtained 28 995 votes or 1.47 per cent of the voters (with 1 seat) (Electoral Commission of South Africa 2009:105). Apart from these parties, like the AMP other parties, which also contested the provincial election in the Western Cape, did not win any seats. The AMP performed badly due to both poor organisation, apathy and the fact that its religious-based politics affected its popularity as it continued to model its goals around Islamic values in the public sphere.

In 2000, under the leadership of Wasfie Hassiem, the AMP gained momentum and concentrated its campaign in the Cape Metropolitan Council area in which it sought to compete in the December 2000 election. However, its organisation and preparations were poor. It began its campaign late; party leaders and members rarely met for meetings in order to strategise for the election; in addition, the party failed to hold public meetings to mobilise the people. Furthermore, party members often communicated informally and had very limited media coverage. The AMP campaigned through posters, the circulation of pamphlets, and appearing on Muslim radio stations less than three weeks before the election date. For example, the party managed to campaign through the Voice of the Cape, a Muslim community Radio Station in Cape Town. Some AMP candidates had to campaign for themselves and could not rely on the AMP's campaigning team or its resources. Some of the official campaign statements of the party were centred on Islam and the projection of religious ethos in the public sphere.

One of the AMP's campaign posters asserted: "a vote for the AMP will give you a reward for here and the hereafter. If you vote for the ANC/DA and they give you gay rights, you share in the sin" (Matthee 2008:212). Some of the party's pamphlets comprised Quranic quotations centred on concepts such as human dignity, religious tolerance, justice, and harmony, absolute service to the people, compassion, mercy and racial harmony. For example, the party's pamphlet *AMP: Your Natural Home in the Western Cape* stated that "A Vote for the Africa Moral Party Is a Vote for: Peace & Freedom/Equality/Women's Rights/Racial Harmony/Religious Values/an End to Injustice" (Matthee 2008:212). Moreover, other messages of the party revolved around the party's disapproval of immorality, gambling, abortion, gay rights, drug abuse, prostitution and so forth.

In its 2000 campaigns, the party strongly appealed to the Muslim community by emphasising its respect for Islamic morality and values. For example, in his political campaign rhetoric, party leader Wasfie Hassiem showed that he was convinced that his party would promote the political aspirations of the Muslim community. Some members of the AMP were convinced that though a minority, the Muslim community had to seek representation from among members of their own religion. Such an emphasis on identity politics in the 2000 campaign indicates the AMP's politics of power on the part of its leaders and supporters. In the 2000 Cape Town Metropolitan Council election, the DA obtained 752 425 votes or 53.55 per cent of the voters (with 107 seats), the ANC won 540 753 votes or 38.49 per cent of the voters (with 77 seats), and the ACDP obtained 54 076 votes or 3.85 of the voters (with 8 seats). Furthermore, the United Democratic Movement obtained 20 329 votes or 1.45 of the voters (with 3 seats), the PAC obtained 6 402 votes or 0.46 of the voters (with 1 seat), the IFP obtained 3 935 votes or 0.28 per cent of the voters (with 1 seat), and the Middle Party acquired 3 857 votes or 0.27 of the voters (with 1 seat).

In the 2000 Cape Town Metropolitan Council election, the AMP came fifth with 14 589 votes or 1.04 per cent of the voters which translated to two seats on the city council. By winning two seats, the party demonstrated to have political influence in society. However, as in the 1994 election, most Muslims in the 2000 election voted for bigger political parties such as the DA and ANC, as opposed to the AMP, although it had a strong religious basis. Muslims in the Western Cape have always identified themselves with non-Muslims, which partly explains the poor performance of the AMP. In the early 2000s, the AMP entered into a coalition with the Democratic Alliance that later led to the appointment of AMP leader Badih Chaaban by the Municipal mayor Helen Zille. But when Badih Chaaban was involved in the corruption financial scandal in which he owed the City of Cape Town about R500 000 related to rates and rentals, he was subsequently expelled and lost his seat as municipal councillor.

After Badih Chaaban lost his councillorship and the AMP suspended him, he then co-founded the National People's Party (NPP) with David Sasman on 30th September 2007. The controversy that arose from the mayhem greatly weakened the position of the AMP in the Western Cape. When the AMP distanced itself from Chaaban, it described his action as contrary to the values of Islam and attributed his shady dealings and flaws to his personality. Another reason for the weakening of the AMP in the Western Cape may well be explained based on the fact that by 2000, there was also a considerable number of Muslims holding prominent positions in the bigger non-Islamic majority opposition parties who appealed to the Muslim population for votes. Despite the poor performance, the results of the 2000 election show that it had gained support by increasing its proportional vote and gaining two municipal seats.

After its participation in the 2000 election, the AMP developed a more secular political outlook to attract more non-Muslims and to gain influence that is more political. Mohamed Salih (2009:195) argues that while the AMP partly resisted endorsing Islamic theological considerations and values in its program, it strongly upheld more broad economic policy-directives such as:

> Local development, simulation of small enterprises, training skills for development, utilisation of Cape Town poverty alleviation, promotion of tourism in poor areas, support of growth initiatives that introduce innovation in environmental sustainability, spatial integration of first and second economies; renewal and regeneration of satellite economic models, and an increase and improvement of the social assets of the poor.

In 2009, the AMP contested the Provincial Legislature election of the Western Cape Province. According to the election results, the Democratic Alliance obtained 1 012 568 votes or 51.46 per cent of the voters (with 22 seats), the ANC won 620 918 votes or 31.55 per cent of the voters (with 14 seats), Congress of the People won 152 356 votes or 7.74 per cent of the voters (with 3 seats), ACDP obtained 28 995 votes or 1.47 per cent of the voters (with 1 seat), and the Independent Democrats obtained 92 116 votes or 4.68 per cent of the voters (with 2 seats). The AMP obtained 4 333 votes or 0. 22 per cent of the voters without any seat. The AMP also competed in the

2011 Western Cape Local Government Elections in which it gained a considerable number of votes and managed to win one seat.

When the AMP tried to contest in the 2016 Local Government Election in the Western Cape, it performed badly, worse than it had ever done in its history. In all provincial municipalities, wards and voting districts, it only managed to obtain 3 263 votes or 0.07 per cent of the total voters (Electoral Commission of South Africa 2016). By 2016, the AMP had lost all the three seats it had won during the 2000 and 2011 elections in the Western Cape. When it tried to contest in the 2016 Local Government Elections, it only won 3 263 votes or 0.1 per cent total votes from all provinces, municipalities, wards and voting districts. Since 2016, the party has been silent, its future blurred. Although the reasons for the steady decline of the AMP are manifold, some of which have already been discussed, Mohamed Salih (2009:195) attributes it to "the inability of the divided Muslim community to become a political force to reckon with". This has led to the formation of Al-Jama-ah, a more influential political party with a more broad and open political agenda. Although the AMP has become inactive, its ability to gain seats during elections and to form coalitions with other political parties shows that the party had substantial political influence in South Africa, especially in the Western Cape which has a larger number of Muslims.

Al-Jama-ah Political Party

The Al-Jama-ah Political Party was the third prominent Islamic party to be established in South Africa, with the head office in Pinelands, Cape Town. It has generally demonstrated a more stable and significant political influence in South Africa. It was registered as a political party on 20th April 2007 with the intention of attracting younger Muslims and contesting in the national and provincial elections. One of the key founding members of the Al-Jama-ah Political Party is Ganief Hendricks, former President of the Muslim Students Association of South Africa who also served as a municipal councillor in the City of Cape Town. Ganief Hendricks is also former First Deputy Chair of the IUC, Executive Committee Member of Majlisush Shura Al Islami (Muslim Parliament), First Chair of

Radio 786 Committee and has also served as General Secretary of the Workers against Regression Trade Union and Member Commission on Racism & Sexism – Transformation Forum. A closer look at Al-Jama-ah Political Party's historical evolution indicates that the party's popularity and influence has been increasing gradually.

Regarding the underlining reason for the establishment of the party, Al-Jama-ah firstly refers to the history of prominent South African Muslims who fought for freedom such as Sheikh Madura, the first renowned political prisoner on Robben Island due to his resistance against colonialism. Party leaders also acknowledge both Tuan Guru (1712-1807) and Shaykh Yusuf of Makassar (1626-1699) who, having been exiled to South Africa, continued to struggle against colonialism, racism and injustice in their respective eras. Similarly, several other Muslims, in their absolute sacrifice for freedom and justice, were detained and executed before and during apartheid. Former President Jacob Zuma stressed the same point in his address to Muslims at the Sultan Bahu Fete organised by the Muslim Sultan Bahu Centre in Mayfair, Johannesburg on 12th April 2009:

> Our struggle has also produced many outstanding and courageous leaders from the Muslim community who contributed meaningfully and sacrificed their lives so that our people could be free. Among the stalwarts of our struggle who were Muslims are heroes such as Dr. Yusuf Dadoo a close companion of Oliver Tambo and leader of the SACP for many years, Ahmed Kathrada who was imprisoned with Mandela during the Rivonia Trial, Ahmed Timol killed by the apartheid regime in prison. Other prominent Muslim leaders included Ismael Cachalia, Dr. Mohammed "Chota" Motala, Ebrahim Ismail Ebrahim, Fatima Meer, Dullar Omar and many others who contributed to make South Africa what it is today. We revere and honour these outstanding leaders of our people. They have equal claim to the successes that we have scored since 1994, when our country moved into an era of peace, freedom and democracy (African National Congress 2009).

For Al-Jama-ah leaders, the historical legacy of Islam in South Africa is the basis of Al-Jama-ah, "a legacy of struggle for peace, justice and freedom" (Al-Jama-ah 2009:1). Like their ancestors who have been historically active in the public sphere in fighting against colonialism, racism and inequality, Al-Jama-ah perceives itself as equally being committed to foster justice, equality and promotion of Muslim values and culture. Apart from its historical legacy, the leaders of Al-Jama-ah claim that the party was created due to the debacles of the AMP, both in terms of its poor performance in elections and uneven relations with the Democratic Alliance. Such a vacuum created apathy among Muslims and the need for a more stable political party that would put Islam on the political platform. In a *Fact Sheet* uploaded on its website in 2009, Al-Jama-ah affirmed:

> While contesting elections for 14 years the AMP failed to win a seat in parliament but in the 2006 local elections it won 3 seats in the Metro using its seats to help put the DA in power and Helen Zille as mayor later being expelled because of the debacles of Badih Chabaan…After these events the apathy in the Muslim community to take part in the political life of South Africa escalated and concerns were raised in many quarters that matter that Muslims will go underground to deal with their issues (Al-Jama-ah 2009:2-3).

Al-Jama-ah has presented itself as a political party that is a viable alternative, geared towards the creation of a government. Moreover, in some of its publications and rhetoric, Al-Jama-ah points to the openness of the democratic South Africa to give religious and non-religious institutions and organisations the freedom to represent themselves and their needs. Regarding why Al-Jama-ah was established, the party's website affirms:

> The Al Jama-ah Political Party was established in 2007 by its Party Leader, Ganief Hendricks, that instead of finger pointing, Muslims could play a sincere and positive role, contributing to the transformation of post-Apartheid South Africa, for the benefit of all South Africans. The Constitution of South Africa supports the system of a multi-party democracy, as opposed to a single party state. According to The African Peer Review Mechanism (APRM), domination of one political party in South Africa will be detrimental to freedom in South Africa. What is best for South Africa is a

diversity of political parties with competing policies (Al-Jama-ah 2019).

The founders of Al-Jama-ah perceived the need to form a political party that has the interests of Muslims at heart, especially the youth. The party's slogan 'Islam is the answer' conforms to its central aim of ensuring that Islam is represented in parliament, and that Shariah law is recognised. In its 2009 manifesto, Al-Jama-Ah emphasised the need for Muslims in South Africa to uphold religious freedom in the public sphere through the creating of constitutionally based religious rights with regards to:

> (1) Muslim Personal Law: Marriages, Family law, protection of Orphans and Children; (2) facilitation of supplementary Religious Education: Madrassas', HIV/AIDS and Abortion (3) better working conditions and wages for the Religious fraternity (Imams), (4) Mu'adhins and caretakers of the mosque; (5) establishment of a pension fund for the Religious fraternity (Imams), Mu'adhins and caretakers of the mosque, and (6) improved communication between the Muslim society and all peoples (Al-Jama-ah 2009:2)

Apparently, the party primarily aims at representing the needs and interests of the Muslim community in South Africa. This is clear in its emphasis on the need for the government's official approval of the Muslim Personal Law, improved working conditions for Muslim religious leaders by including *Imams* in the Basic Conditions of Employment Act and the maximum representation of Islam in the public sphere. Moreover, Al-Jama-ah seeks to persuade the government to repeal regulations that undermine the centrality of cultural and religious values in society, to the extent that it suggests the African value of "Ubuntu and religious teachings must be subjects in school and at work" (Salih 2009:197). Concerning the Islamic finance system, Al-Jama-Ah promises alternative banking systems for Muslims based on the economic system stipulated in the Quran and the practices of Prophet Muhammad.

Moreover, some of Al-Jama-Ah's objectives and goals present the party as part of the broader transnational Islamic network and movement. In its foreign policy, the party calls for the liberation of the people in Palestine based on the idea that the freedom South

Africans enjoy cannot be fully realised if some people are tormented by oppressive regimes. On that basis, Al-Jama-ah promises that it will:

> (1) Struggle for the liberation of Masjidul Aqsa in Palestine. Masjidul Aqsa is the first Qibla and the third holiest mosque of Muslims, (2) struggle for the self-determination of the Palestinians and the freedom from occupation of the Waqaf lands in broader Palestine, and (3) support the One State Solution in Palestine (Al-Jama-ah, 2009:4).

An analysis of such a policy leads one to affirm that Al-Jama-ah identifies itself with international Islamic organisations that call for the common cause of Muslims across the Islamic world. Apart from its emphasis on Muslim interests, the party also sought to address issues affecting South Africa as a whole. *Al-Jama-ah's* ability to address the issues and problems affecting South Africans such as poor service delivery and unemployment in general have enabled the party to have significant political influence in South Africa. Regarding the problem of unemployment and lack of opportunities, Al-Jama-Ah promises that it will make full employment a constitutional right and ensure that the Employment Equity Act 55 of 1998 is redressed to guarantee equal opportunities for all. The 2009 party manifesto affirms that a programme will be created which would ensure employment for first time school leavers; and that it would "secure 100 000 jobs in state-sheltered employment for sensory and physically disabled persons including cadres maimed by the apartheid regime inside and outside South Africa" (Al-Jama-ah 2009:2). For Al-Jama-Ah, full employment for all citizens including matriculants ought to be a constitutional right. The party promises to reform the legislation on employment so as to guarantee young people between sixteen and twenty-two years of age first time jobs "through accredited skills training, according to a ten-year development plan, leading to full employment in the country" (Al-Jama-ah 2009:2).

Based on its observation that the South African healthcare inadequately responds to the health needs of the elderly, vulnerable and disabled, Al-Jama-Ah promises to revisit the healthcare system so as to ensure that necessary attention is given to these groups rather than subjecting them to queues and long waiting hours. The terminally ill and those in extreme poverty and destitute will be treated freely, without medical aid. Regarding the education system, Al-Jama-Ah promises to ensure equal educational opportunities for all, devise lower Teacher-Learner ratio standards and give unbiased opportunities to all leaners in the representation of the country in world sport events. Moreover, the party seeks to make the criminal justice system more conducive so that the rehabilitation of offenders may be more effective. For example, instead of exposing non-violent and first-time offenders to harsh prison conditions which promote crime and violence, they can be rehabilitated by reintegration into civil society. In Al-Jama-Ah's domestic and broader economic policy, the party promises the elimination of poverty through various means; for example:

> Putting a strong case before the government for a guarantee for every family of an income above the poverty line, which it believes is R2 000 per month for a family of four. The wealth of the country must filter down to grassroots levels unlike present empowerment laws and codes, which keep the wealth among the elite (Salih 2009:197).

Al-Jama-ah reaffirms the right of all people to enjoy dignified lives to the extent that both government and society cannot overlook or ignore the vulnerable, refugees and people with disabilities. Similarly, the government should regulate staple food prices and bread so that all children have the right to basic needs, especially food. Finally, the party perceives a need to encourage women-owned businesses, interest-free loans, and viable enterprises for those living with disabilities. For Al-Jama-ah, the equal participation and opportunities in the access of natural resources and equality in the local and international exports of finished products is central in a democratic setting.

Although Al-Jama-ah has a particular emphasis on Muslim interests, it has continued to emphasise its inclusive nature by arguing that it seeks to represent all South Africans. The objectives of the party show that its 'inclusive' element is reflected in its emphasis on the need for the full employment, quality healthcare and equal opportunity to education for all South Africans. Such an attitude has helped the party to acquire political influence in society. Soon after the party was created, it formed a National Working Committee to commence on the campaigns in all provinces. *Al-Jama-ah* distributed flyers in mosques and had discussions with Islamic religious leaders throughout the country. Since its formation, Al-Jama-ah has tried to campaign and win votes from both Muslims and non-Muslims.

Al-Jama-ah's first major public appearance was in October 2008, when the party leaders filed a complaint to the Independent Communications Authority of South Africa (ICASA) on the Draft Regulations on Party Election Broadcasts, Political Advertising and Equitable Treatment. In the complaint, the party upheld the need for political parties to have equal advertising space on government media. In the April 2009 General Election, Al-Jama-ah contested in both the national and provincial elections. According to the election results of the National Assembly, the ANC obtained 11 650 748 votes or 65.90 per cent of the voters (with 264 seats), the Democratic Alliance obtained 2 945 829 votes or 16.66 per cent of the voters (with 67 seats), the Congress of the People obtained 1,311,027 votes or 7.42 per cent of the voters (with 30 seats), the IFP obtained 804 260 votes or 4.55 per cent of the voters (with 18 seats) and the Independent Democrats obtained 162 915 votes or 0.92 per cent of the voters (with 4 seats) (Election Resources on the Internet 2009).

Moreover, the United Democratic Movement obtained 149 680 votes or 0.85 per cent of the voters (with 4 seats), the FF-VF Plus obtained 146 796 votes or 0.83 per cent of the voters (with 4 seats), the ACDP obtained 142 658 votes or 0.81 per cent of the voters (with 3 seats) and the United Christian Democratic Party obtained 66 086 votes or 0.37 of the voters (with 2 seats). Four political parties; namely, the PAC, Minority Front, Azanian People's Organisation and the African People's Convention obtained one seat each. Al-Jama-ah obtained 25 947 votes or 0.15 per cent of the voters and managed to perform better than other political parties such as Christian Democratic Alliance, South African Democratic Congress and the Women Forward Party. Nevertheless, it did not manage to win a single seat at the national level. Closer analysis shows that 9 808 (37 per cent) votes came from Western Cape; 6 392 (25 per cent) votes came from Gauteng, and 6 392 (24 per cent) votes came from KwaZulu Natal.

The remaining 14 per cent of the voters came from other provinces such as North West, Eastern Cape and Mpumalanga. At the provincial level, the party also gained some votes. For example, in its two stronghold provinces it obtained 7 612 votes or 0.22 per cent of the voters in KwaZulu Natal and 9 039 votes or 0.46 per cent of the votes in Western Cape, totalling to 16 652 votes or 0.10 per cent of the voters in the two provinces alone. It performed more than three times better than the AMP which obtained a total of 4 333 or 0.03 per cent of the voters in the two provinces. In the 2011 municipal elections, Al-Jama-ah again contested in only two cities; namely Johannesburg and Cape Town. The party considered this election a huge victory since it managed to win two seats, one in Johannesburg under Abdul Razak Noorbhai and the other in the City of Cape Town under the party leader Ganief Hendricks.

In July 2011, Al-Jama-ah through Ganief Hendricks, its national leader and Sheikh Abduragiem Abderoef, its general secretary made a submission to the Portfolio Committee on Justice and Constitutional Development. In the submission, they proposed the need for a separate court to deal with Muslim marriage matters so that the Constitutional Court may stop hearing appeals on Muslim Marital Law. For example, the document proposed an amendment to clause 3, section 167(3)(b)(1) of the Constitution 17th Amendment Bill suggesting that it should read: "...and issues connected with decisions on constitutional matters excluding religious marriage doctrinal matters so that faith matters from the holy texts are not declared unconstitutional" (Parliamentary Monitoring Group 2011). Based on such attempts, Al-Jama-ah has been trying to get the support of established Muslim organisations and bodies in South Africa. For example, on 26th November 2011, party leader Ganief Hendricks met leaders of the Jamiatul Ulama – KwaZulu Natal (Council of Muslim Theologians) on the need for Muslims to support the party.

During the meeting, Al-Jama-ah "made a direct call for the Ulema to call on Muslims especially Muslim women voters to register to vote and to vote for the Party which is a national Muslim

Party with a national footprint" (Al-Jama-Ah 2011). The party leader shared with the KZN Jamiatul Ulama leaders its vision of representing Muslim interests, upholding the values of the Shariah law, and enacting policies that would benefit all people. In 2012, the party leaders proposed to the South African Human Rights Commission that the two official Islamic holidays; namely *Eid Al-Fitr* (Festival of Breaking Fast) and Eid Al-Adha (Festival of Sacrifice) be recognised as paid public holidays. Concerning the issue, the Al-Jama-ah website affirms:

> June 2012, Cllr. Ganief Hendricks proposed to the 'Rights Commission' that the two Eids be recognised, in accordance with legislation of the Public Holidays Act (Section 2.2), as paid public holidays. Many employers fail to implement Chapter 3 (Section 15.2B) of the Employment Equity Act (Act 55 of 1998), depriving employees of their basic labour rights, not granting them equal dignity in celebrating their respective religious and cultural holidays (Al-Jama-ah 2018).

After some campaigns, Al-Jama-ah contested the 2014 National and Provincial elections. According to the results, the ANC obtained 11 436 921 votes or 62.15 per cent of the voters (with 249 seats), the Democratic Alliance obtained 4 091 584 votes or 22.23 per cent of the votes (with 89 seats), and the Economic Freedom Fighters obtained 1 169 259 per cent votes or 6.35 per cent of the voters (with 25 seats). Moreover, the IFP obtained 441 854 votes or 2.40 per cent of the voters (with 10 seats) and the National Freedom Party obtained 288 742 votes or 1.57 per cent of the voters (with 6 seats). The United Democratic Movement and the FF-VF Plus each won four seats while the Congress of the People, ACDP and African Independent Congress won three seats each. Finally, Agang SA obtained two seats while PAC and African People's Convention obtained one seat each.

The election results indicate that Al-Jama-ah party fared quite well with 25 976 votes or 0.14 per cent of the voters at national level which demonstrated the party's popularity and a certain degree of political influence in the country. However, like other small parties such as the Minority Front and the United Christian Democratic Party, it did not obtain any seat nationally. As compared to the results of the 2009 General Election, Al-Jama-ah received less votes in the

2014 election. Al-Jama-ah also contested at a provincial level in some provinces such as the Western Cape where it performed quite well – it came fifth out of over 25 parties that contested. Based on the 2014 Western Cape Provincial election official results of the top four parties, the Democratic Alliance obtained 1 259 645 votes or 59.38 per cent of the voters (with 26 seats), the ANC obtained 697 664 votes or 32.89 per cent of the voters (with 14 seats), the Economic Freedom Fighters obtained 44 762 votes or 2.11 per cent of the voters (with one seat) while the ACDP obtained 21 696 votes or 1.02 per cent of the voters. In its fifth place, Al-Jama-ah obtained 13 182 votes or 0.62 per cent of the voters without winning any seat.

Despite the lack of substantial popular support and inability to win a seat at national and provincial levels, after the 2014 election results, the party made it clear that it had made significant success, given its limited resources. In the 2016 municipal election, the party contested in three provinces; Gauteng (greater Johannesburg municipality and Ekurhuleni municipality), Western Cape (Cape City Town municipality), and Kwazulu Natal (for example, Pietermaritzburg, Ethekwini and Estcourt municipalities). In its campaigns, the party tried to gather support from Muslims. In an interview with Radio Islam based in Johannesburg just before the 2016 elections, Party chairperson Abdul Razak Noorbhai asserted that "a Muslim voice from a Muslim-led party is best suited to have Muslim interests at heart", since non-Muslim political leaders seem to ignore the interests of Muslims in South Africa.

Moreover, the party appealed to non-Muslims for votes. In mid-2016 at the launch of its election manifesto for the 2016 municipal elections, party leader Ganief Hendricks claimed that the party had gained wide support from non-Muslims who perceive Al-Jama-ah with its Islamic ethos as a viable alternative. The party leader emphasised that the party was geared towards the transformation of society especially in the Western Cape where residents are neglected. In its 2016 campaigns, the party promised that it would ensure that municipal ward budgets would be put in place in Cape Town where only corporate budgets exist. According to the results of the 2016 Local Government Election from all provincial municipalities, wards and voting districts, Al-Jama-ah obtained 36 891 votes or 0.10 per cent of the voters out of a total vote cast of 39 236 786 (100 per cent) – out of which 718 803 were spoilt votes.

In the election, Al-Jama-ah managed to acquire 9 seats at the local municipal level: "six in KwaZulu Natal, one in Gauteng and two in the Western Cape" (Ebrahim 2019). The support obtained by the party in the election reaffirms its ability to gather support from both Muslims and non-Muslims, thereby pointing to its strong political influence in South Africa. Since 2016, the party perceives its vision beyond the parameters of the Islamic values. Based on the comments made by Suleman Dangor in a Muslim newspaper, Al-Jama-ah contends that:

> The support the Party got in the 2016 Municipal Elections shows that many voters outside the Muslim faith in looking for an alternative political Party to vote for place a premium on a leadership they can trust who come from a community that is very charitable and for whom alleviating poverty knows no religion (Al-Jama-Ah 2017).

According to Al-Jama-ah, while its vision still emphasises the need to represent the interests of Muslims, including fighting against moral issues such as alcohol and drug abuse, it treats the pressing issues being faced by non-Muslims with seriousness. For example, the party insists that it seeks to devise fresh and balanced means for service delivery, a transparent and more collaborative law-making process and new strategies to reduce the high poverty levels. In September 2017, the party leaders claimed that "Al-Jama-Ah is now a Party for all communities" and that "the days of an easy ride in politics just to promote Islamic values are over" (Al-Jama-Ah 2017). The party has affirmed that the nine councillors it obtained in the 2016 municipal elections, are inadequate for it to deliver. Consequently, the party aims at winning more seats in the 2021 municipal elections. According to Al-Jama-Ah's website, "the parallel focus is the 2021 LGE and it is within the reach of the Party to win 100 council seats in the 2000 municipalities. This will enhance the sustainability of the National Office" (Al-Jama-ah 2018). Al-Jama-Ah intends to contest in the 2019 National and Provincial election so as to win a seat in Parliament.

On 8 May 2019, general elections were held in South Africa, and Al-Jama-ah contested in both the National Assembly and Provincial Legislatures of some provinces. In the period leading to the election, Al-Jama-ah campaigned based on its manifesto which the party published on its website on 10 March 2019. The manifesto began by stressing that:.

> South Africa currently finds itself in the grip of poverty violence, economic instability, unemployment and corruption. The very moral fibre of our society is being eroded. Our people are crying out for fundamental change, but those pleas are falling on deaf ears. Al Jama-ah will position itself as the alternative to the bigger parties and will see to the needs of all sectors of society, not only an elite few. Our goal is to boost the institutions of democracy, so that the people of South Africa are enabled to proudly be active citizens of this country. Our democracy is being destroyed by corruption. We are greatly disturbed that the public protector budget is not adequate we will push for full funding, to address each and every case – so that we stop the corrupt and wealthy from getting richer, whilst the poor continue to suffer (Al-Jama-ah 2019).

Al-Jama-ah formulated its manifesto based on six major elements; namely, safety and security, youth participation, health, business development and entrepreneurship, sustainability and employment. Concerning safety and security, the party noted that inequality, violent crime, gangsterism and substance abuse continue to escalate in most South African communities. The party promised to address these issues by strengthening law enforcement agencies, police departments, curtailing substance abuse, supporting rehabilitation centres and lowering the crime rate. In its manifesto, the party also emphasised the need to involve youth in the political sphere. The party announced that it had been joined by the Congress of South African Students (COSAS) and Progressive Student Movement (PSM) which would help it to have a direct link with the youth and their challenges.

The party stressed the need for youth empowerment initiatives, employment, boosting the deteriorating education system and creating platforms for developmental skills. To ensure adequate political involvement of youth, Al-Jama-ah appointed Aisha Nontobeko Mkhwanazi, a 20-year-old second-year student from KwaZulu-Natal as the party's second candidate in their parliamentary candidate list. While reaffirming the need to integrate youth into the politics of the country, Al Jama-ah president, Ganief Hendricks hoped that as a black female Muslim, Aisha Nontobeko Mkhwanazi would appeal to the broader Muslim community and its youth. Ganief Hendricks stated that "young people may be politically active in their high school years but once they get into varsity, they lose interest in politics" (Okoye 2019).

Regarding health and business development Al-Jama-ah promised to "fight for a health service which provides its patients with proper care and treats them with dignity and compassion" and to boost entrepreneurship by co-ordinating "business development and entrepreneurial workshops all over the country, so that the dependency on pie in the sky jobs decreases and people are the masters of their own destiny" (Al-Jama-ah 2019). Concerning sustainability, the party manifesto emphasised its passion for a safe and sustainable country, the need for clean drinking water and the centrality of curtailing all forms of pollution. For example, the manifesto noted that "Our planet is precious and needs to be protected at all costs…We will lobby to save the environment, rivers and seas from chemical poisoning as well as protecting our waterways from sewage pollution" (Al-Jama-ah 2019).

Finally, Al Jama-ah stressed the need for the creation of employment opportunities through developmental programmes, construction, equipping people with basic business skills and the creation of accessible job advertising platforms. Although Al-Jama-ah's manifesto was inclusive and addressed the needs and aspirations of all South Africans, it stressed its primary aim to represent the needs of the Muslim community based on its slogan 'Deen first' and its claim that Al-Jama-ah was a Muslim party with Muslim leaders. Regarding its slogan ('Deen first'), the 2019 Al-Jama-ah's manifesto started:

> Is the moral compass which will guide us in the manner in which we conduct ourselves, and especially the decisions we take on your behalf? It is our commitment of honesty

and transparency in all that we do. It is not exclusive. Rather it is inclusive to all those who wish to build a South Africa on justice, fairness and a high moral fibre as its foundation. More importantly it indicates that we are proudly Muslim. In this democracy, it is something we will not be apologetic for. From Halaal to Hajj issues, there needs to be a party with the political will and Islamic ethos to take up the concerns of our members and our communities at the highest level. Al Jama-ah is a Muslim party – not just a party with Muslim leaders (Al-Jama-ah 2019).

Despite its emphasis on the Muslim interests and Islamic ethos, the party's manifesto stated that Al-Jama-ah members "believe in the hard-won democracy of our country and in no way want to move any sort of Islamic state" and that its leaders "have the expertise and the political will to take forth and lobby for issues which affect Muslims, and the communities we live in" (Al-Jama-ah 2019). Further, one of the party's campaign posters stated that "Al-Jama-ah is a people's party that will represent and reflect your activism and commitment towards justice, compassion, morality, upliftment and development of all South Africans. Vote Al-Jama-ah" (Al-Jama-ah 2019). In the 2019 general election at the national level, there were 26,779,025 registered voters out of which 17,671,615 cast their votes thereby representing a 66.05 % voter turnout.

According to the election results of the top four at a national level, the ANC obtained 10 026 475 votes or 57.50 per cent of the voters (with 230 seats), the Democratic Alliance obtained 3 621 188 votes or 20.77 per cent of the voters (with 84 seats), Economic Freedom Front obtained 1 881 521 votes or 10.79 per cent of the voters (with 44 seats), Inkatha Freedom Party obtained 588 839 votes or 3.38 per cent of the voters (with 14 seats) (Electoral Institute for Sustainable Democracy in Africa 2019). Moreover, Vryheidsfront Plus obtained 414 864 votes or 2.38 per cent of the voters (with 10 seats), the African Christian Democratic Party obtained 146 262 votes or 0.84 of the voters (with 4 seats) and the United Democratic Movement obtained 78 030 of the votes or 0.45 per cent of the voters (with 2 seats).

In this election, Al-Jama-ah secured the 14th place at the national level having obtained 31 468 votes or 0.18 per cent of the voters with 1 parliamentary seat under its founder and leader, Ganief Hendricks. At the provincial legislature level, Al-Jama-ah managed to receive some votes especially in Eastern Cape (3 007 votes or 0.15 % of the voters), Gauteng (7 606 votes or 0.18 % of the voters), KwaZulu-Natal (9 899 votes or 0.28 % of the voters) and Western Cape (17 607 votes or 0.86 %). In the Western Cape Provincial Legislature, Al-Jama-ah managed to win one seat. This means that in the 2019 general election, Al-Jama-ah secured one seat in the National Assembly and one seat in the Western Cape Legislature which can be regarded as a major success in the political aspirations of the party. After winning the parliamentary seat, Ganief Hendricks told *Daily Maverick* that the Muslim population has often been ignored in politics: "Muslims don't have a voice. Our marriages are not recognised, our children, when they're born, are illegitimate and when you die your death certificate says, 'never married'" (Mafolo 2019). Ganief Hendricks also lamented that Muslim people's rights had not been prioritised by Muslim lawmakers in Parliament:

> They [Muslim parliamentarians] toe the party line, they didn't want to be seen to be pushing the Muslim agenda. We're talking about personal law rights, we're not talking about the other big stuff, like the Sharia which is the criminal law of Islam (Mafolo 2019).

The success of the party in the 2019 general election can be attributed to four major reasons: the gentrification of the Bo-Kaap area, the inclusivity of Al-Jama-ah's manifesto which most likely attracted some non-Muslim votes, the party's strong appeal to the Muslim community, and its strong and broad campaign networks. Firstly, Al-Jama-ah gained votes in the Bo-Kaap because some residents who traditionally voted for the Democratic Alliance 'punished' the party for the gentrification of the Bo-Kaap where houses were being purchased by wealthy families some from outside the country thereby changing the entire character of the area. Formerly known as the 'Malay Quarter,' Bo-Kaap is an old neighbourhood that has, to a greater extent, remained a historical and cultural centre for Malay Muslims or Cape Malays, a group that partly introduced Islam in the country.

Based on the cultural and historical significance of the Bo-Kaap, attempts have been made by residents to have the place declared a heritage area. In November 2018, the Muslim Judicial Council issued a statement affirming that "years of pleas to declare Bo-Kaap a heritage site has fallen on deaf ears. It is for this reason that the residents have decided to peacefully protest...against gentrification in the area" (Gerber 2018). This statement is based on the fact that there have been attempts geared towards the redevelopment, rejuvenation and gentrification of the Bo-Kaap, which might affect the cultural significance of the area and also lead to the displacement of some poor residents:

> The Bo-Kaap is an older inner-city, working-class neighbourhood in Cape Town, South Africa. ...The area with its colourful housing units and 11 mosques is part of Cape Town's cultural heritage and a very important tourist attraction. As in the case of De Waterkant, a gentrified neighbourhood adjacent to it, the area has seen a large number of housing units renovated and upgraded. Property prices have increased dramatically, although they are still relatively low, while the number of properties sold is also on the rise – so much so that the community leaders and especially the Muslim residents are in a constant battle to preserve the neighbourhood's cultural identity (Kotze 2013:124).

Some Muslims in the Bro-Kaap voted for Al-Jama-ah since the DA had failed to address the gentrification problem in the area. For example, some residents claimed that the DA in the Western Cape had not been ardent at enabling the area to be recognised and conserved as a unique historical and cultural place where the process of gentrification should not occur. On that basis, the vote for Al-Jama-ah in the Bro-Kaap was partly motivated by politics rather than the Muslim party itself.

Secondly, the party in the period prior to the 2019 general election managed to appeal to both Muslims and non-Muslims by emphasising on the challenges and problems such as employment, healthcare and poor water and sanitation facing all South Africans. Although the party integrated an Islamic ethos in its manifesto, it nevertheless emphasised the needs and contextual problems facing the country and its ability to offer a solution. The party also emphasised that "voting for Al Jama-ah doesn't necessarily mean endorsing Muslims only to take up political positions" but that "the party is open to qualifying anyone participating in political decision-making provided that they are members of the party" (Ebrahim 2019). Since most key leadership positions were occupied by Muslims, this presented a challenge to the party's goal in integrating non-Muslim into its hierarchy.

Thirdly, the party appealed to the Muslim population for support by emphasising its ability to prioritise the needs of the Muslim community which are not being addressed by broader non-Muslim political parties such as ANC, EFF and IFP. Based on the 2013 General Household Survey on the South African religious demography, out of the 1 042 043 Muslims in South Africa (2.0 % of the total population), the majority of the Muslim population is concentrated in the Western Cape, followed by KwaZulu-Natal and thirdly by Gauteng province. This explains why the majority of the votes which the party obtained came from Western Cape which consists of a substantial number of Muslims thereby enabling the party to gain one seat in the Legislature of the same province.

Shortly before the 2019 general election, Abubakr Thapelo Amad, one of Al-Jama-ah's councillors in the City of Johannesburg, noted that although the party is inclusive, it is at the same time faith-based: "We are an inclusive political organisation which is founded on the basic fundamentals of Islam and Ubuntu… there are certain disciplines of Shariah that can be adapted for this country to move forward" (Ebrahim 2019). Similarly, in the 2019 general election aftermath, Ganief Hendricks commended the fact that most votes came from Western Cape Province where the party was formed:

> I was very happy (because) most of our votes came from Lansdowne. The place where we started the party and launched the party. They were the founding members…So, for 12 years they stuck with us and the only way you can measure that is by their vote (Mafolo 2019).

The party's advocacy of the principles of shariah law and attempts to present the Muslim interests such as constitutional and religious rights of Muslims enabled it to gain some votes among Muslims especially in places where Muslims are a majority. Finally, in its campaigns, Al-Jama-ah used various platforms and networks in an attempt to gather broader support for the 2019 general election. Apart from its website and the usual platforms such as newsletters, posters and Muslim radio stations, Al-Jama-ah made use of informal social networks:

> Al Jama-ah may have started out in the Western Cape, but the party was able to replicate its support in other provinces and communities with its focus on the religious and constitutional rights of Muslims. Its appeal to a subset of South African Muslims is analogous to the ACDP's prioritisation of religious Christians... Al Jama-ah benefited from communal and cultural networks. It was able to campaign through closed WhatsApp and Facebook groups affiliated to religious communities. These networks allowed the party to market its message directly to potential voters – at a fraction of the cost of traditional advertising and campaigning. In a crowded election market, it is critical for smaller parties to cut through the noise and appeal to their markets. It's also a huge advantage to be associated with informal social networks where there's a high level of trust and credibility that comes from being within the ground (Berkowitz 2019).

Based on its campaign strategies Al Jama-ah has created an important roadmap and framework for "any party that would be a contender on the national or provincial stage: First, identify your base. Ideally, it's urban, closely knit, and aligned to your party's values. Second, contact your base directly through informal, communal networks" (Berkowitz 2019). Therefore, the ability to uphold a manifesto that creates a balance between the needs of the Muslim population in the country and the general aspirations facing all South Africans such as employment and healthcare based on strong campaign strategies and networks enabled Al-Jama-ah to gain support in the 2019 general election. If the party is to continue with the same campaign strategies and trends, it will be able to provide a Muslim voice in the political landscape of the country, and consequently, maintain political influence in its strongholds.

Support for Islamic political parties

As shown, Islamic political parties have been to some extent successful due to their ability to acquire seats and a substantial number of votes during elections. The success of Muslim political parties in gathering support from Muslims and non-Muslims and to win seats has enabled them to have political influence in South Africa. Nevertheless, the attempt by Islamic political parties to focus on the issues that solely affect the Muslim community such as Muslim Personal Law has partly contributed to their poor performance during elections. In that way, most South Africans prefer to vote for non-Muslim political parties that represent the interests and aspirations of everyone rather than a specific community of faith.

Despite their poor campaign strategies and lack of resources, Islamic parties have generally concentrated their campaigns in provinces with greater Muslim populations. This partly explains why almost all Muslim political parties were founded in the Western Cape. In virtually all election results in which the AMP and the Al-Jama-ah have contested nationally, the highest number of votes has always come from Muslim majority provinces. Some of these political parties engaged in discussions with Islamic bodies, organisations, religious leaders and the local Muslims in their attempts to gain support. All three Islamic parties have at some point campaigned or attempted to campaign through Muslim community radio stations, mosques and some Muslim gatherings. This strategy is still being employed by Al-Jama-ah, the major Islamic political party today. Muslim political parties have also used the fact that they support Muslim values to gain Muslim support.

The voting patterns from all elections in which the three political parties have participated indicates that most people who voted for them are from provinces that have the larger Muslim populations. Clearly, the geographical distribution of the votes already shown indicates that most voters who voted for Al-Jama-ah in the 2004, 2009, 2016 and 2019 elections are Muslim. Like the Islamic party and the AMP, Al-Jama-ah relies on the Muslim population as its support base. For example, these political parties have confined themselves to provinces with the highest Muslim populations such as KwaZulu Natal, Gauteng and Western Cape. Clearly, all elections in which Islamic parties have contested at the national or provincial levels, the highest number of votes have come from those three provinces. For example, based on the results of the 2009 General Election in which Al-Jama-ah contested in almost all provinces, 37 per cent of its votes came from Western Cape, 25 per cent of its votes came from Gauteng and 24 per cent of its votes came KwaZulu Natal. It is interesting to note that both the Northern Cape and Free State which have the smallest Muslim populations only obtained 2 per cent of the votes for Al-Jama-ah. Similarly, in the 2019 general election, the majority of Al-Jama-ah's votes came from provinces such as Gauteng, KwaZulu-Natal and Western Cape where most Muslims are concentrated.

Although the majority of South Africans who support and vote for Islamic parties are Muslim, most Muslims do not actually vote or support these parties. The strategy of Muslim political parties to uphold the Islamic identity to mobilise popular support and win votes from Muslims has not produced much results. This is because most Muslims do not find the idea of having exclusively Islamic political parties appealing in a democratic South Africa (Hassan 2011). By emphasising on Muslim values and interests in their political discourse, Islamic political parties have employed identity politics. Identity politics refers to a politically motivated group, institution or organisation within society whose political participation is based on self-interests or exclusively religious, cultural or racial convictions.

Such an understanding resonates with Christina Späti's (2016:6) conception of the notion as "a struggle over the qualities attributed, socially and institutionally, to individuals and groupings of individuals." Thus, identity politics involves notions such as recognition, misrecognition, exclusion and inclusion. While identity politics may be based on race, religion, gender or ethnicity, in some cases it arises when a statistically minority or segregated group seeks to voice out or project its values or ethos in the broader society. One may question whether the particular 'needs' and 'interests' of Muslims which Islamic political parties claim to address are not being considered or addressed by non-Muslim majority political parties.

The *Al-Qalam* newspaper in 2007 featured an article by Manjra which described the formation of Islamic parties as "a betrayal to the secular democracy" since this "would contribute to isolate Muslims instead of getting them to be involved more actively in the broader debates and questions" (Hassan 2011:88). On that basis, the formation of Islamic parties hinders Muslims from engaging with the broader society on general key issues such as the eradication of poverty, economic and political transformation. Yusuf Dhala, a member of the Islamic Da'wa Movement in his interview with Hassan Rasnia, expressed the same idea and stated that "the manifesto they used was more on the *imams* and things like that. The whole country is not a Muslim country. If I go to campaign and started to talk about *imams* and *zakat*, people won't understand" (Hassan 2011:91). Clearly, some Muslims perceive the founding of Islamic political parties with their emphasis on Muslim identity as irrelevant and irreconcilable with the principles of democracy. Moreover, other concerns from Muslims relate to the viability and practicality of religious political parties. For example, in 2008, Inayet Said, one of Rania Hassan's interviewee, stated:

> You are a minority, you created an exclusive club by having and creating a Muslim party, you'll have very few people who would support a Muslim party, and at the end of the day when you are talking about politics, it is numbers that count (Hassan 2011:91).

It appears that religious-based political parties have not been viable in the democratic South Africa due to limited support. Moreover, some Muslims do not know that Islamic political parties actually exist. Among other reasons, some of these parties such as the AMP have not been engaging in serious campaigning and the organising of public meetings to gather support and publicise themselves. Generally, this is due to the lack of resources, lack of good leadership networks and organisation. For example, the attempts that have been made by some Islamic parties to campaign through Muslim community radio stations such as Voice of the Cape (Cape Town) and Radio Islam (Johannesburg) have not produced tangible results because some Muslims do not actually listen to these radio stations. This contradicts the claims by some leaders of Muslim political parties that they have a wide support from Muslim communities.

However, Muslim political parties have sometimes expressed themselves and their goals as broad and inclusive to attract the votes of Muslims and non-Muslims. Islamic parties have partly presented themselves as being open to all people, and some of their goals testify to this fact. Theoretically, this points to their commitment to the democratic value of political participation and inclusiveness. For example, when the Islamic Party was formed, it claimed that it was "open to all South Africans, irrespective of religious affiliation" (Mahida 1993:143), which was apparent in the party's inclusive political, economic and social policies. The AMP also emphasised the same idea, by including issues such as better education, housing, health services and improving the economy for all.

Similarly, Al-Jama-ah, the most open of all Muslim political parties in South Africa, also upholds the same inclusive conception. Nevertheless, I have already substantiated the idea that these parties primarily uphold Islamic principles. The fact that these parties seek to base their goals on Islamic values or to project religious ideologies in the public sphere instead of exclusively addressing the needs and challenges of the society at large has substantially affected their ability to gain support from both Muslims and non-Muslims. At the same time, this makes one question the extent to which Muslim political parties are actually inclusive.

Some Muslims who have not been supportive of Islamic political parties have actually been voting for non-Muslim political parties for two reasons. Firstly, some non-Muslim political parties have inclusive and broad objectives and goals that shy away from identity politics; and secondly, Muslims are well represented in larger and broader non-Muslim parties. For example, several Muslims hold key government positions both at local and national levels. Muslim individuals such as Essop Pahad, Mawlana Cachalia and Mosy Moolla supported the ANC by committing themselves to the broader struggle for all South Africans, rather than the limited interests of their own faith community.

Rather than aligning themselves with Islamic parties that promote Muslim interests, most Muslims have opted to support and vote for non-Muslim political parties. Following Rania Hassan, the same opinion was expressed by the MJC, which stated that "since many political parties stood for broad principles which Muslims were in agreement with, there was no reason why Muslims could not vote for non-Muslim parties" (Hassan 2011:100). Major political parties such as the ANC have historically worked hard at winning Muslim votes. Apart from having inclusive goals and ideas, they also seek to address the needs of particular communities. Khan gives two explanations that were cited by Lubna Nadvi concerning the reason why the ANC managed to gain considerable votes in the 2004 General Election from Chatsworth and Phoenix, the Indian Muslim majority townships in KwaZulu Natal:

> The ANC got the Muslim vote because they had the support of the Muslim leaders. Some of them took out newspaper advertisements calling on Muslims to vote ANC. The second major factor for the Muslim vote going to the ANC could be related to the conflict in the Middle East. The DA has no clear-cut policy, and this convinced many Muslims to vote ANC (Khan 2004).

Without attempting to generalise Lubna Nadvi's position, most non-Muslim political parties in South Africa have tried to express goals that exhibit the values of the democratic society that are not based on race, ethnic group, religious convictions or the interests of a particular group. In other words, most people today do not vote based on racial grounds or religious affiliation but based on the policies of a particular political party and its ability to deliver. In the post-apartheid period, the pluralistic and democratic nature of the country has made it difficult for identity politics to be successful. Even the most religious and traditional people perceive issues from a broader and open perspective, rather than from a limited, racial or religious angle. Such reasons explain why the number of Muslims who vote for non-Muslim political parties is far bigger than those who either support or actually vote for Islamic political parties.

Identity and Islamic Political Parties

South African Muslim political parties have all emphasised the centrality of an Islamic ethos and principles in their campaigns and manifestos. Although this has resulted in these parties receiving support in some cases, the same factor has negatively affected their election performance. In most cases, Muslims and non-Muslims have opted to support political parties which are primarily inclusive and clearly address the needs of all South Africans, rather than the interests of a specific faith community, ethnic group or race. A general examination of the manifestos and goals of the three Islamic parties carried out in section three indicates that they all emphasise the centrality of Islamic identity through identity politics in their political discourse. Muslim political parties in South Africa have employed identity politics in two ways; firstly, by trying to project Islamic values in the public sphere, and secondly, by using identity politics to win the support of the Muslim population.

All three Muslim political parties; namely, Islamic Party, Africa Muslim Party and *Al-Jama-Ah* have advocated Muslim interests and identity in their objectives and aims. Some Islamic parties have openly claimed that Muslims in South Africa should not vote for non-Islamic parties since Muslims as a minority and marginalised group ought to be represented by Muslims. Primarily, the goals and objectives of virtually all Muslim political parties that have been formed in South Africa have emphasised the interests of the Muslim community. As discussed in the third section, when the Islamic Party and the Africa Muslim Party were formed, their manifestos were simply a reproduction of the Islamic religious texts elaborated by slogans such as 'the Quran is our constitution'. The parties also sought to address the specific needs of the Muslim community as reflected in their campaign discourse and statements which even claimed that voters would be rewarded in the afterlife if they voted for Islamic parties. The mission statement of *Al-Jama-Ah* primarily advocates the need for the freedom of Muslims to practise their religion to the extent of having a constitutionally approved Muslim Personal Law which would regulate marriage and family issues based on the principles of Shariah law, without the interference of the secular legal system.

The main principles of the Islamic Party were rooted in the ideology of Islam so much so that it even proposed total independence of the Islamic judicial system, media, and educational institutions by being fully regulated by a religious moral policy. The Africa Muslim Party promised to ensure that Muslim interests are thoroughly addressed in the government's decision-making structure. The emphasis on the need to represent Muslim interests indicates the desire of these political parties, or at least some of their leaders and supporters, to influence society. In this case, identity politics exhibits elements of the politics of power in which some Muslims in South Africa are believed to have the ability to either influence society with religious values or that they must be constitutionally allowed to exercise such values outside of the general legal system.

Al-Jama-ah, for example, has often argued for the need of a separate Muslim court to deal with Muslim family law issues. A key question is whether the party's emphasis on Muslim identity and its attempt to present the aspirations of Muslims in South Africa have enabled it to gather the support of Muslims. Apparently, such an approach has partly caused the political party to receive limited support. One of the reasons why Islamic parties have lacked support can be attributed to their emphasis on Islamic values and identity and the fact that some Muslims prefer to vote for established political parties such as ANC, DA and EFF. From this perspective the objectives and goals of Muslim parties are rooted in the Islamic faith, and virtually all key leaders have been Muslim. It is for this, among other reasons, that Muslims and non-Muslims have preferred to vote for the mainstream political parties such as DA, ANC and EFF instead of voting for Islamic parties which seem to set Muslims apart from other South Africans. Suleman Dangor makes a vital contrast between Islamic parties which claim to represent Muslim interests and anti-apartheid Muslim individuals who embraced a broader political outlook:

> If we contrast this development with Muslim involvement in politics five decades earlier, we find individuals such as Dr Yusuf Dadoo, Mawlana Cachalia, Ahmed Kathrada, Essop Pahad, Mosy Moolla and others had committed themselves to the ideas and goals of the African National Congress (ANC) and did not concern themselves only with their specific faith

community. They were committed to struggle with and on behalf of the majority disenfranchised South Africans. The Muslim parties, in contrast, perceived as their primary function the promotion of Muslim interests. Interestingly, though, the majority of Muslims opted to join and/or vote for the well-established political parties (Dangor 2009:118).

Clearly, the rhetoric of 'Muslims voting for Muslims' has not been appealing to average Muslims in the country. In contemporary South African society with its emphasis on pluralism and unity, the notion of 'Islamic political parties' isolates the Muslim community from the broader and more inclusive political landscape. This has contributed to the lack of progress in political engagement and in winning the support of the Muslim voters. One might question why the interests and needs of the Muslim community which Muslim political parties claim to represent cannot be considered as part of the aspirations of all South Africans. One of the reasons is that non-Muslims don't share them. The attempt to gather support to form a common Islamic identity by encouraging Muslims throughout South Africa to vote for Islamic parties based on the Muslim label has been problematic. Although democracy permits religious-based parties, such parties are unlikely to succeed in pluralistic and non-theocratic states like South Africa given that they often represent the interests of a more limited group rather than the aspirations of all citizens.

While that might be the case, from the perspective of political participation, Muslim political parties are not a betrayal of democracy, but an important aspect that promotes the democratisation process and political transformation of the country. The South African model of religion and state which is based on the principle of separation with interaction supports the active participation of religious organisations in the public sphere. (Mutelo 2021:26). Above all, the mere presence of Muslim political parties demonstrates the interest of Muslims in South Africa's politics. Further, the fact that Muslim political parties such as *Al-Jama-Ah* affirm that they are inclusive and address challenges that every South African encounter such as poverty, unemployment and poor service delivery indicate they are a credible alternative to the ANC-government. Such an argument explains why a few Muslims still vote for Muslim parties as shown by the election result statistics in the third section. The lack of support and poor performance during elections show that the insistence on Islamic identity has not helped Muslim political parties to grow.

Muslim Judicial Council of South Africa

As one of the major Muslim organisations claiming to represent the majority of Muslims in South Africa, the political involvement of the MJC in the country is important. Although during the early phase of its existence the organisation was generally apolitical and silent on public issues; the 1980s witnessed the resurgence of the MJC as an influential religious organisation in the public sphere through its involvement in the political struggle against apartheid. The organisation distributed pamphlets, released statements, made declarations, organised public meetings, participated in anti-apartheid rallies, and supported anti-apartheid liberation movements such as the UDF. Some of the key members of the MJC such as Sheikh Abubakr Najjar, Ali Gierdien, Gassan Solomon, Imam Abdullah Haron, and Sheikh Nazeem Mohamed were personally prominent anti-apartheid activists. In the post-apartheid South Africa, the organisation has continued to occasionally participate in political issues although it has tended to focus on issues affecting Muslims.

Establishment of the Muslim Judicial Council SA

The MJC was established as a Muslim Faith-Based Organisation in 1945 in Cape Town, Western Cape. The MJC's (2022) website claims that the organisation has since remained "one of the oldest, most representative and most influential religious organisations in South Africa and enjoys local, national and international credibility". The MJC was formed out of the need to create a Muslim representative body comprising of Muslim religious scholars (*ālims*) and religious leaders (*imāms*) primarily responsible for regulating Islamic judicial and religious matters in the Western Cape. Before the formation of the MJC, individual Muslim religious scholars and religious leaders often regulated religious matters for their own congregations and constituencies. For example, there were influential *imāms* whose authority on the interpretation of Islamic religious issues was limited to their congregations or individual mosques.

Although most Muslim scholars in South Africa have been graduates of local and international Islamic institutions, most of them follow the *Ḥanafī* and the *Shafī* Islamic Schools of Law. Dawood Terblanche (2015:27) asserts that differences in "religious thoughts were often debated in a public platform where these *'ulamā'* presented their divergent points of view on religious practices and interpretation of doctrine". Although such debates were important because they gave Muslim scholars the latitude to share views and enrich each other about various religious issues, there was a need for a representative body that would act as a central authority in regulating such issues. The aim of establishing the MJC comprising of Muslim religious scholars of diverse educational backgrounds was to bring unity of opinion on major Islamic issues:

> The primary reason for the MJC's establishment in 1945 was as a body that would bring together the 'ulama of Cape Town as they went about addressing issues of mutual concern and seeing to the religious needs of their community. In fact, the MJC still sees itself as a 'bay-tul 'ulama' – a home for all *'ulama'* (Rafudeen 2013:152).

The proposal of forming a Muslim representative body was initiated by Dr Abdurahman Abrahams and other members of the Muslim Progressive Society, an organisation that focused on issues relating to welfare and social relief in Cape Town. Most members of the Muslim Progressive Society were convinced that the establishment of a representative Islamic religious body would unite Muslim religious scholars who would speak authoritatively on judicial issues on behalf of the Muslim community. Thus, a substantial number of senior Muslim religious scholars and members of the Muslim Progressive Society initiated discussions regarding the possibility of forming a judicial council with clear religious principles and goals. The inaugural meeting, at which the leadership of the council was elected, was open to all Muslim religious scholars in Western Cape. It took place on 10 February 1945 with 62 founding members during which the MJC was officially established. The gathering elected an Executive Committee of 18 people with Sheikh Mohammad Shakier Gamieldien as its chairperson. Important attendees at the meeting included Sheikh Muawiyyah Sedick, Sheikh Mogamat Salih (Abadie) Solomons and Imām Noor Hassiem.

Among the primary aims and objectives of the MJC were "to consolidate and strengthen the spirit of unity amongst the *ulamā*" and also "to strive and attain the spiritual, educational, intellectual, moral, social, cultural and economic aspirations of the Muslim community" (Mahida 1993:67). Thus, the MJC perceived itself as a body that would provide rulings on religious matters and guidance to Muslims in the Western Cape. It adopted a ten-point programme which has continued to be its hallmark. A feature of the programme was to engage in dialogue with the government. The MJC was also to introduce uniformity in Islamic educational institutions, monitor the educational methodologies, encourage the publication of Islamic literature, support religious education and represent the interests of the Muslim community in South Africa to the government. The aim of producing and distributing Islamic literature in South Africa was to strengthen Islamic identity through certain guiding laws and principles.

Muslim Judicial Council during Apartheid

During the first two decades of its existence, the MJC generally did not comment on public matters but focused on issues affecting Muslims in Western Cape. However, there were individuals within the MJC such as Sheikh Abubkr Najjar, Ali Gierdien and Imam Abdullah Haron who explicitly expressed opposition against apartheid during this early period of the organisation's existence. According to Ursula Günther (2004:120), in an interview on 17 July 2000 in Cape Town, Ali Gierdien remarked that the MJC and the Muslim community in South Africa were:

> Scared of the government ....Where Haron, like myself, we were outspoken people. We were associated even with the Black Sash and people like that. [...] By and large, the Muslim

community was very reticent and very a-political at some stage. [...] That time we were very annoyed with the leadership of the MJC because they were, the majority at that time, the older guard, they were apolitical...they would be friends with the Coloured Advisory Council, and the Coloured Affairs Department and things like that.

Although the MJC remained passive and politically distanced in the first twenty years of its existence, this changed in the 1960s due to political upheavals. The 1960s witnessed the Sharpeville massacre which involved the killing and wounding of several protesters, the banning of political organisations and imprisonment and detention of various leaders of liberation movements. The Sharpeville massacre on 21 March 1960 was followed by various political disturbances such as the banning of political organisations and liberation movements such as the African National Congress and the imposition of other draconian legislations such as the 90 Day Detention Act. Already existing apartheid laws such as the Group Areas Act of 1950, the Group Areas Development Act of 1955, the Natives Resettlement Act of 1954, the Unlawful Organisations Act of 1960 and the Industrial Conciliation Act of 1956 intensified the situation. Given such political changes, many Muslim scholars and religious leaders in Western Cape began to emphasise the need for Muslims to be more active in the struggle for liberation.

Based on the political changes, the MJC issued a statement in March 1961 declaring that 'Islam could not condone apartheid', and active propagation of Islam began in the locations. The declaration known as the *Call of Islam Declaration* was drawn up and issued by the MJC together with other Muslim organisations in Western Cape such as the Claremont Youth Association and the Cape Town MYM. Not all members of the MJC supported the declaration as they perceived it as being too political. The statement challenged apartheid legislation:

> For too long a time now we have been, together with our fellow-sufferers, subjugated, suffered the humiliation of being regarded as inferior beings, deprived of our basic rights to earn, to learn and to worship according to the Divine Rule of Allah. We can no longer tolerate further encroachment on these, our basic rights, and therefore we stand firm with our

brothers in fighting the evil monster that is about to devour us – that is oppression, tyranny and *basskap* (supremacy) (Meiring 2005:163).

The declaration was a direct attack against apartheid legislation which strived to racially separate people in almost all spheres of life. The *Call of Islam Declaration* openly opposed apartheid segregationist laws concerning job reservation, population registration, detention without trial, pass laws and unjust economic policies. On 7 May 1961 in Cape Town, just two months after the release of the Call of Islam Declaration, the MJC convened a well-attended meeting to discuss the situation further. During the meeting, the MJC boldly declared that "apartheid in any form could not be condoned by Islam" (Solomon 1999:2). The meeting opposed the Group Areas Act that racially separated Muslims thereby denying them the religious right of places of worship, homes and established Muslim communities. In his speech at the meeting, Imam Abdullah Haron, an executive member of the MJC, remarked that the Group Areas Act was "inhuman, barbaric and un-Islamic... [they are] designed to cripple us educationally, politically and economically... We cannot accept [this type of] enslavement" (South African History Online 2011).

The MJC upheld the centrality of freedom of movement and other related rights which opposed all forms of racial segregation. The organisation appealed to all Muslims in South Africa to unite in the struggle against oppression and injustices. Between 1961 and 1965, the MJC organised several meetings and released statements against apartheid. Prominent individuals within the MJC such as Imam Abdullah Haron and Sheikh Nazeem Mohamed protested against the Group Areas Act and advised Muslims in Western Cape to defy the Act by refusing to comply with the racial-based residential relocations. While such individuals played a central role and protested against apartheid policies more directly, the MJC as an organisation did not go further than organising meetings and issuing statements and declarations. When certain areas were declared 'white areas' in the early 1960s, this affected Muslims since relocations meant that most Muslims had to abandon their places of worship.

The MJC organised a national conference in March 1964 where it protested against relocations by encouraging Muslims never to abandon their mosques. While some members of the MJC felt that the organisation was not doing enough in opposing the Group Areas Act, others affirmed that the discussions, declarations and public statements were enough. Some members of the MJC such as Sheikh Mohamed felt that the organisation's stance against the Group Areas Act was too passive. He challenged the MJC during the Annual General Meeting in June 1965 to express its grievances against apartheid laws directly to the government. Due to his strong opposition to the Group Areas Act and involvement in the Coloured People's Congress and PAC, Imam Abdullah Haron's political activism experienced challenges. Abdullah Haron's political career began undergoing problems in the aftermath of March 1966 when it became clear that he belonged to a liberation movement whose cause was to overthrow the apartheid regime. Having been kept under surveillance for one year, he was subsequently arrested in May 1969 under the Terrorism Act and died in detention in September 1969. Whilst other Muslim leaders and organisations protested the detention and death of Imam Abdullah Haron, the MJC remained silent about the event although he was the chairperson of the organisation at the time of his death. The MJC did not publicly condemn the detention or death of Imam Abdullah Haron. It remained silent on the issue while other Muslim organisations organised marches and issued strong statements.

The 1976 Soweto uprising where several demonstrating school children were killed on 16 June 1976 in Soweto, Gauteng for protesting against apartheid laws such as the use of Afrikaans as a medium of instruction in schools received a more substantial response from the MJC. Regarding the number of protesters who were killed during the series of protests led by school children, Sifiso Ndlovu (2006:347) affirms:

> From the official records, the para-military police who had arrived in Soweto during the day were given orders to shoot to kill; law and order were to be maintained 'at any cost'. The police shot dead another 11 people before that day. Ninety-three more people were shot dead by police over the next two days.

After the Soweto uprising, the MJC issued a statement strongly condemning the apartheid regime and the killing of the protesting school children. The MJC also condemned the brutal method used by security forces against the peaceful protesters and upheld that "sovereignty is vested in the Almighty alone and recognised as such by all Revealed Religions (and) Islam stands for the dignity and freedom of all people" (Lubbe 1989:79). During this time, the MJC was experiencing leadership challenges due to differences of opinion regarding the best approach to the political upheavals. While some members thought that the organisation should not be too involved in the political situation, others maintained that the MJC ought to play a central role in the political struggle because Muslims were part of the oppressed and suffering masses in the country.

The 1980s marked the phase in which the MJC acquired considerable political influence. In 1980, the MJC organised a symposium where social, economic and political issues affecting the country were deliberated. During the symposium which was attended by various Islamic organisations in South Africa, the South African Student's Association criticised the MJC for its inability to give direction and emphasised the need for Muslims to take a more active political role rather than being complacent. In the same year, school boycotts by thousands of black African, Indian and Coloured students spread in places such as Cape Town, Durban and Port Elizabeth. Students protested against the apartheid education system, poor infrastructure and learning conditions in their schools and upheld the need for 'education for liberation.'

The MJC released a statement stating that the organisation supported the students' actions in boycotting classes. However, the MJC did not make any direct criticism of the education department or the minister of education. Clearly, the MJC was reluctant to become too involved in the political struggle and thus did not go further than releasing a general statement supporting the boycotts. While Sheikh Abubakr Najaar as president of the MJC released a general statement on the school boycotts, some members of the organisation thought that a more direct challenge to the government was necessary. The election of Sheikh Nazeem Mohamed as President of the MJC at the 1980 Annual General Meeting signalled change and more direct participation of the MJC in the political struggle. In 1980, Sheikh Nazeem Mohamed succeeded Abubakr Najaar who had been president of the MJC since 1978. By the end of 1982, Imam Gassan Solomon and Maulana Farid Esack, two progressive Muslims who had already been actively involved in the struggle for liberation were formally integrated into the MJC. Imam Gassan Solomon and Maulana Farid Esack served on the executive of the MJC after their formal acceptance as members of the MJC.

In 1983, the MJC joined other Islamic organisations such as the Islamic Council of South Africa and the Muslim Assembly in rejecting "the division of Muslims into racial groups and the Tricameral Parliament, which would exclude blacks" (Matthee 2008:93). Between 1983 and 1984, the MJC became involved in the fight against the Tricameral Parliament by affiliating itself to the UDF. When the UDF was formed in 1983, it became a major anti-apartheid liberation movement. As a non-racial coalition against the racial-based Tricameral Parliament of 1984 and the apartheid regime, the "UDF brought together some 700 community, trade union, cultural, sporting, religious, student and political organisations, representing over two million members, in a common front" (Wolpe 1990:78). For example, the UDF encouraged school learners and workers to boycott by staying away from work and school. Affiliating itself to the UDF forced the MJC to play a more prominent role in its opposition to apartheid and fight for justice and freedom for all South Africans.

Most members of the MJC became actively involved in the activities of UDF to the extent that some of the organisation's members acquired leading positions within the UDF. For example, Sheikh Mohamed, the President of the MJC became part of UDF's national patrons while other members of the MJC such as Sheikh Gabier addressed some UDF's gatherings. When the MJC affiliated itself to the UDF, it released a statement emphasising that Muslims in South Africa ought to join other oppressed South Africans in the fight for justice and freedom. The statement emphasised that the MJC was convinced "that it cannot divorce itself from the rest of the oppressed and those with the same ideals in the formation of a united democratic front, to oppose a system of apartheid in South Africa"

(Solomon 1999:3). The statement was reported in the *Muslim News* on 12 August 1983. The MJC released the statement to justify why it had affiliated itself to the UDF. The MJC participated in various protest activities of the UDF and made various statements in support of the need for a non-racial South Africa, liberation from segregationist institutions and policies, and the need to reject the racially based Tricameral Parliament.

The MJC also distributed pamphlets at mosques encouraging Muslims not to vote and to protest against apartheid policies. Through its involvement in the UDF, the MJC provided platforms for UDF to reach out to people at the grassroots through marches, the distributing of pamphlets at mosques and the Muslim media. By collaborating with UDF and actively participating in the struggle against apartheid, the MJC's political influence became preponderant. While supporting the 'UDF Unites, Apartheid Divides' slogan of the UDF, the MJC strongly appealed to all Muslims in South Africa to boycott the 1984 tri-cameral elections. On 23 March 1984 the *Muslim News* featured a strongly worded statement from the MJC:

> Any type of support for the racist Tricameral system of government is a blatant violation and denial of the *Kalimah* or *Tauheed'* and thus an outright denial of Islam. To support materially, verbally or by 'voting for the Tricameral racist system on 22 August is an act of Haraam' (Pandy 1994:38).

The active participation of the MJC in the struggle against apartheid and especially its involvement in the activities of the UDF clearly indicated its ability to work with liberation movements during the struggle for democracy in South Africa. Consequently, the MJC's affiliation to the UDF drew criticism from the Muslim community as well as organisations such as the MYM and MSA. Although most members of the MJC continued to participate in the activities of UDF, the MJC as an organisation withdrew its affiliation from UDF in July 1984. Some members of the MJC continued to participate in activities of UDF after officially withdrawing from the organisation. Between 1985 and 1886, there was an upsurge of mass mobilisation against the racially exclusive apartheid system in which the MJC actively participated. In 1985, several violent and non-violent forms of protests and resistance against apartheid laws brought many South Africans to the centre of the struggle for liberation in the country. Prominent anti-apartheid activists and organisations began openly to defy the apartheid system and the government's use of extreme force to promote law and order.

During this period, the MJC voiced its position against apartheid and called for Muslims in the country to openly call for a non-racial and free South Africa where all people are equal and treated with dignity regardless of race, colour or religion. It also organised various public addresses and distributed pamphlets and documents within Muslim and non-Muslim communities in support of the anti-apartheid resistance. In August 1985, thousands of people from different parts of Cape Town including Muslims attempted to match to Pollsmoor prison for the release of the then-imprisoned Nelson Mandela and other political prisoners. When the police became aware of the march, they immediately banned it in terms of a magisterial edict. The massive march continued and led to arrests and detentions after violent clashes between protesters and police in which some people died while many others were injured. In the process, the MJC's Chairperson Sheikh Abdul Gamied Gabier, along with other religious leaders and prominent anti-apartheid activists who took part in the march were arrested and detained. the response of the MJC concerning the unjust apartheid laws and detention of political activists by the police during the Pollsmoor March was explicit and robust:

> The MJC then issued a strong statement on the unjust detention of its Chairperson and all other religious leaders. The statement further condemned the cruel, brutal and inhuman actions of the armed forces as well as their presence in the black townships and declared that the policy of apartheid, segregation and oppression was un-Islamic, abnormal and contrary to the laws of Allah (Solomon 1999:3).

Clearly, the MJC portrayed an influential role in the political sphere by participating in the march and later issuing a strongly worded statement demanding the release of the detainees. The MJC described the way police dealt with protesters as unfair, heartless and cruel and demanded the unconditional release of those detained. During the 1985 upheavals, the MJC also provided material support to the affected communities, especially black communities in Western Cape. In the same year, the MJC condemned the Trojan Horse Massacre where many people protesting against the apartheid government were killed on 15 October 1985 in Athlone, Cape Town. Apart from responding to the killings through a statement, the MJC organised a public meeting at a mosque in Sunnyside, Cape Town that was attended by hundreds of people where prominent Muslims such as Dullah Omar and Sheikh Nazeem Mohamed were speakers.

During the meeting, the security forces with teargas canisters, casspirs and a police van raided the mosque with the aim of disrupting the gathering. The MJC condemned the actions of the police as a desecration of the mosque and a violation of the freedom of religion. The MJC also challenged Muslim religious leaders and the Muslim population in South Africa to oppose apartheid in whatever way possible. The participation of the MJC in public protests influenced Nelson Mandela in March 1985 to write a letter to the organisation, pointing out the two evils that confronted society and applauding the organisation for its fight against these evils:

> In my mind the current situation in which I cannot express myself fully and fairly, except to let you know that I consider the Muslim Judicial Council to be fully committed to the elimination of these evils. This is the reason why the MJC is an inspiration to us all, yours sincerely, signed N. R. Mandela (Solomon 1999:3-4).

When the apartheid government announced its intention of holding the municipal elections on 26 October 1988, the MJC was among the first organisations to urge the public to boycott the elections. The MJC also appealed to the Muslim community to boycott the elections, which denied the values of justice, freedom, and equality since it would put segregationist local leaders into office. This contributed to the failure of the municipal elections where most Black electorates boycotted the election. In 1989, the MJC participated in the Defiance Campaign that was organised by organisations and movements such as the ANC, the UDF and the Congress of South African Trade Unions (COSATU). The Defiance Campaign was regarded as the Mass Democratic Movement (MDM) due to the national reach and support it received. The MDM was launched based on the alliance of anti-apartheid groups to form an anti-apartheid coalition nationally. The campaign involved acts of civil disobedience, openly challenging segregation policies within healthcare and educational institutions and deliberately breaking offensive laws. The MJC fully supported the Defiance Campaign that was meant to end the oppressive apartheid laws and policies:

> Referring to the Defiance Campaign, the MJC said that it supported the Campaign. The MJC said that the division of South Africans on racial lines was an evil sin and that all the suffering of the people was the result of the repression of the racist government. It denounced the brutality displayed by the police against innocent and unarmed people, committed to a peaceful and non-violent campaign of defiance. The MJC called upon people to join the struggle to destroy Apartheid and build a non-racial and undivided South Africa (Pandy 1984:70).

The MJC appealed to Muslims and non-Muslims throughout the country to join the Defiance Campaign and publicly protest against unjust apartheid regulations. Moreover, the anti-apartheid rallies which the MJC organised at mosques under the banner 'Islam defy Apartheid' were often attended by hundreds and sometimes thousands of Muslims and non-Muslims. Throughout the 1980s, the Annual General Meetings of the MJC, which are still held regularly since the establishment of the organisation, featured many discussions and deliberations on the need for justice and freedom in South Africa. Key members of the executive such as Sheikh Nazeem Mohamed and Imam Ali Gierdien gave speeches at various public rallies, protest marches and gatherings. By 1989, the MJC had become an influential organisation in the public sphere based on its strong leadership which comprised of the General Council, Supreme Council and sub-committees which were elected based on their knowledge, expertise and experience as Johannes Lubbe (1989:66) clearly attests:

> The MJC SA consists of two main bodies, namely the General Council and the Supreme Council. The General Council to whom all *shuyūkh, moulānas* and *imāms* belong is sub-divided into a *halāl*-committee, a welfare committee, a committee for relief work and a committee for matrimonial

affairs. The members of these sub-committees are elected annually during the Muslim month of Muharram when all office bearers of the MJC are elected. With the exception of administrative staff and social workers, all members of sub-committees come from the ranks of the MJC itself and are elected on the basis of competence and experience.

The period between 1990 and 1995 was a complex time of revision and transition in terms of the political involvement of the MJC in the changing political scene. With the release of political prisoners, the unbanning of liberation movements and commencement of political negotiations, the orientation of the MJC changed. During the period of transition to democracy, the MJC appealed to the apartheid government to hasten the process of transition and participated in discussions regarding religious freedom and the place of Muslims in a democratic South Africa. For example, the leaders of the MJC aligned with the World Conference on Religion and Peace, a multi-religious organisation which deliberated on issues such as the relationship of state and religion and the notion of religious freedom during the transition period from apartheid to democracy. In the early 1990s, the World Conference of Religions for Peace South Africa had representatives from diverse religious groups such as the Pretoria Buddhist Group, the South African Catholic Bishops Conference, the Jews for Social Justice, the Sikh Council of South Africa and the Spiritual Assembly of Baha'is. In December 1990, it organised a conference in Johannesburg during which Sheikh Mohamed participated as President of the MJC.

Muslim Judicial Council's Public Engagement Post-1994

The MJC post-1994 has retreated to the private sphere, focusing on issues that directly affect or concern Muslims, although it has continued to have a minimal political influence in South Africa generally. According to Sindre Bangstad and Aslam Fataar (2010:829) "[t]he shift has been dramatic. The MJC has primarily positioned itself as the defender of Muslim 'interests' both with regard to the national and the international context". Despite its inactive stance on public issues, the MJC has remained one of the most representative Muslim organisation in South Africa and directly controls more than 150 mosques in the Western Cape which are considered as its primary affiliates. Other mosques in the Western Cape are affiliated to other *'ulama* organisations such as the Islamic Council of South Africa based in Cape Town. In the new South Africa, the MJC continues to perceive itself as the custodian of Islamic jurisprudence through its rulings on issues concerning Islamic faith and practices at the Cape. Although the MJC's primary influence has been in Western Cape, it has historically represented most Muslims nationally and has occasionally tackled issues faced by South African citizens generally. The MJC has also continued to reach out to Muslim communities through its various departments dealing with social development issues, Quranic affairs, poverty alleviation, Muslim cemeteries, prison welfare, environmental issues, the issuing of *fatwā*, providing mediation and arbitration services and *ḥalāl* certification and monitoring. The MJC has also been active in promoting the religious rights of Muslims such as the need for recognition of Muslim marriages by South African law in the country.

The MJC has several Muslim scholars who are registered as official members and attend the organisation's monthly general meetings. In 1999, the organisation had 149 Muslim religious scholars who were registered, members and 8 associate members. The number rose to over 250 in 2004. Most of these Muslim religious scholars are from diverse educational backgrounds having studied at different Islamic educational institutions in Arab countries, India, Pakistan and South Africa. The MJC comprises six structures which can be considered as its power base:

> (1) The *Imārah* upon which the senior *'ulamā'* serve, (2) The Presidency which comprises of the elected President of the organization, his first deputy and the second deputy, (3) The Executive Council, (4) The General Majlis which is the greater membership of the MJC SA, (5) The Secretariat, [and] (6) The Treasury (Terblanche 2015:33).

The term of office for the president of the MJC has been five years. In 2020, the presidency of the MJC was under Shaykh Irfaan Abrahams who had been elected in 2016 having replaced Maulana Igsaan Hendricks. Although the MJC through its diverse departments and projects has historically been attempting to reach out to Muslims in Western Cape and beyond on various issues affecting the Muslim community, it has mainly focussed on issues relating to the Muslim Personal Law and the MJC Halaal Trust. Apart from attending to matrimonial issues within the Muslim community, the MJC has been engaging with the government regarding the need to recognise Muslim marriages legally. Since its foundation, one of the major programmes of the MJC has been "to demand that the Government recognise Muslim marriages as legal when performed in conformity with the laws of the Holy Koran" (Lubbe 1989:65). Although Muslim Family Law has been practised since the 17th century in South Africa, South African law has not recognised its validity due to inherent factors such as polygamy. In 2003, the MJC supported a submission of the draft of the Muslim Marriages Bill by the South African Law Reform Commission to the Ministry of Justice and Constitutional Development.

The submission appealed to parliament to legalise the status of marriages conducted and regulated under Islamic law officially. The MJC, like other organisations such as the MYM and the Women's Legal Centre has continued to appeal to the government for recognition of Muslim marriages as valid and to promulgate the rights which such legal recognition would entail. Thus, the MJC and other Muslim organisations have continued to participate in lobbying the government to pass the Muslim Marriages Bill which would be a regulatory framework for Muslim marriages in the country. Apart from religious rights concerning the Muslim Family Law, the MJC has been instrumental in promoting the religious rights of Muslims such as the wearing of religious attire at workplaces.

The MJC intervened in 2006 when Mrs Fairouz Adams, a prison social worker, was dismissed from work when she refused to remove her headscarf so as to wear a uniform at Breede River Community Corrections Office in the Western Cape: "she wore a headscarf, considered a security risk by the Department of Correctional Services, and refused to tuck her blouse into her skirt or trousers" (South African Press Association 2006). When Mrs Fairouz Adams was fired for refusing to conform to the official dress code which according to her was against her religious beliefs, she then appealed against her dismissal. The MJC represented her to the department by pointing out why the department must accommodate her, and "after a series of interventions by the MJC, an agreement with the Department of Correctional Services (DCS) which meant that Adams returned to work was reached in 2006" (Bangstad and Fataar 2010:829).

In July 2019, the MJC intervened when Fatima Isaacs, an army major constitutionally challenged her employer, the South African National Defence Force (SANDF) over the wearing of a Muslim headscarf at work. Fatima Isaacs who had been serving in the army for ten years was charged for defying the military code after refusing to stop wearing her headscarf. According to SANDF's spokesperson Mafi Mgobozi, the "charges are not about wearing the headscarf" but about "defying the military command. In the military, we have lawful command. If the OC has demanded you to do something and you don't want to do it, the charges emanate from that" (eNCA, 2019). By refusing to remove a headscarf as part of her uniform at work, she was charged of wilful insolence and disobeying a direct lawful command by a military court.

Fatima Isaacs questioned why a female Muslim member of SANDF should be prohibited from wearing a headscarf under her army beret, especially as the scarf beret does not cover the face and ears. In this case, the MJC intervened claiming that SANDF violated Isaacs' religious rights. The MJC entered into dialogue with the SANDF which led to the signing of an agreement emphasising that the two organisations would work together in resolving the matter. Regarding the case, Etheridge (2019) reported:

> The MJC, SANDF and legal representatives held talks on Tuesday to discuss the situation of Major Fatima Isaacs, who faces a military court hearing for her refusal to remove her headscarf, also known as a hijab... The parties said the talks were 'amicable and constructive' and the SANDF made a commitment to address the headscarf issue in their policies within a set time frame. 'The SANDF has categorically declared that Islamophobia and discrimination has no place in the SANDF, since it is representative of all peoples of our rainbow nation,' the joint statement read. The MJC first deputy president Moulana Abdul Khaliq Ebrahim said they

were happy that all the parties were working out a pathway for the future. Second deputy president Shaykh Riad Fataar added his appreciation for the issue not being brushed aside. 'We don't expect the military to be soft and easy, we expect them to be tough. But we also expect justice,' he said.

On 8th August 2019, SANDF and MJC reached an agreement on the issue when the former highlighted that though its employees may wear a Muslim headscarf, they are required to follow the strict policies to ensure that a professional dress code is maintained. The SANDF and MJC agreed that a headscarf does not necessarily impede the policy of the former, which means that female Muslim workers may now wear under-scarves. The SANDF provisionally permitted Muslim women to wear headscarves under their army berets as the organisation continues the process of revisiting its policy on dress code. The MJC considers this as a landmark case in its ongoing enforcement of Muslim religious rights and general freedom of religion.

Although the MJC has focused on the general interests of the Muslim community since the advent of the democratic dispensation, there have been attempts made by the organisation to participate directly in the political sphere. The MJC has been involved in the debates on the participation of Muslims in the political process especially concerning voting. While some Muslims questioned whether they should participate or boycott the democratic but secular elections in 1994 and 1999, some questioned the legitimacy of the new political order. The MJC was clear in its position that Muslims should participate in the democratic elections as South African citizens. Ahead of the first non-racial general election in 1994, the MJC indicated that it was not aligned to any political party although most of its key leaders were more supportive of the ANC. For example, MJC's key executive members such as Sheikh Nazeem Mohamed, Imam Gassan Solomon and Sheikh Abdul Gamied Gabier attended ANC meetings, delivered opening prayers and pledged their support for the party. Sheikh Nazeem Mohamed was himself a friend of Madiba Nelson Mandela. When Sheikh Nazeem Mohamed was asked why he would opt to vote for the ANC as opposed to other parties, he affirmed:

> I will vote for the ANC. I have great admiration for (the) ANC President Nelson Mandela. He is a strong leader of a strong party and I believe that the ANC has the necessary clout and support to bring about change in South Africa - the change we all need, and to bring about justice, and freedom and democracy in this country. As Muslims, we have spoken to ANC members and have been given the undertaking that Muslims will be respected as part of tile Islamic religion. The ANC stands for freedom of religion and will protect the religious rights of Muslims and secure a right to exercise our religion (Pandy 1994:88).

While the MJC encouraged Muslims in South Africa to participate in the first democratic and non-racial elections, it emphasised that they should not vote "for those groups, and their surrogates, who have been guilty of the crimes of apartheid" (Bangstad & Fataar 2010:226). The MJC also issued a statement directed at Muslims in South Africa ahead of the 1999 elections encouraging them to participate actively in the election. While the IUC, under Achmat Cassiem, implored Muslims not to participate in the 1999 elections, the MJC aligned itself with Muslim organisation such as the United Ulama Council of South Africa and the MYM by appealing to Muslims in South Africa to vote for the party of their choice. Unlike the MJC, the IUC felt that participating in non-Islamic politics meant approving unIslamic policies and practices of government. As such, the MJC has played a vital role in encouraging Muslims and non-Muslims to participate in the elections and democratic process, thereby securing political influence within Muslim communities and beyond.

In the 2004 general election, the MJC did not directly encourage Muslims to vote for the party of their choice, rather it provided comprehensive guidelines on how they should choose a party to vote for. A closer analysis of the guidelines indicates the MJC's preference for the ANC as opposed to other political parties. In 2008, the MJC participated in a workshop, which dealt with Muslims, and their political participation in democratic South Africa, organised by the Institute for the Study of Current Islam based at the University of Cape Town. During the workshop, the MJC presented its findings on the various approaches and strategies that are being employed by the organisation in South African politics based on Islamic principles. Such workshops have been helping the MJC to reflect on its political involvement after the demise of apartheid which has witnessed the organisation's retreat into internal religious affairs.

In 2008, the MJC had a meeting with former President Jacob Zuma in which the organisation discussed issues concerning the political direction of South Africa and the ongoing contribution of Muslims in the society. Although the MJC's President, Maulana Ighsaan Hendrieks insisted that the organisation was non-partisan, *Cape Argus* reported that after the meeting with Jacob Zuma on 25 June 2008 he affirmed that "MJC members would welcome Zuma as president of our country" (Bangstad & Fataar 2010:287). This shows that although the MJC has been focusing on religious issues in post-apartheid South Africa, it has continued to be politically influential through its engagement with government officials and engagement with political issues such as those concerning elections. The MJC has also been participating in international issues in its effort to represent the interests of Muslims and participate in public space. After reports about al-Qaeda terrorist attacks in the United States in September 2001, the MJC responded to the event by condemning the attacks and how militant groups employ the Islamic faith to fulfil their own political goals. The statements of the MJC against the attacks were so strong that they caused its offices to be attacked by an arson a few days later. When the United States began deliberating its plans of attacking Afghanistan and emphasising the anti-terrorism campaign, the MJC joined the Congress of South African Trade Unions and other organisations in organising an anti-war rally in Cape Town.

Regarding the conflicts in the Middle East, the MJC has maintained its support for Palestinian rights by organising several demonstrations and protest marches in the Western Cape. In his address to a gathering with former President Jacob Zuma on 21 July 2016, Shaykh Irfaan Abrahams upheld the international concern of the MJC (2016):

> As a people who stand with the oppressed in other parts of the world, we appreciate the definitive position the ANC took when it invited the leader of Hamas, Comrade Khalid Mish'al

as its official guest in October 2015. Comrade Khalid went on record and said that the South African Government has been one of the greatest supporters and friends of the people of Palestine. Of particular concern to us is the escalating conflict in Syria that has destroyed an entire nation and caused the biggest refugee crisis the world has ever seen. As freedom and peace-loving people, we would encourage our government through our International Forums to play a meaningful role in bringing to an end this devastating conflict.

In March 2018, Shaykh Irafaan Abrahams, President of the MJC, issued a statement to all South African Muslims and non-Muslims encouraging them to participate actively in the voter registration ahead of the 2019 national elections. He appealed to all Muslim individuals, organisations and mosques to encourage their communities to make a difference by participating in the voter registrations. According to Daries (2018), Shaykh Irafaan Abrahams affirmed that the "political landscape nationally and internationally compels us to play a leading role in the '*fiqh* of citizenship'" and that "our participation in elections ensures we influence those who represent our values and aspirations to serve humanity". In his statement, Shaykh Irafaan Abrahams also advised Muslims on the documents that were required for voter registration.

Islamic Identity and the MJC

The Muslim Judicial Council has been the most influential and Muslim representative theological body in the Western Cape. Although the MJC has occasionally participated directly in politics, it has primarily continued to focus on the general interests of the Muslim community. Since its establishment, the organisation has maintained its Islamic identity by promoting the interests of Muslims, advocating the government's recognition of Muslim rights such as Muslim Personal Law and the regulation of various aspects of Islamic life in South Africa. The MJC adopted a more conservative and passive stance towards the political situation at a time when some Muslims expected the organisation to be vocal and progressive as one of the most representative bodies of the Muslim community in South Africa.

It is apparent that the need to secure a uniquely Islamic identity in the Western Cape was one of the major reasons why the MJC was formed in the first place. For example, from its early stages, the MJC sought to produce "Islamic literature to assist Muslims to find their Islamic identity in a secular setting like South Africa through designing a specific codification of laws for minority Muslims" (Terblanche 2015:28). The MJC clearly outlined its objective to promote Islamic life and identity. Although the MJC partially resisted certain apartheid laws such as the Group Areas Act, participated in certain anti-apartheid strategies and even affiliated itself to the UDF, some members of the organisation failed to oppose the legitimacy of the system. More progressive and politically vocal members such as Hassan Solomons criticised the passive role of the MJC in the apartheid resistance politics which was partly motivated by the organisation's quest for Islamic identity. The MJC slightly moved away from its apolitical stance in the 1980s when the organisation became more involved in the anti-apartheid struggle.

It has already been noted that the MJC secured links with the UDF and used various strategies that were employed by the Call of Islam, Qibla and the MYM to resist the apartheid system in the struggle for justice and freedom for all South Africans. By unequivocally declaring that apartheid is against the spirit and values of Islam, Islamic organisations such as Call of Islam and the MJC gave direction to South African Muslims. In post-1994 the MJC has maintained a passive public profile on issues that continue to affect society generally, apart from its minimal contribution in the political sphere by engaging with government officials and encouraging Muslims and non-Muslims to participate in elections and the democratic process. The MJC has focused on representing and addressing the needs and interests of the majority of the Muslims in the Western Cape. However, the ten-point programme of the MJC portrays it as primarily a religious organisation established to focus on religious issues with a traditional religious outlook rather than a political one. The MJC's political involvement continues to be generally motivated by its attempts to defend Muslim interests at local and international levels:

> In the national context, the MJC has been instrumental in supporting and promoting the religious rights of Muslims,

whether these relate to the right of female Muslim prison employees to wear the Islamic headscarf,83 to demanding religious rights for Muslim inmates in prisons in South Africa, to supporting the recognition of Islamic marriages in South Africa, to raising the issue of South African Muslims illegally detained in other countries in Africa in the era of the so-called 'war on terror,' to attempts at regulating the pilgrimage (*hajj*) industry, or to regulating the certification of Islamic food and drink products. In the international context, the MJC along with other 'ulama' and advocacy organisations were instrumental in preventing the publication of the so-called 'Muhammed cartoons' in South Africa in 2006 and have been outspoken defenders of Somali, Iraqi and Palestinian rights to self-determination, among many issues. Particularly on issues relating to conflicts in the Middle East, the MJC has expressed its appreciation for the government's stance in attempting to chart an independent course in international politics (Bangstad and Fataar 2010:829).

Due to the MJC's emphasis on Muslim 'interests', its political influence in the democratic process through the creation of political and social awareness and promoting human rights and social justice for all South Africans continues to be minimal. Although based on its website (MJC 2022) it considers itself the "most representative and influential Muslim religious organization in the Western Cape, recognized locally, nationally and internationally for the religious, cultural and organizational roles it plays in South Africa", the organisation has primarily remained a judicial agency for Muslims with a religious objective. By and large, the MJC has maintained a dominant role in addressing the needs of the Muslim community and as a custodian of the Islamic faith and law in Western Cape and beyond. As such, its political involvement especially in advocating for human rights and equality has been geared towards the need for greater religious freedom, with some minimal political involvement in the broader society.

The People Against Gangsterism and Drugs (PAGAD) in Western Cape

The formation of People Against Gangsterism and Drugs (PAGAD) is rooted in the history of gang and drug activities in the Western Cape which can be traced back to the mid-nineteenth century. Before 1950, there were already reports of gangsterism and inter-gang wars and conflicts in the Western Cape, especially in the Coloured residential areas of Cape Town. The issues of crime, drugs and gangsterism have historically been a huge problem in Western Cape. Unlike in other areas such as Soweto in Johannesburg where gangsterism and drug-violence was controlled early enough, gangs and drug-lords in the Western Cape had a more stable existence, which attracted the attention of the youth. PAGAD attempted to participate in the public sphere through various strategies. The loss of popular support from the community, the backing of the state and police, and religious organisations from 1996 onwards meant that PAGAD would struggle to maintain hegemony over the escalation of drugs and gangs which has historically perpetrated crime and terrorised the community.

Background to the Emergence of PAGAD

The strict implementation of the Group Areas Act of 1950 intensified gang activities in South Africa. In the Western Cape, gangsterism and crime have been rooted in the social, economic and historical conditions created by the apartheid system. The removal of non-whites from places such as Lower Claremont, Simon's Town, District Six, Windermere and Newlands can be perceived as one of the key factors that precipitated gang activity and crime in the areas of relocation such as Cape Flats:

Perhaps one of the most devastating and long-lasting of the social costs of forced removals on the communities that now form the Cape Flats is that of gangsterism, which is accounted for by several researchers as a legacy of the forced removals during the apartheid era (Du Toit 2014:1-7).

Following the Group Areas Act and the notion of separate development, the racial classification system and relocations broke families, thereby resulting in distress and poverty among the politically and economically marginalised non-whites. As already stressed in the second section, during apartheid, hundreds of thousands of black Africans, Coloureds and Indians were relocated. For example, District Six, which had been a prominent Coloured area in the Cape Peninsula, was demolished to create white settlements, which drastically or significantly affected the family life of communities that had resided in the area for many years. This contributed to the higher levels of crime and disruption of social structures among black Africans, Coloureds and Indians who had been relocated to underdeveloped and highly impoverished areas, often on the periphery of the city.

Apart from factors such as unemployment, poverty and other effects of relocations, the proliferation of drugs, gang activities and crime in the 1990s can be partly attributed to certain apartheid regulations and policies which did not monitor people for crime and its prevention. For example, the police used their time and resources to control the movement of people and arrest the violators of apartheid administrative crimes while ignoring the actual crimes in Black and Colou red settlements. In some cases, street gangs and illegal smuggling clusters were co-opted by civil authorities to help curb anti-apartheid mobilisations:

> In the 1980s, gangs like the Hard Livings were still limited to their neighbourhood. Money, in addition to drugs, came from gambling and extortion. The gangs did not only rely on naked force and fear to embed themselves in communities. Often, they would distribute food parcels to the needy and give assistance at funerals. Many in the community would also rely on the gangs to buy 'cheap' television sets, VCRs and the like. There were cruder tactics too. Rashaad Staggie, for example,

would drive through the streets and throw money from his car (Desai 2004:17).

Regarding the popularity of urban street gangs in the 1980s in some parts of Cape Town, Schäft holds that most Coloured residential areas have always had a high and more stable number of gangs as compared to black African, Indian and white communities. From the outset, gangs have never operated based on ethnicity or religious affiliation; their operations have been rooted in the socio-economic life of Cape society. Before the demise of the apartheid regime in 1994, "different gangs with thousands of members ruled by intimidation, bribery and the provision of services like protection and credit guarantees" (Matthee 2008:141) had control over certain major drug markets. Different drug groups were linked to divergent drug networks in most neighbourhoods. The use of Mandrax was more intense in Phoenix, Sea Point and around the Cape Flats. While the Phoenix area was predominantly Indian, the usage of Mandrax was intense on the Cape Flats among Coloured communities.

By 1994, a distinction between drug merchants and street gangs already existed in Cape Town, especially in Coloured areas. Superficially, drug merchants were distinguished from gangsters, although some drug-lords have been involved in gangsterism and some gangsters have been distributing drugs in streets. There has been a strong link between gangsterism and drug networking in the Coloured communities of Cape Town:

> Street gangs are mostly involved in street-level pushing of drugs, an activity which is seldom very lucrative. Prison often serves as a conduit through which street gangsters establish the networks and the status required for becoming drug-dealers. Drug dealing requires an advanced network and infrastructure and stratified, corporate gangs are often the medium through which drug-lords organise their activities in Cape Town's Coloured communities (Bangstad 2005:197).

In most Coloured communities in the 1990s, different gang groups fought over territories to create stable drug networks. A substantial number of key drug dealers, mostly gang members and leaders, were Coloured and Muslim. In 1994, *Boorhaanol Islam* affirmed that "the ultimate irony for Muslims though, in the prohibition of these social vices, is that their own brethren, as in drug trafficking, become its chief exponents" (Boorhaanol Islam 1998:2-3). Although many Muslim drug merchants were Nigerian and Moroccan immigrants, several local Muslims played a central role in the drugs and gangsterism syndicate. The Hard Livings gang whose prominent members were Muslim controlled the distribution of drugs in the Cape Flats, especially in residential areas such as Manenberg. In 1994, the Hard Livings became part of a network of drug merchants that had been regulating the influx and supply of drugs in the Cape Flats since its foundation in 1992.

An equally influential gang known as the Americans was also prominent with smaller networks in the Cape Flats. Unlike the Americans who did not have strong links, the Hard Livings had created strong connections with smaller gangs. Moreover, some non-Muslim immigrants have also been involved in the drug trade. Sindre Bangstad (2005:197) mentions "the Nigerian criminal networks that have established a foothold in Cape Town since 1990 have mainly focused on the niche of supplying the market with cocaine and heroin instead". Most gangs and drug-lords on the Cape Flats generated their income from illegal activities related to crime and the supply and distribution of drugs such as Mandrax and marijuana. From 1994, the major causes of crime, which was on a rise in most neighbourhoods in Cape Town, were gangsterism and drugs.

Based on the findings of the City Victim Survey conducted by the Institute for Security Studies in 1998, people in the affected Coloured areas claimed to be at risk due to the proliferation of violent crime even prior to 1994. The fight against gangsterism and drugs in Cape Town, especially among Coloured communities by police has been inadequate. Heinrich Matthee (2008:140) highlights three key areas of the Cape metropole based on the status of law reinforcement and cases of violent crime between 1994 and 2000:

> Firstly, in the business and tourist areas of central Cape Town and the northern and southern suburbs, violent crime occurred sporadically but was more or less containable by the police. Secondly, in the more hazardous areas of Woodstock and Athlone and on the Cape Flats, protection by the police was uneven. Thirdly, in some highly-populated, high-risk Cape Flats areas like Manenberg, Elsies River and Mitchells Plain,

the police at best monitored an uneasy peace during the day. However, the Cape Flats area was not socio-economically homogeneous, and areas like Grassy Park and Mitchells Plain included less troubled neighbourhoods.

The relationships between the police personnel and drug merchants contributed to the failure of the police force to curb the problem of drugs and gangs. In the 1990s, some drug merchants and gangs established strong links with law enforcement agencies, local corrupt police officers, and sometimes with senior and high ranked police officers for the sake of protection on the Cape Flats. Because some gang leaders had been informers prior to 1994, some "senior police officers were forced to proceed cautiously against some gang leaders lest information about their past relationship might jeopardize their careers" (Matthee 2008:142). Such reasons contributed to the incapability of the local police to curb the high rates of crime originating from gangs and drugs thereby causing the public to lose trust in the ability of the police force to enforce the law and protect the troubled neighbourhoods.

However, some reasons for the proliferation of drugs and crime in the Cape Flats and other areas are attributed to the changing political milieu after the 1994 elections. Apart from the changes that came with the fall of apartheid in 1994 such as the adoption of more flexible and democratic regulations, there were problems that came with the amalgamation of the different police forces to form the South African Police Service:

> The fall of apartheid met neo-liberal globalisation, with its accompanying paradigm of deregulation, dropping of exchange controls and privatisation, facilitating the porousness of borders. And so, the flow of illegal substances was facilitated in South Africa. There were also other factors at play. The transition saw the coming together of 11 former police forces into the SAPS, providing all kinds of co-ordination problems. This was exacerbated in the Western Cape by the fact that the police were controlled by the New National Party (NNP) and the Department of Justice by the ANC; the lack of co-ordination was compounded by politicking (Desai 2004:17).

The police force had to adapt to the new changes in structure through coordination that made it difficult to curb crime and influential gangs. The changing political environment also gave way to some international drug syndicates who saw opportunities for business markets in South Africa, especially in Cape Town. Because of the weakness of the police force, a good transport system and the presence of strong drug networks, "drugs poured into the country and the criminal justice system offered little resistance" (Schärf & Vale 1996:33) which led to the founding of a drug cartel known as The Firm. The establishment of the cartel meant that gangsterism and the drug market had become more organised, with some gangs playing the role of coordinators for the drug markets and collecting revenue.

PAGAD's Phases and Methods of Protest

Prior to the formation of the PAGAD, systematic community efforts against crime and gangsters existed in the Western Cape. Peacemaker-groups geared towards the curbing of gangsterism, drugs, and crime can be traced to the early 1970s with the formation of the Manenberg Residents' Movement which later became known as 'The Peacemakers'. When the Peacemakers' methods of dealing with the situation were seen as ineffective, the Neighbourhood Watches' (NWs) model developed from the early 1980s. Like the Mitchell's Plain Neighbourhood Watch Association (MPNWA), several Neighbourhood Watch groups existed in other parts of the Western Cape such as Surrey Estate and Manenberg. Most communities in the Western Cape felt unprotected and were unsatisfied with the way the police and other local law enforcement agencies dealt with problems relating to the drug trade, crime and gang violence from early 1994. Regarding the high level of crime in South Africa in the mid-1990, Sigrid Funke (2004:215) affirms:

> In 1996 the country's crime record was labelled one of the worst in the world: 45 out of every 100000 South Africans were murdered each year, eight times the international norm of 5.5 (Canada 2.0; New York City 26.5), a woman was raped every six seconds and nearly 200 armed robberies were committed on a daily basis. Tourists were hit regularly, and foreign investors were increasingly losing confidence.

THE PEOPLE AGAINST GANGSTERISM AND DRUGS (PAGAD) IN WESTERN CAPE

Although most anti-drug and gang community-based groups worked with the police to curb the problem, such groups organised themselves into Neighbourhood Watches and increased pressure for crime culprits to be apprehended. Most Muslim anti-drug clusters had been formed in places such as Surrey Estate and Bo-Kaap. There were also efforts being made by some Muslims who "conducted anti-drug education campaigns from the mosques" (Matthee 2008:142) and in streets. The first major public appearance by a Muslim anti-drug cluster was early in 1995 when a group of Muslims under the Bo-Kaap Anti-Drug Coordinating Committee peacefully marched to Parliament as a response to the worsening situation of drugs and gangs in Western Cape. However, such peaceful initiatives remained generally unsuccessful in the worsening situation of drugs, crime and gangs. Further, such community protection initiatives by the local Muslims did not receive much support from Muslim leadership organisations such as the MJC. The unsuccessful efforts of the peaceful community-based protection initiatives and the worsening situation regarding gangsterism, crime and the drug trade brought about the formation of vigilante groups after 1994. The People Against Gangsterism and Drugs, which later became known by its acronym 'PAGAD,' was among the vigilante groups that were formed in the mid-1990s in the Western Cape:

> The PAGAD movement was initiated by a handful of NW members from a few coloured Cape Town townships who decided to organize public demonstrations to pressure the government to fight the illegal drug trade and gangsterism in South Africa more effectively (Fourchard 2011:617).

With the zeal of Neighbourhood Watches, concerned community members and isolated anti-crime and anti-drug community-based groups came together to mobilise the community against gangs and drug lords, leading to the formation of PAGAD. Although the exact month of the formation of PAGAD has remained debatable, the organisation was most probably formed in the Western Cape in November or December 1995. The lack of clarity regarding the actual date of the formation of PAGAD can be attributed to the view that the organisation was not yet referred to as 'PAGAD' prior to 1996. By the end of 1995, PAGAD was still a small movement without extensive structures or organised leadership, although it "held three house meetings in December 1995" (Matthee 2008:144). When such meetings began to be attended by greater numbers of people due to the escalating community support, in December 2015, Ebrahim Francis one of PAGAD's founding member and leader made an important remark about the group: "we are ordinary people and we are against gangsterism and drugs. So why not call ourselves People Against Gangsterism and Drugs?" (Monaghan 2004:4). When the group was formed in 1995, it focussed on raising consciousness through awareness programs, meetings and placard displays against gangsterism and drugs in the Western Cape, especially the Cape Flats. Before September 1996, there were different groupings that characterised the initial ideological perspectives of the organisation; namely:

> Populist moderates that included Nadthmie Edries and Farouk Jaffer; Islamic political extremists symbolised by the involvement of Qibla; populist militants with reference to the involvement of some G-Force members, and concerned citizens, in particular the larger Muslim community (Botha 1999:11).

The organisation had gained considerable momentum by the beginning of 1996 when more structured public meetings and candlelight vigils began to be held, pamphlets distributed and staider conscientisation programs were organised. Some key members of PAGAD also began appearing on Muslim community radio stations such as Bush Radio and Radio 786 for interviews and panel discussions. In its initial phase, PAGAD gathered support from the community through mass mobilisations, organisation of peaceful protests and petitioning the police and government to curb the problem of drugs, violence and crime on the Cape Flats. The success of its marches and public meetings enabled PAGAD to gain widespread support from the community, thereby becoming a broad community movement initially accepted by most Muslims and some non-Muslims in the Western Cape.

PAGAD's initial strategy was non-confrontational based on the popular mobilisation of the community against gangsters, crime and drugs, including the issuing of memorandums to the authorities after peaceful protests, thereby enabling the organisation to gain political influence. The organisation petitioned the government and police to act against drugs and gangs on behalf of the community. The non-confrontationist approach characterised the organisation in its initial phase between 1995 and mid-1996; afterwards, other strategies were introduced. From 1995 up to mid-1996, the organisation also engaged in various educational and awareness programs geared towards the control of crime, thereby acquiring substantial positive political influence in society. For example, PAGAD leaders and supporters lobbied the community, youth groups, civic groups, religious groups and other organisations to gather support in the struggle against drug lords and gangsters.

The organisation became a civil society movement with concerned community members who wanted to stop crime, gangs and drugs in the Western Cape. Such activities gave the organisation political influence by its ability to positively attempt to stop crime, drugs and gangsters from controlling the community. According to Tayob, the leaders of PAGAD insisted that the organisation should follow the rule of law, maintain a disciplined focus, and "asked members to ensure that only licensed firearms be used in the marches" (Tayob 1996:32). During this initial stage, non-violent popular mobilisation through marches and protests was one of the defining features of the organisation:

> Initially, PAGAD's mobilization occurred through house and public meetings, a candlelight vigil in March 1996 at the time of the first big public protest march, also promoted on Radio 786, and other protest marches and motor cavalcades. According to law enforcement officials, between 1996 and 1999, PAGAD held 29 motor cavalcades, of which 24 occurred without any violence (Matthee 2008:162).

The organisation also engaged with the government and police in its efforts to stop crime. Constructive dialogue with police and government departments such as the Department of Justice was an initial defining strategy of the organisation. On 6th March 1996, PAGAD made its first public appearance through a protest match it organised to the residence of the Minister of Justice, Dullah Omar, demanding the government's urgent solution to the problem of gangs and drugs. This protest came after PAGAD's consultations with Minister Dullah Omar were unproductive. During the protest, the group chanted: 'Who are we? We are people against gangsterism and drugs'. The relationship between PAGAD and the authorities indicates the positive response that it received from the police and government during its initial stage. The methods of protest and non-confrontationist strategies employed by PAGAD during its initial phase gave the organisation significant political influence through its ability to maintain hegemony in the fight against drugs, gangs, violence and crime in the Western Cape.

The years between mid-1996 and early 1999 can be considered PAGAD's phase of extreme vigilantism and confrontation when the organisation secured a mixture of positive and negative political influence. After a public meeting on 11th May 1996, PAGAD supporters marched *en masse* to Parliament in Cape Town where they handed over an ultimatum to the government demanding "swift action against gangs and drug lords within sixty days" (Botha 1999:45). Approximately 3 000 PAGAD supporters, including prominent Muslims such as Shaykh Ebrahim Gabriels from the MJC, Achmad Cassiem the Qibla leader, and Thafier Najjaar, attended the march. Shaykh Ebrahim Gabriels later became president of both the United Ulama Council of South Africa and Muslim Judicial Council (The United Ulama Council of South Africa was established in 1994 as a collective body of all the major theological bodies and can be assumed to represent the majority of Muslims in South Africa whereas the MJC was formed in 1945 and safeguards a substantial representation of the Muslim community at the Cape). PAGAD warned that if no substantial action was taken regarding the situation, then the organisation would take its own action. Though the organisation was largely Muslim, the march was also joined by a handful of non-Muslims including Father Christopher Clohessy, a Catholic priest from Tafelsig. When PAGAD felt that the government's action was insufficient and ineffective, it undertook the initiative to combat crime by confronting crime perpetrators. Two major reasons for popular justice which can be directly linked to PAGAD's confrontationist strategy can be highlishted:

> (i) the crime perpetrated in the community gives rise to a strong sense of vulnerability among members of the community; and (ii) the local structure of the community encourages the involvement of the community, especially in

socially and ethnically homogeneous communities that facilitate communication and trust between participants and which encourage identification with the victim (Botha 1999:10).

PAGAD's critique of the authorities' inability to deal with crime resulted in its supporters taking matters into their own hands. As Anneli Botha shows, the escalation of crime – in this case, perpetuated by drug lords and gangs – caused the community to feel vulnerable and unprotected. As such, the community itself then creates forums, which show concern for the problem and calls for participation to control the problem. To confirm this, Clohessy one of the leaders of PAGAD asserts that the birth of a confrontationist approach was based on PAGAD's realisation that a non-confrontation and non-violent strategy was largely unsuccessful:

> A non-confrontational approach to this particular problem (activities of gangsters and drug dealers) is no longer a viable route - and that those who are empowered by law to confront these social evils are simply not able to function in a way that bears real fruit. There is no doubt, therefore, that PAGAD arose with an agenda that included both confrontation and force. In itself, force can be classified as extreme pressure, and is not necessarily violent (Botha 1999:10).

Clohessy's view exposes the underlining factor as to why PAGAD employed popular justice as a strategy, especially in the Western Cape. PAGAD supporters felt that the community had been left defenceless, and because the response and action of the authorities was largely inadequate, the community itself had to 'take the law into its own hands'. The influence of Qibla was one of the motivating forces behind the militant strategies of PAGAD. Individuals who were key Qibla supporters and leaders such as Achmat Cassiem became part of PAGAD's leadership. Based on her interview with Sheikh Achmat Sidique, leader of the MJC in May 1998, Anneli Botha argues (1999:20):

> The leadership of PAGAD, those who make the real decisions are all members of Qibla or, as they would say, the IUC. The reason why Qibla is using PAGAD and other organizations is to build support by involving its members. When one looks at the leadership hierarchy of PAGAD and other organizations

(for example the IUC) the same individuals always feature as being, Qibla supporters. The reason for this is that Qibla developed a name for themselves over the years: 'They have been labelled as a militant group. But their strategies and methodology could be found in that of PAGAD'.

The strong relationship between Qibla and PAGAD was not only demonstrated in the ideological strategies which the two organisations shared, but also in the fact that the two shared several top leaders. Thus, Qibla partly influenced the establishment and militant elements of PAGAD. Nevertheless, whatever influence Qibla had on PAGAD, the escalation of drugs and gangs and the inability of the authorities to constructively deal with the problem was the major motivating factor regarding the formation of the organisation and the militant strategies it has historically employed. Due to the government's inability to act, from June 1996 onwards PAGAD's mass mobilisation was increasingly being characterised by popular justice and a decrease in the initial non-violent and non-confrontationist schemes. To combat crime, PAGAD adopted the strategy of force and confrontation directed at both the government and the perpetrators of crime. The confrontation directed at the government was based on the authorities' incompetence in dealing with the escalating crime and violence while confrontation directed at those who perpetrate violence and crime meant taking the law in their own hands to instil the order and safety of the community.

By July 1996, PAGAD had become an almost structured organisation with a cohesive leadership and defined objectives. It established its formal organisational structure and began referring to itself by the acronym 'PAGAD' both in print and on radio programmes. Due to the success of PAGAD in the Western Cape, similar anti-drug and crime groups were created in Eastern Cape, Gauteng, Eastern Cape, Northern Cape and KwaZulu Natal provinces. These were the People Against Drugs and Violence (PADAV) from the Eastern Cape, People Against Crime and Drugs (PACAD) from Gauteng and the People Against Gangsterism and Drugs (PAGAD) from the Northern Cape. Because of the need for consolidation and creation of a national leadership and anti-crime body, a conference was organised on 9th December 1996 in Port Elizabeth, Eastern Cape. At the conference, Abdus-Salaam Ebrahim was elected as the National Chief Co-ordinator, Abidah Roberts as the National Secretary and Aslam Toefy as the National Chief Commander. The conference decided that the name 'PAGAD' was to be used by all provincial bodies.

In December 1996, PAGAD organised a rally at Athlone Stadium on the Cape Flats in Cape Town which was attended by about 10 000 PAGAD supporters during which the organisation was formally launched. Although PAGAD's leaders often denied the association of the organisation with Islam, it was predominantly a religious group. The objectives of the group clearly reflected its religious nature, and the emphasis on certain Islamic principles in the organisation was apparent. Although its founders had hoped that it would become "a multi-religious organisation, but because its dominant membership was of Muslim people, it became an Islamic front" (South African History Online 2011). From the beginning, the organisation observed key Islamic festivals and certain Islamic values, and reference to the Quran was part of its public and private discourse. Most of its gatherings were held in Mosques, Muslim prayers were sometimes used, and the Quran was at times recited. In 1999, the organisation produced an *Eid al-Fitr* bulletin in which it emphasised the need for almsgiving and charity for those in destitution. A survey published in November 1996 found that:

> 62 per cent of the Muslims contacted in Cape Town expressed support for PAGAD three months after it had received general public attention with the lynching of Rashaad Staggie. The survey also found that a mere 17 per cent of the Christians surveyed supported PAGAD. Significantly, 26 per cent of those surveyed thought PAGAD represented Muslims, 15 per cent that they represented 'the community' and 1 per cent that they represented Christians (Bangstad 2005:199).

Although the fact that PAGAD has been primarily an Islamic-oriented organisation is undeniable, it has never presented itself as Islamic, but rather as a community-based organisation which has been open to welcome non-Muslims. Nevertheless, because the majority of its supporters and all its leaders and key ideologues have been Muslim, the organisation can be perceived as being Islamic. In July 1996, PAGAD's leaders such as Farouk Jaffer and Abdussalaam Ebrahim indicated that confrontations between the organisation and drug dealers were looming due to slogans such as 'kill the merchant' and 'one merchant, one bullet. One gangster, one bullet' slowly began to be used both on posters and in the organisation's discourse. PAGAD began organising 'ultimatum marches' to residences of identified gang leaders and drug merchants who would be given the ultimatum: 'We are giving you 24 hours to clean up your act, or we will come back for you'.

The ultimatums required that a perpetrator stop all illegal activities within 24 hours or else 'face the mandate of the people', especially through the G-Force, its armed wing. PAGAD supporters and members began engaging in militant activities such as violent paramilitary styles, shootings at the houses of alleged drug merchants and exploding pipe bombs. In August 1996, PAGAD's G-Force group perpetrated ten violent attacks on the homes of alleged drug leaders and crime suspects while only nine non-violent marches were made. One of the violent confrontations between PAGAD and drug dealers resulted in the death of Rashaad Staggie, a prominent drug merchant and a co-leader of the Hard Livings gang. On 4th August 1996, a group of PAGAD supporters "pulled notorious gang leader Rashaad Staggie from his car, threw a flaming Molotov cocktail into his lap and shot him dead" (Erasmus 1996:217). From then up until 2000, PAGAD entered into a stage of extreme vigilantism and violence thereby being implicated in many killings, shootings and bombings of many crime syndicates and sometimes police. Heinrich Matthee (2008:162) outlines the major protest marches of PAGAD between 1996 and 1999:

> There were a total of 17 legal and 16 illegal protest marches between 1996 and 1999: two legal and 10 illegal protest marches in 1996, of which eight involved violence; eight legal and five illegal marches in 1997, of which four involved violence; and two legal and one illegal march in 1998, of which two involved violence. By 1999, all five marches were legal, and none involved violence.

Between 1996 and 1999, there were several attempted assassinations, pipe and petrol bombs on houses and offices of drug merchants and prominent gangsters organised by or at least linked to PAGAD supporters. Some members of PAGAD engaged in armed training which included the procurement of both illegal and legal firearms, explosives and grenades. Further, most of "PAGAD's marches and meetings were characterised by the open display of firearms by its supporters, the use of armed marshals and military-style discipline" (Botha 1999:56). Such violent and confrontationist approaches caused the South African government to consider PAGAD a terrorist organisation and the police to consider it as a 'gang' and a crime accomplice.

Although PAGAD initially gathered support from the community, the government and some Muslim leaders and organisations thereby gaining political influence, by 1999 its membership and popularity drastically dwindled. There are many reasons for this. The violent tactics employed by the organisation especially between August 1995 and 1999 forced most of its supporters to withdraw their membership or support and forced some of its leaders to resign. They felt that the organisation had diverted from its original goal and had become another crime abettor. The decreasing number of marches "from 12 [marches] in 1996 and 13 in 1997 to three in 1998 and five in 1999, the attendance at marches and meetings declining from thousands in 1996 to the low hundreds by 1999" (Matthee 2008:162) indicates the drop in public support. Rachel Monaghan (2004:7) highlights the findings of a crime survey conducted in June 2003:

> A victim survey conducted in Manenburg (June 2003) found that of those people living in the Cape Flats when PAGAD was an issue, only 34 per cent of respondents expressed support for the organisation. Furthermore, 25 per cent of those who had supported PAGAD withdrew their support due to the violence used by the group, especially the violence directed at others within the community.

The support PAGAD initially received from established religious organisations was eroded drastically and some Muslim organisations described the organisation as being anti-Islam by 1999. Because of PAGAD's militant activities, most Muslim clergy, scholars and organisations such as the MJC, MYM and the Islamic Council of South Africa became dissatisfied with the organisation and launched several criticisms. For example, the *Majlisush Shura Al Islami*, the Islamic Council of South Africa and the MJC persuaded Muslims in South Africa to "shun extremes' and condemned those among us who have glorified violence and have put aside reason and rationality in the search for solutions" (Gottschalk 2005:3). The lack of support from Muslim religious establishments significantly affected the popularity of the organisation, especially because it had been primarily a Muslim organisation with religious principles from the start. In response to the criticisms, PAGAD saw other Muslim organisations as not doing enough:

> PAGAD was very critical of the role that the religious bodies were playing in the lives of Muslims, and particularly in facing and addressing the social ills like drugs, crime and gangsterism, either because the community was growing faster than the capacity of the religious institutions to actually help, or because the approaches the religious establishments adopt were outdated (Hassan 2011:112).

PAGAD became critical of most Muslim religious clergy and leaders of the MJC by describing the leaders of the organisation as 'hypocrites' and 'religious gangsters' due to their inability to act against the evils of society. Such intolerance of PAGAD towards Muslim clergy, institutions and scholars contributed to the failure of the organisation to maintain the extensive support it had originally gathered. With the declining popular support, and most of its leaders under prosecution or in prison, PAGAD became a small organisation by 2001. For example, Abdus Salaam Ebrahim who had been national coordinator of the organisation encountered several arrests and latter imprisonment. By January 2000, "110 people with PAGAD links were facing charges in connection with 55 urban terror cases" (Monaghan 2004:9) while many others had been convicted of several cases relating to the illegal possession of ammunition, bombs and explosives, intimidation, murder and attempted murder. Thus, by 2001 PAGAD was perceived by the "South African state and the United States as 'an urban terror group threatening not just the State's monopoly on the use of coercive force but the very foundations of constitutional democracy'" (Rabasa 2006:39).

When PAGAD's strategy become confrontationist and linked to illegal activities in its dealings, the state became critical of the organisation especially since some of its members were now taking the law into their own hands. After classifying PAGAD as a terrorist group, the state later envisioned a "threefold strategy aimed at denying PAGAD political space, religious space and financial access" (Hassan 2011:110) which negatively affected the growth of the organisation. To weaken PAGAD, the government in the Western Cape organised anti-PAGAD campaigns, discouraged the funding of the organisation by donors and petitioned religious leaders to isolate themselves from PAGAD. The state's attempt to curtail the public display of firearms and the tight conditions for marches and demonstrations demobilised the organisation.

Further, when the government began infiltrating PAGAD through state agents, the organisation began to drift into smaller cells. The state's move to weaken the organisation extended to the religious sphere. According to Ashwin Desai (2004:23), "the ANC co-ordinated a programme to 'squeeze' PAGAD from meeting spaces in mosques and encourage leading Muslims to denounce PAGAD". On its part, PAGAD criticised the state for channelling its resources towards the prosecution of PAGAD leaders and members rather than putting an end to crime by apprehending the actual perpetrators – gangsters and drug lords. In a public statement, Zolissa Lavisa the then-acting National Commissioner of police stressed that PAGAD was no longer the solution to the problem of crime in the Western Cape but that its confrontationist tactics made it part of the problem. For example, the launch of Operation Good Hope tasked to investigate and stop urban terrorism in the Western Cape in 1998 clearly targeted PAGAD. Operation Good Hope was a special police unit that was created to "investigate PAGAD and crimes against the state" (Gottschalk 2005:9) and by 1998, key PAGAD members especially those belonging to the G-Force had been arrested and imprisoned.

Despite a considerable decrease in the number of supporters, PAGAD has continued to maintain a presence on the Cape Flats as a crime control organisation mainly using non-violent strategies in the struggle against gangs and drugs. Post 2000, the organisation has continued to protest against crime, drugs and gangsterism around Cape Town. The absence of drug dealers in Surrey Estate was attributed to the efforts of PAGAD. As of 2004, the organisation continued to hold public demonstrations to protest against drugs and gangsters and to conduct drug and crime awareness programs on the

Cape Flats. In August 2005, PAGAD's Regional Safety co-ordinator Salie Abader stated that "the anti-drug and gang group still had enormous community support and was contacted regularly by people from Bishop Lavis to Bishop's Court fed up with the government's inability to combat crime" (Bamford 2005). Salie Abader also noted that the problem of drugs and gangs was still a big issue in the Western Cape which required that the community work with the local police to stop drug lords and gangsters.

Although PAGAD continued to insist that violence was not part of the organisation's strategy, by 2004 the rhetoric of some of its leaders such as Abader indicated that both confrontationist and non-confrontationist methods were still being employed. While PAGAD continued to lobby the community to join in demonstrations and marches during which petitions were submitted to the government, some of the marches continued to turn violent. On 1st August 2015, PAGAD led a peaceful march and motorcade in Manenberg demanding that authorities take more action against the escalating crime and violence in the city. The march turned bloody due to the clash between protesters and gang members: stun grenades were detonated, bottles and rocks were thrown on the driveway, and as messages of warning to drug merchants and gangsters were being delivered, the crowd shouted 'Viva Pagad, viva!' and 'One merchant, one bullet!'. During the mayhem, a police officer was injured, and police vehicles were damaged. In an interview with *Daily Maverick* after the incident, Haroon Orrie a PAGAD representative affirmed:

> We don't want to blame the authorities but today, the SAPS themselves came under the crossfire from gangsters. Some were injured, and vehicles were damaged. If they had worked with us from the beginning, they would not have had this problem...If SAPS does not work with us, gangsters will take advantage of that...We are saying yes, we can fill that gap (where police cannot reach). History can testify to this. Gang tactics will not deter us. We will be back (Van Der Merwe 2015).

On 17 October 2015 in Cape Town, PAGAD led a match against drugs, the escalating crime and gangsterism. The march, which was also supported by the Azanian People's Organisation, the PAC and the Economic Freedom Fighters, started in Gugulethu and finished at the Athlone Police Station where a memorandum was handed over to the authorities. The peaceful match was motivated by the problem of gangsters and drugs that continued to escalate without constructive action on the part of the authorities. Similarly, on 25th September 2017, PAGAD supporters held an anti-gang and drug motorcade in Kensington, Cape Town when "members of PAGAD clashed with alleged gangsters, causing the surge in shootings" (Daily Sun 2017). While calling for an end to the shootings, killings, and ongoing violence, PAGAD has continued to appeal to the authorities and the local community to join in order to put a stop to the gangs and drugs. The organisation continues to perceive itself as filling in the gap in case the authorities cannot do it, though its marches have generally been peaceful and less in number since 2000. The organisation has also not been content with the manner of the government and police and has often accused the government of unfairly treating its leaders as criminals while they are trying to protect the community and the actual perpetrators move about freely.

In conclusion, the ideology of PAGAD was initially unclear; the group espoused the approaches of the Neighbourhood Watches, the Qibla movement and the strong need to strengthen the safety of the community. Nevertheless, from its small beginnings, the objectives of PAGAD have been tied to the background of drugs, violence, crime and gangsterism for which it was formed in the first place. The ineffective legal system, moral decay and high levels of crime motivated the formation of the organisation in the Western Cape. Therefore, when the organisation was formed, it was meant to combat and eradicate drugs and gangsterism that was perpetuating violence, crime, immorality on Muslim children and the lack of safety on the part of the community. The emphasis was initially on the negative impact of drugs and crime on the wellbeing of the community and its values which were perceived as central to a safe and peaceful community.

PAGAD's more coherent vision and objectives became clearer in its documents, speeches, discussion programmes on Radio 786 and memorandums submitted to the authorities under the leadership of Abdus-Salaam Ebrahim. The memorandum submitted to the Minister of Correctional Services during one of its mass protests on 26th September 1996 clearly illustrated its key objectives:

> One of the most important functions of the government is to see to the safety of all its citizens and non-citizens. Unfortunately, this is not the case ... We, The People Against Gangsterism and Drugs, have embarked on this mass demonstration to: (1) Inform the people of South Africa of the escalation of drug addiction and gangsterism. (2) Make the people of South Africa aware that something is being done about the cancerous growths of drug addicts and gangsterism. (2) Alert the government that urgent and drastic steps must be taken to curb, stop and eradicate the upsurge of gangsterism and drug addiction. (3) Galvanize the entire population to be prepared to take alternative steps if the situation does not improve in the near future. (4) Inform the entire population of the extent of corruption within the Police and Judiciary (Botha 1999:21).

PAGAD members were concerned about the escalation of drugs, the illegal dealings and addictions associated with it and the gangs that continued to terrorise the community. Thus, making the community aware of the problem and its proliferation was considered a vital objective of the organisation from its small beginnings. Apart from its willingness to eradicate and combat the problem, the organisation found that alerting the authorities of the need for an urgent solution to curb the situation was imperative, especially that the local police were ineffective. As indicated in their document submitted to Parliament after a mass protest on 11th May 1996, PAGAD supporters were ready to act if the government did not resolve the problem, since the non-confrontational strategies often ended up inconclusive. Thus, the initial objectives of PAGAD were based on the daily problems encountered by the community as a result of drugs and gangs and the inability of the state to ensure safety and curb the problem. Conforming to the objectives handed to Parliament in September 1996, the National Executive Committee in March 1997 convened and approved the following objectives for the organisation:

> (1) to propagate the eradication of drugs and gangsterism from society, in accordance with the divine will of The

Creator; (2) to co-operate with and to co-ordinate the activities of people and people's organisations which have similar aims and objectives [to those of PAGAD]; (3) to make every effort to invite/motivate/activate and to include those people and peoples' organisations who are not yet part of PAGAD; and (4) to raise funds for the aforementioned aims (Kalidheen 2008:94).

The first three objectives highlighted above formed the core of PAGAD's strategies and approaches towards both the perpetrators and the government. The objectives of PAGAD aligned with its initial mission statement which states that the organisation is a "caring people's movement, proceeding from a foundation of truth, unity, justice and fearlessness, with the ultimate aim of eradicating the evil scourge of gangsterism and drugs from society" (Funke 2004:231). Despite having well-defined objectives, from 1998 onwards some of the leaders of the organisation began emphasising the need to represent Muslims in the South African political sphere and for the need to defend Islamic values.

Nevertheless, from mid-1996 up to 2000, PAGAD's objectives were generally based on its eagerness to combat crime, drug trafficking and gangsterism rooted in its dissatisfaction with the way the authorities dealt with the situation and welfare activities. For almost five years between 1996 and 2001 based on its initial objectives the organisation "led a campaign ... to wipe out prominent gangsters, expose illegal activities and protest against the lack of government commitment to curb drug- and gang-related activities" (Lambrechts 2013:120). In 2000, Abiedah, Roberts PAGAD's National Secretary, emphasised that the objectives of the organisation had not changed and promised stringent actions against gangsters and crime perpetrators. PAGAD supporters upheld the same sentiment during a march on 17th October 2015 in Cape Town where they pointed to the presence of drugs, crime and gangsterism as the major reason why the organisation continued to have a presence.

PAGAD, State and Impact in the Western Cape

Although PAGAD's major objective to fight against drugs, gangs and crime has remained the same since its inception in 1995, this section has demonstrated that the strategies it has historically employed to achieve its objectives have not been the same. The initial strategies of PAGAD were that of non-confrontation, which enabled the organisation to have substantial political influence. Notably, PAGAD initially received a positive response from the ANC government and some sort of collaboration with the local police. Although without much success, meetings were held between PAGAD leaders and some ANC ministers such as Minister of Justice Dullah Omar, to see how the organisation could contribute to solving the problem of drugs and gangs. On 25th June 1996, a meeting between PAGAD representatives and Minister of Justice Dullah Omar was held. In its consultations with the state, PAGAD also held meetings with George Fivaz, National Police Commissioner, to explore the possibility of cooperation in the fight against crine and gangs. In a statement released on 4 November 1996, the ANC government in the Western Cape "perceived PAGAD as a 'popular movement' and acknowledged that those who joined it 'wanted to find solutions (to the problem of drugs and gangs) together with the government'" (Hassan 2011:109).

The organisation also created various rehabilitation programmes for drug addicts and educational programmes in the Western Cape, which contributed to the positive reception of the organisation by the government and police. PAGAD members raised awareness regarding the problem of gangs and drugs in the Western Cape and lobbied religious and social groups to participate in the campaign. Clearly, PAGAD received positive support and affirmation from leaders of the government who endorsed its agenda and initiative to curb crime since the organisation's slogans and strategies reaffirmed such a goal. For example, based on the relationship between the state and PAGAD in the initial stages of the organisation in 1996, Na'eem Jeenah (1996:21) affirmed:

> Partnerships are now possible between the community and the State together to combat the threats to peace and stability. It is true that peace cannot exist without justice, but the struggle

for justice does not have to be a struggle for the overthrow of the state.

From the discussion on the phases and strategies of PAGAD, it is apparent that the organisation began employing a militant approach from mid-1996 when it adopted a dual strategy: it continued to engage in its 'overt' activities which were largely legal and at the same time began to employ illegal and violent 'covert' activities. It has been indicated that the violent and confrontationist approach was adopted during the latter part of 1996 when PAGAD supporters began taking the law into their own hands due to the government's failure to act and when the negotiations between the organisation and the authorities did not yield concrete results. While crime continued to escalate, the formal legal channels were considered as inadequate and slow. The courts and police personnel were also regarded as corrupt and not strong enough to represent and address the public concerns adequately. As such, PAGAD employed political radicalism to practically curb the problem. When an organisation employs political radicalism, it uses revolutionary and militant measures and strategies to instil socio-political change at grassroots level, through violent pressure and intimidation.

As an organisation, PAGAD positioned itself not only as an alternative agency of law enforcement with regard to crime and drugs but also as activists who challenged the injustices and violence that was being inflicted on most communities in the Western Cape. As such, PAGAD partly exposed the government's inability to act effectively on drugs and gangsterism. Some government officials perceived PAGAD as a threat since it questioned the willingness of the State to eradicate crime "by passing the corporatist structures set-up by the State" and "managing at the same time to sustain mass mobilisation, embarrassing Muslims who were ANC leaders and questioning the very legitimacy of the State" (Desai 2004:24). The results of a survey conducted in 1996 on the Cape Flats revealed that only 26 per cent of those surveyed thought that the police could be trusted, 75 per cent thought that some police personnel were involved in corrupt activities linked to drugs while 55 per cent were not happy with the way SAPS was handling the problems affecting their community.

In August 1996, Sydney Mufamadi, Minister of Safety and Security identified police corruption as the main reason for the escalation of crime by gangs in Cape Town. Regardless of its initial relevance and on-going initiatives to combat crime, the government, especially due to the organisation's militancy tactics, was increasingly overlooking PAGAD's achievements. For example, in 2009, Jeremy Veary the police station commander of Mitchells Plain downplayed the achievement of PAGAD:

> PAGAD has not closed a single shebeen or drug outlet in their history. PAGAD is a non-entry as far as we are concerned and [is] average in size compared to our street committees …We don't recognise PAGAD, they are irrelevant. We have structures we work with, like street committees and sector policing. PAGAD did not bring any value to the table (Hassan 2011:110).

Although Jeremy Veary's opinion clearly overlooks many achievements and efforts of PAGAD as an organisation, it nevertheless, shows the disapproval of its militancy strategies on the part of the government and police. While the illegal and violent activities which the organisation employed to achieve its objectives from mid-1996 were based on the practical problem of crime that many communities in the Western Cape were facing, and the inability of the state to provide a solution to the problem, the drug dealers and gangs themselves undermined the peaceful and non-confrontationist strategies of PAGAD. The physical attacks on targeted drug lords and gangsters that some of PAGAD's members employed, were based on the fact that these culprits were unwilling to relinquish their criminal operations even under threat.

However, one wonders whether the violent and illegal 'covert' activities PAGAD employed justified its branding as a terrorist group by the South African government and the United States Department of State. The general characteristics of terrorism include the unauthorised use of violence and force in an extreme way, and the presence of a political or social motive. Regarding terrorism, the emphasis is on the illegal use of force or violence aimed at terrorising and instilling fear rather than the intended deliberate attempt to achieve a certain political or social goal. Because terrorism often aims at modifying behaviour using force or violence in order to manipulate behaviour, the targeted group is coerced to comply with the demands presented by those undertaking the action. Given that terrorism aims at terrorising and instilling fear, although PAGAD employed features of terrorism, it was primarily a vigilante organisation that used certain elements of violence to put an end to the problem of drugs and gangs in the Western Cape. While its aim is not to terrorise, vigilantism involves a certain degree of violence which is directed towards the establishment of the socio-political order within a community. Monaghan (2004:11) maintains that:

> Crime-control vigilantism is directed against those individuals who are suspected of committing acts that would be punishable by the formal system but who are not punished due to inefficiencies, corruption or leniency within the formal criminal justice system. Examples of this type of vigilantism would include the elimination of suspected petty thieves or drug dealers by groups of private citizens.

The activities of PAGAD during the phase of extreme vigilantism were focused on crime-control whereby drug dealers and gangsters were identified and punished by the community, given the inability of the law enforcement channels. As concerned and threatened citizens, PAGAD supporters felt that they had the power to put an end to the problem encountered by their community even to the extent of taking the law into their own hands. Apart from the education programs, rehabilitation initiatives and dialogue with the government, the use of crime-control vigilantism was an important approach which the organisation used to achieve its objectives between 1996 and 2000. Since PAGAD supporters felt threatened by the increase in crime in their community, they were convinced that their self-help action would enable their targets to give up their criminal activities. Nevertheless, if all the incidents of bombings, shootings, murder and clashes with the police and justice system that have been linked to PAGAD since its inception are taken into consideration, then one can conclude that the organisation has exhibited elements of terrorism in its approaches.

PAGAD has been directly involved in illegal strategies using violence by taking the law into its own hands, as was the case in the public lynching of Rashaad Staggie. At the same time, the organisation has historically tried to control crime by employing other non-violent means possible to stop drug dealers and gangsters who were roaming freely in the community. On several occasions, PAGAD has denied some of the bombings, runaway shootings and other acts of terrorism that have been linked to some of its supporters and leaders. The argument that between 1996 and 2000 the state was more concerned with controlling PAGAD's strategies and prosecuting some of its key members rather than targeting the actual crimes committed by gangsters and drug dealers is to some extent justified.

Although PAGAD's major aim to fight against drugs, gangs and crime has remained the same since its inception in 1995, the strategies the organisation has employed to achieve its objectives have not been the same. The factors that motivated the formation of the group and the initial shape it took indicate the practical basis upon which the group was established. The earliest marches, demonstrations, anti-crime awareness campaigns and public meetings were generally pacifistic, which actually caused the government and local law enforcement agencies such as the police to perceive PAGAD as a positive community initiative. PAGAD emerged as a community initiative with positive political influence to curb the practical problem of drugs and gangsterism in Cape Town, because the people felt the need to do something about their situation. Thus, from its formation towards the end of 1995 until mid-1996, the organisation gained widespread support from the community and the government.

The government initially supported the organisation because during this period it had neither developed anti-state sentiments nor began employing militant and confrontationist strategies. The ability of the organisation and its leaders to cooperate with the authorities especially by initiating dialogue and several crime awareness initiatives was a clear sign that PAGAD initially perceived itself as a community based anti-drug and anti-gangsterism organisation that sought to make a positive contribution to society. Because PAGAD was initially thought of as an organised popular movement advocating for a crime-free society, the government perceived its supporters as those "who wanted to find solutions (to the problem of drugs and gangs) together with the government" (Hassan 2011:10).

THE PEOPLE AGAINST GANGSTERISM AND DRUGS (PAGAD) IN WESTERN CAPE

Apart from public support, the backing it got from prominent academics, clerics and leading Islamic organisations such as the Islamic Council of South Africa, the MJC and other academics clearly contributed to the initial success of the organisation.

Therefore, during its initial stages, PAGAD was a peaceful and non-violent organisation which sought to rid the Western Cape of the challenge of drugs and gangs both through its own efforts and by working with the government and other organisations. Within a few months of its formation, PAGAD managed to achieve some of its objectives through its constructive covert activities which were done within the legal framework, though the problem of gangs and drugs did not disappear. Its mere foundation shows the conviction of ordinary citizens to do something fruitful about their community, in line with the law and in collaboration with other role players such as the local authorities. This is confirmed by Manjra who asserts that "PAGAD gave hope to these people where they saw none ... PAGAD represents the response of civil society who clearly feel alienated from the political process" (Manjra 1996:38-39).

Although the organisation did not change its overt approach, which necessitated operating within the framework of the law, from mid-1996 it began employing illegal and violent strategies to achieve its objectives, a strategy that I have referred to as political radicalism. Such a change in strategy can be attributed to the escalation of drugs and gangs on the Cape Flats, the lack of constructive action on the part of the government from the dialogue which PAGAD had initiated, and the organisation's need to employ a more potent approach to the problem. Frustrated by the proliferation of crime and drugs in the Western Cape, dissatisfied with the response of the relevant departments of the government and the police, PAGAD began engaging in the issuing of ultimatums and visiting the houses of targeted drug dealers which caused the organisation to be implicated in many shootings, killings and murders.

The government's rigid and pressing measures against PAGAD in terms of "denying PAGAD political space, religious space and financial access" (Hassan 2011:110) were an attempt to curb PAGAD's 'terrorist' activities related to the organisation such as shootings and killings. The main question is whether PAGAD achieved its objectives during the phase of extreme vigilantism and confrontation between mid-1996 and 2000. While reports from police and other government officials seem to have largely been negative by focusing on the illegal and violent activities of PAGAD, it is apparent that the organisation did achieve its primary objective – to rid the city of the problem of drugs and gangsterism. The militant approach the organisation adopted, especially the threatening ultimatums it was issuing and attacks on the houses of suspected gangsters and drug dealers, was part of the organisation's efforts to achieve its objective. Although the authorities focused on the illegal and violent activities of the organisation to the extent of claiming that it had "become 'just another gang' and 'part of the crime problem'" (Dixon & Johns 2001:15), the organisation did manage to achieve its objective through its numerous activities such as marches, the drug and gang awareness programmes, the issuing of ultimatums and its appeal to the authorities to curb the problem.

Despite the evidence that some members of PAGAD, especially those belonging to the G-Force, were implicated in 'urban terror' in the Western Cape, the organisation was clearly a force which drug dealers and gangs had to reckon with, and thus helped to control the problem of crime on the Cape Flats. Further, the efforts of the organisation in solving the problem of crime in the Western Cape was itself a challenge to the inability of the law enforcement agencies and the government in addressing the problems which tormented society. PAGAD continues to be a formidable challenge which exposes the government's failure to fulfil its constitutional obligation to create a safe and crime-free society for its citizens. This shows that where the government cannot fulfil the affirmed obligation, the citizens, through their initiative and effort, have the power to protect themselves in an open and democratic context. Although the violent and militant means that PAGAD has historically employed might be questionable, it is apparent that the organisation continues to help the government to deal with the problem of drugs and gangs through its crime awareness campaigns, marches and submission of memorandums to police stations and departments such as the Department of Justice. The fact that the organisation during its phase of extreme vigilantism and confrontation disregarded certain systems and structures of the government in its methods of protest and demonstrations against drugs and gangs does not undermine its constructive success in curbing the problem of crime and fostering a safer community in the Western Cape. Apparently, PAGAD was a formidable challenge to the authorities in that it sought to propagate its ideologies by partly bypassing the established law enforcement system and some of its members took the law into their own hands.

Muslim FBOs and their Public Engagement

The issues of poverty, unemployment and economic disparities continue to affect millions of South Africans. In post-apartheid South Africa, several Muslim Faith Based Organisations (FBOs) have been specialising in building houses for the poor and homeless, providing medical facilities and business opportunities to the disadvantaged, distributing food, clothing and blankets, and many other necessities, thereby helping the poor and needy in many impoverished communities throughout South Africa. There are three prominent Muslim FBOs in South Africa; namely the GOG, the Islamic Medical Association and Minara Chamber of Commerce. The partnership of these organisations with the government and their influence in the public sphere from the perspective of socio-economic empowerment, especially with reference to their humanitarian activities and the provision of medical and business-oriented facilities and opportunities. This section indicates that the political influence of Muslim FBOs has been based on their social welfare initiatives and political activism.

Muslim Faith-Based Organisations in South Africa

While the government is the major agent in the process of poverty alleviation, economic development and disaster relief provision, several civil society organisations play a central role in this regard. In South Africa, NGOs have roots dating back as far as the 1970s when several private humanitarian organisations began sprouting with a global outreach in their services and operations. Most religious NGOs and groupings that are involved in the provision of humanitarian aid and other poverty alleviation programmes can be classified as Faith-Based Organizations (FBOs). As voluntary and non-profit making groups, FBOs are largely religious-based or at least faith-inspired. The values of FBOs are primarily based on certain beliefs or core principles of a religious group that is often reflected in the vision and mission. The founders and members of FBOs are united based on religious beliefs, having been inspired by their religious faith to play a role in the social, political, economic or spiritual welfare of their members and society. Most Muslim FBOs in South Africa concentrate on poverty alleviation projects, disaster relief response and providing aid to the poor and disadvantaged communities across the country.

Muslim non-profit FBOs provide relief, charity, humanitarian aid and other poverty alleviation initiatives in both disaster relief and poverty-stricken areas throughout the country. There are approximately 43 Muslim non-profit FBOs in South Africa. These FBOs specialise in providing humanitarian disaster relief and charity. The Directory of Muslims Institutions and Mosques in South Africa produced in 1997 asserted that there were about 43 Muslim FBOs in South Africa. The major Muslim FBOs registered as independent NGOs include the Al-Imdaad Foundation, Islamic Relief South Africa, Muslim Hands South Africa, the South African National Zakah Fund, Minara Chamber of Commerce, Islamic Medical Association, GOG Foundation and the Africa Muslims Agency. Muslim FBOs seek to uplift the living conditions of the needy and poor by providing humanitarian services, empowerment of marginalised communities through poverty alleviation schemes and emergency response in cases of natural disasters.

The Gift of the Givers

The Gift of the Givers (Arabic, *Waqf al-Waqifin*) was founded by Dr Imtiaz Sooliman who has been chairperson since its establishment. Dr Imtiaz Sooliman was born in Potchefstroom, North-West province in 1962 and matriculated in 1978 at Greyville's Sastri College in Durban. The Soolimans arrived in South Africa in the early 1900s from the coastal region of India in search of economic opportunities. Dr Imtiaz Sooliman's grandfather, Joosab Gani Sooliman became the owner of a shop in Potchefstroom, a town in the North-West Province. As a young boy, he was exposed to works of charity through a family shop where his father Ismail Sooliman and grandfather Joosab Gani Sooliman generously offered lower prices and loans to impoverished customers. After matriculating, he enrolled at the University of Natal Medical School where he studied medicine and graduated as a medical doctor in 1984. Having completed his internship at Durban's King Edward VIII Hospital, he became a private medical practitioner in Pietermaritzburg in 1984. He subsequently became part of the Islamic Medical Association, a non-profit organisation aiming at providing medical and healthcare services to underprovided, underprivileged and impoverished communities. Having been founded in the early 1980s in South Africa, the Islamic Medical Association has branches around the country. It is primarily made up of Muslim health and medical professionals committed to the belief in the responsibility and need to serve the community.

In 1990, Dr Sooliman and other members of the Islamic Medical Association visited the Nacala Hospital in Northern Mozambique. The visit had been motivated by a severe drought and the grips of civil war in Mozambique. During the visit, Dr Sooliman was greatly inspired to focus on humanitarian work when he watched children desperately digging for water in the sand. Dr Sooliman describes this experience as a turning point in his life:

> The difficulty that ordinary Mozambicans experienced in their daily lives touched my heart ... I went to Mozambique because I wanted to help. I'd never done anything like that before in my life. I saw two frail and malnourished kids in a riverbed digging a half-metre-deep hole and using their tiny hands to scrap out muddy drinking water. That freaked me out (Morton 2014:10).

The Mozambican experience and his involvement in the Islamic Medical Association inspired Dr Sooliman to devote the rest of his life to the humanitarian cause. As soon as he returned to South Africa, Dr Sooliman began raising funds to provide humanitarian aid in Mozambique. Within a few days, he managed to raise enough money so that 30 boreholes may be dug, and malaria medication and relief may be delivered to Mozambique. This was Dr Sooliman's first major humanitarian outreach shortly before he founded the GOG. In 1991, he went on a humanitarian trip to the Gulf War in Iraq, before going to an area ravaged by a cyclone in Bangladesh in 1992. On his way to Bangladesh in August 1992, he passed through Istanbul, a major city in Turkey where he met a prominent Muslim Sufi teacher, Shaikh Muhammed Saffer Effendi al-Jerrahi. Dr Sooliman recalls every detail of his encounter with Shaikh al-Jerrahi which changed his life forever:

> It was 6th August 1992; I was 30 years old and it was a Thursday in Istanbul. The Shaikh's manner was so gentle, so soft, so accommodating…his face was engulfed in such light, his deep eyes were filled with such compassion and his presence was so magnetic – you just couldn't help being drawn to him, falling in love with his personality (Morton 2014:11).

During this encounter, Shaikh al-Jerrahi instructed Dr Sooliman to establish a charity organisation known as the GOG, and through it to serve the needs of all people unconditionally. The instruction was explicit: "My son, I'm not asking you. I'm instructing you to form an organisation that will be called the Gift of the Givers. You will help all people …" (Ritchie 2016). The spiritual teacher instructed Dr Sooliman to help all people regardless of race, class, religion, geographical location, political affiliation or culture. He was also instructed to help people unreservedly without expecting anything in return – he was to do this with compassion, mercy and love. He was told to do this for the rest of his life, since the 'best among people are those who benefit mankind'. This axiom, which the spiritual master employed in his instruction to Dr Sooliman, has since then become the motto and foundational principle of the organisation. Thus, based on the instruction of al-Jerrahi, Dr Sooliman founded the GOG on 6th August 1992.

As a Muslim FBO focusing on relief-giving and poverty alleviation projects, its headquarters have remained in Pietermaritzburg, KwaZulu Natal province with offices in places such as Cape Town, Johannesburg, Durban and Malawi. The GOG continues to draw its inspiration from the Islamic faith as signified by its logo. The capital letter 'G' on the logo symbolises the Almighty God who sustains and protects all creation while the small letter 'g' represents created humanity. According to the website of the GOG Foundation (2022), "the Logo symbolises the 'Hand' of Almighty

God over the hand of man signifying Positivity and Hope" and that "the Gift of the Givers Foundation and its Donors strive to be that symbol of Hope, God Willing". Since only the Almighty God is the absolute Sustainer and Provider of all creation, the GOG and its donors are metaphorically facilitators of God's aid, which they merely distribute to the needy and poor. Such sentiments portray the GOG as having profound spiritual origins, inspiration and motivating factors.

This marked the humble beginnings of the GOG, which has now grown and expanded its projects and outreach both within and beyond the borders of South Africa. It has worked in many countries worldwide such as Zimbabwe, Pakistan, Haiti, Syria, Somalia and Bosnia providing food items, aid materials and rescue teams. Since the 1990s, Dr Sooliman has earned many accolades and honours such as the Order of the Baobab which he received in 2010 in recognition of the organisation's work. Imtiaz Sooliman was among the local heroes who were honoured by former President Jacob Zuma on Freedom Day ceremony in Pretoria in April 2010. He was awarded with Silver, the Order of Baobab in recognition of the work of his organisation in disaster relief operations. In 2016, Dr Sooliman was awarded the prestigious Global Citizen Award in London for his humanitarian work through the GOG. The Global Citizen Award is an international award given annually by the international advisory firm 'Henley and Partners' to individuals whose contribution to the global community is inspirational and extraordinary.

By the end of August 1992, Dr Sooliman and the GOG team found themselves intervening with aid in the Bosnian crisis helping the needy. The organisation sent about 780 tons of blankets, clothes and food to Bosnia through Croatia and Turkey. By 1994, the GOG began developing containerised healthcare clinics to provide primary healthcare to be used in rural areas. The organisation managed to have twenty-three such clinics developed and deployed mainly within South Africa. Between 1994 and 2003, the GOG developed from being an organisation geared towards the alleviation of poverty and disaster relief response to providing many humanitarian activities and projects including psychological support. For example, the Careline was formed in 1997 by Dr Sooliman and his first wife Zohra primarily to address the psychological challenges, especially of the disadvantaged. Its mission statement emphasizes a commitment to the unconditional service of all humankind. Careline offers counselling services and training to various underprivileged communities in South Africa. The GOG has undergone tremendous growth and development in its humanitarian operations. Although the GOG has been active in many international operations, it has also been fully engaged in various disaster relief and humanitarian operations within South Africa.

When Impendle, a town in Umgungundlovu Municipal District, KwaZulu-Natal province was hit by a Hurricane on 24 December 1994, GOG assisted about three hundred poor families with blankets and food parcels. The Gift of the Givers carried out the relief with Provincial Traditional Authorities Minister Nyanga Ngubane, Provincial Social Welfare Minister Gideon Zulu and Premier Frank Mdlalose. On 25th December 1995, the floods in the Edendale Valley in KwaZulu-Natal province, an informal settlement that comprised several slum communities and squatter camps, left about 130 people dead and 1000 others homeless. The GOG responded to this disaster by providing "500 food hampers, cooking pots, eating utensils, blankets and new clothing to homeless victims" (Morton 2014:29). Apart from Edendale Valley, the organisation provided carpets and mattresses to the flood victims in areas such as Mpumuza, Kwa Pata and Slangspruit.

The organisation also placed several containerised mobile clinics in places such as Atteridgeville Township, west of Pretoria and Tembisa Township on the East Rand, Gauteng province which help provide primary healthcare facilities to poor communities. From 1994 onwards, the organisation also began assisting with fires, diseases, floods, droughts and tornadoes throughout South Africa, especially in poorer areas such as townships, informal settlements and rural areas. The organisation slowly created contacts and secured stable suppliers and donors who were willing to contribute and support its humanitarian work. As such, the GOG managed to start opening other projects to help disadvantaged communities. For example, the Education Support Programme was launched in 1997 to contribute to the educational transformation of the country.

Since its establishment in 1997, the Education Support Programme has been empowering young people by providing learning materials in poverty-stricken communities across South Africa. It provides learning materials such as computers, stationery, books and supports cultural activities, sports, science laboratories and uniforms for learners in schools. By 2000s, the GOG became the largest NGO focusing on humanitarian disaster relief operations with headquarters in Africa. In May 2008, Xenophobia ignited violence through several riots which started in Gauteng settlements such as Alexandra where several foreign nationals from countries such as Zimbabwe and Mozambique were attacked and killed. The violence spread to many parts of South Africa especially Free State, Mpumalanga, KwaZulu-Natal and the North West.

Thousands of foreigners deserted their homes due to xenophobic attacks and took refuge at police stations, often without clothing, bedding and food. The GOG provided basic needs such as food parcels, tents and blankets to xenophobia victims. For example, Desai and Vahed (2010:6) affirm that Allauddin Sayed Gauteng's head of the GOG operations "immediately organised for 400 loaves of bread and 200 blankets to be sent to the Alexandra Police Station". Although the xenophobia victims were based at police stations, the GOG continued to provide financial aid, clothing, food, baby goods and sanitary facilities when they were moved to refugee shelters and city halls where they were housed. The GOG continued to provide relief support to such places for over three weeks in many parts of the country that had been affected by the violent xenophobic attacks.

The GOG has also begun providing bursary schemes to financially stranded young South Africans. According to (Morton 2014:29), "in 2009 Gift of the Givers disbursed R1.2 million on bursaries and by 2012 that figure was more than R5 million annually". The bursary scheme has since continued to help impoverished youths find employment and fund their studies. The GOG was also among the first to respond to disasters between December 2010 and February 2011 when different parts of South Africa experienced a series of floods which led to material loss and destruction of houses and drinking water infrastructure. The most affected areas included Orange River, Bloemsmond, Upington and

Keimoes communities in the Northern Cape Province, Bella Vista in Western Cape, and the Ladysmith and Newcastle regions of KwaZulu-Natal. The response of the government through disaster management activities was inadequate. Several district municipalities struggled to cope with the situation due to the lack of proper disaster management structures and professional skills. The GOG, through its team, intervened by first conducting assessments of the impacts of the floods, and then distributing the much-needed relief to flood stricken victims. The GOG distributed food parcels, clothing, hygiene packs and household goods to many parts of the country during the period of the flood crisis. The Gift of the Givers used trucks and a helicopter to transport its rescue teams and supplies to victims of floods in many parts of the country. It also catered for about 50 isolated families in places such as George Island, Eksteen Island and Lanklaas. Clearly, the GOG began responding to many other crisis situations to support the relevant government arm such as local municipality.

In 2011, the GOG launched the Jumpstart Schools Entrepreneurial Programme, another youth empowerment project aimed at addressing the challenge of unemployment by supporting youth entrepreneurship. In 2011, the Jumpstart Schools Entrepreneurial Programme awarded 148 Grade 11 learners with Jumpstart marketing packages consisting of crucial elements for an emerging entrepreneur such as a business card, an e-brochure, an invoice document and access to mentoring services. Such elements areessential in assisting youth to develop the communication, marketing and transactional aspects of running businesses. The program is also meant to inspire the spirit of entrepreneurship in an age of technology and where business is central to human activities. On the inauguration of the Jumpstart Schools Entrepreneurial Programme, Dr Imtiaz Sooliman stressed the importance of sustanined economic growth in south Africa. When the programme was launched, it targeted several participating schools in Durban and Pietermaritzburg's marginalised communities in KwaZulu-Natal. The program aimed at supporting and stimulating the entrepreneurial zeal amongst youth, especially those in high school. In 2011, the GOG also responded to the high poverty levels in Verdwaal, a populated area in North-West province, where four children died from hunger and starvation. Dr Sooliman was astonished by the incident and lamented in a press release:

> Could it really be happening here, that four children die from starvation in a country which is the economic powerhouse of the African continent? ... [We have] a distraught mother, an impoverished community, a lack of education, a lack of opportunity, unemployment ... these are factors that could lead to a crisis, but they should not lead to death ... As a nation we all have failed; our morality, our spirituality ... these are OUR children, in OUR Africa, who died a preventable death in OUR presence. This is extremely painful. But moaning, blaming and complaining is counter-productive in the absence of an appropriate response (Morton 2014:152).

When the GOG dispatched its team to the Verdwaal's rural areas, it found that thousands of people lived in extreme hunger and destitution due to lack of access to basic human needs and unemployment. The GOG instituted feeding schemes to supply food parcels, cooked meals, bottled water, including blankets, detergents and washing powder for thousands of people. The GOG also appealed to the Department of Home Affairs to provide identity documents to hundreds of people in the region who did not have access to social grants. Furthermore, the organisation constructed a kitchen at Motlhatswa Primary School in Verdwaal to be used by the local community in memory of the four children and a plaque as a symbol of poverty in a country rich of mineral resources. The essential needs such as food that the organisation dispatched to Verdwaal over a few months and the construction of the kitchen cost over R2.2 million. The kitchen constructed by the Gift of the Givers at Motlhatswa Primary School was opened on 21 September 2012. During the event, the plague was unveiled and over 3000 people were fed by the organisation.

The GOG in 2012 responded to what has since become known as the Marikana massacre, which occurred at the Lonmin Platinum Mine in Marikana, North West province. Although the tragedy occurred between 11 and 16 August, a series of deaths and casualties of miners, police and security guards followed until 20 September 2012. The massacre had been preceded by peaceful protests over wage disputes between the mine management and the mineworkers that later led to fatal clashes with police. The South African Police Service (SAPS) used lethal force and opened fire on a group of mine strikers, wounding and killing workers. The dispute which started by a wage disagreement between the Lonmin mine management and mine workers was intensified by a further dispute between the Association of Mineworkers and Construction Union (AMCU) and the National Union of Mineworkers (NUM). On 8th September 2012, the GOG commenced its aid delivery of food parcels, blankets, children's toys and paints to the miners and their families whose unpaid strike had lasted for over three months. The GOG teams also rendered psychological support to the victims of the traumatising events in Marikana.

The Gift of Givers has also historically responded to drought and water crises in South Africa. The organisation responded to the dire condition of the people in the informal settlements near the Randfontein dump in Gauteng province were as of 2012 about five thousand people lived in sheer poverty and indignity. The residents lacked proper housing, good water sanitation, toilets, and endured the horrifying smell from the dumpsite with no access to healthcare, schooling and employment. In May 2012, the organisation delivered JoJo water tanks and taps to the Randfontein dump, during a water crisis and continued to fill up the tank once a week. The organisation also constructed a shelter as a central point for medical examination and distribution by doctors and nurses and provided meals for people. Apart from medical care, daily meals and blankets, the organisation responded by providing:

> Five additional toilets, five more taps, two 10 000 litre Jojo tanks, new clothing, shoes, personal and domestic hygiene packs, toys, educational items, food parcels, sweets, biscuits, fruit, mattresses, sanitary pads, disposable nappies, bottled water and plastic dishes are all on the way (Gift of the Givers Foundation 2021).

In April 2013, the GOG responded to a fire in Khayelitsha's informal township located on the Cape Flats in Western Cape. The residents of informal settlements in Khayelitsha face huge challenges such as high crime levels, unemployment, and lack of opportunities for livelihood. The shacks in Khayelitsha are built close to each other with iron sheet metal and timber, and more than half of the population have little or no access to clean water and food, with poor healthcare services and public transport. The severity of poverty, overpopulation, lack of alternative livelihood and poor infrastructure continue to produce high levels of crime, drug abuse and violence in the area.

On 1 January 2013, an accidental fire set many informal houses ablaze in Khayelitsha's Barney Molokwane (BM) section which destroyed over 800 shacks, leaving about 4000 people homeless (Brink 2014 48-53). The rapidly spreading fire left most residents without property, housing, food and clothing. Having provided the homeless victims with clothing, blankets and food parcels, the GOG built about 100 permanent houses which were handed over in April 2013 at an event that was attended by former President Jacob Zuma. The organisation also provided beds, mattresses, brooms, crockery, and other house material to the houses. The project cost the Gift of the Givers R4 million. They were built by professional builders, with a stable foundation, fitted with windows, solar panels and painted. In the same year, the GOG responded by providing food parcels, blankets and tents to the victims of storms in KwaZulu Natal townships such as Molweni, Vulindlela, Imbali, Msinga and Sweetwaters.

Moreover, in view of the 2013 Mandela Day, the GOG began the Alexandra Housing Scheme to provide houses for poor people living in informal settlements in Alexandra Township, Gauteng province. Dr Sooliman remarked that the aim of the GOG was "not just to establish a home, but a village in a healthier environment. Alex would be our third housing project" (Morton 2014:187), after the houses the organisation constructed in Khayelitsha and Duduza. With the help of the Gauteng Provincial Disaster Management and local municipal council, the GOG also constructed houses, paved driveways, a communal kitchen and a children's park with a security system for the new settlement. The newly constructed residence was officially opened on 11 October 2013 by Cornelia September, Minister of Human Settlements.

In November 2015, the GOG responded to another fire that left one person dead and about 100 people homeless in Alexandra

Township, Gauteng. The fire destroyed about 100 shacks, affecting over 110 people who readily needed assistance. The GOG responded by providing blankets, food, clothing and so forth. In 2016, the GOG responded to storm disasters by providing aid to the victims of a storm in Ennerdale, Gauteng and Ottawa and Shallcross communities in Durban, KwaZulu-Natal provinces respectively. Between April and May 2016, the GOG also responded to the violent protests in Vuwani, Limpopo province where roads were blocked, and schools set alight.

The residents were protesting the announcement made by the Municipal Demarcation Board to integrate Vuwani into a new municipality. In its response to the destroyed Vuwani schools, the GOG employed an education support programme to help pupils and teachers whose schools had lost textbooks, and other learning and teaching materials. During the violent protests, teaching materials such as printers and projectors were seriously ruined, while desks and windows were smashed and destroyed. Due to the efforts of the Gift of the Givers, the number of pupils returning to school after the protests increased. The GOG delivered "80 000 pieces of stationery, 100 litres of Dulux paint, paintbrushes, food parcels, mealie meal, printer cartridges" (Gift of the Givers Foundation 2016). The and other essential materials to several affected schools in Vuwani area. The GOG also employed programmes such as mind-set educational materials, videos and internet to help learners catch up with their work. Furthermore, the organisation participated in the repairing of schools such as Radzambo Secondary School in the area.

In 2017, the GOG responded with food parcels to two fires, Knysna and Hout Bay areas in the Western Cape where it catered for over 2500 families with hygiene packs, food parcels and blankets. The organisation also distributed stationery, food and uniforms to learners at Silikamva and Imizamo Yethu High Schools who had lost school items in the fires. Similarly, during the 2017 drought that struck most of Western Cape, the GOG intervened by developing the Beaufort West Witperd Aquifer Development Project to deliver two million litres of water to Beaufort West daily. The Beaufort West Witperd Aquifer Development Project was a massive programme initiated by the Gift of the Givers with the help of specialists. The project was meant to pump water delivered by the GOG into the town's water reservoir, thereby helping the local authorities to curb the water shortage. In the wake of 2018, the GOG found itself continuing to supply water in many parts of Western Cape due to continued droughts. For example, the GOG donated bottled water to schools in Malmesbury and to residents in places such as Moorreesburg, Breede Valley and Klapmuts Communities.

In June 2018, the GOG responded with a R15 million borehole intervention to save the people of Sutherland, a town in the Northern Cape province which highly depended on water for sustainability. The GOG delivered bales of fodder to Sutherland whose several boreholes had dried out. The organisation also established new boreholes in the area, a project that cost millions of Rands. The delivery of fodder was followed by "food parcels, blankets, hygiene packs and warm clothing for the farm labourers, the general population and school children (who will be provided with 5000 specially formulated nutritious meals)" (Gift of the Givers Foundation 2018). Furthermore, in 2018 the GOG responded to fires in Dunoon Township, Western Cape in March 2018 and in Cato Manor informal settlement in Durban, which destroyed many shacks in May 2018.

The organisation's projects are centred on disaster response, management and other poverty alleviation projects. Through its disaster relief response and management, the organisation provides emergency supplies of various needs such as medical teams, counselling teams, food, medicines and shelter. The organisation also responds through poverty alleviation projects to various communities where unemployment and poverty are severe. Since its origin in 1992, the GOG has developed various operations and projects as demonstrated in its historical development. As of July 2018, the GOG Foundation's (2018) website lists its projects and activities:

> Commencing as a disaster response agency, the organisation now has 21 categories of projects which include bursaries, agricultural self-sustainability, water provision, counselling and life skills services, entrepreneurship and job creation, establishment of primary health care clinics and medical support to hospitals, winter warmth and supply of new clothing and shoes, sports development, feeding schemes and

food parcel distribution, supply of household and personal hygiene packs, educational support and toy distribution, provision of housing, care of the physically and mentally challenged, orphans and the elderly as some of our diverse activities.

In the medical and healthcare sphere, the GOG has provided aid to impoverished communities, and in cases of natural disasters through the provision of medical personnel, rescue teams, medicines, medical equipment and children's vaccines. One of the primary ways the organisation has used to address the medical and health concerns of impoverished communities in South Africa has been using containerised healthcare clinics. The GOG's containerised clinics which fall under the primary healthcare unit was the first of its kind to be developed in the world. Developed in 1994, the containerised mobile health care has become one of the key means used by the GOG to reach out to the poor and underprovided communities. The fact that containerised mobile clinics of the GOG are easily transportable, waterproof and conveniently accessible makes it easy for the organisation to transport them to rural areas where they are effectively utilised by many. According to the GOG Foundation (2018), the containerised primary health care clinics cater for many needs and services:

> Services include minor ailments, immunisations, integrated management of childhood infections, wound treatments, burn care, screening for hypertension and diabetes, pap smears, antenatal care, counselling services, specialist psychiatric care for the elderly, TB patient follow up and a range of primary care services.

Over the years, the organisation deployed various containerised clinics to various parts of South Africa where the service caters for thousands of poor South Africans each year. For example, since 1995 the organisation has transported containerised clinics to many towns and townships in provinces such as Gauteng, Northern Cape, KwaZulu Natal and Free State. The majority of the targeted places have been rural areas, townships and informal settlements where people have little or no access to medical care due to socio-economic reasons such as unemployment, poverty and lack of accessibility due to poor public transport. The Gift of the Givers through containerised primary health care facilities has, over the years, been able to reach out to them for free, based on the organisation's conviction that "if the people cannot get to health services then the health services must get to the people" (Gift of the Givers Foundation 2018).

Through the GOG, vulnerable populations and disadvantaged communities throughout South Africa have been able to have access to medical and healthcare facilities. For example, in 1999 the GOG deployed two containerised primary healthcare clinics to Tembisa, a large impoverished township in Gauteng province. The GOG also provides medical support to hospitals and clinics by contributing necessary items such as antiseptics, medicines and medical equipment, disposables, hygiene packs and providing access to ambulances. One of the hospitals that the GOG has funded over the years is Sarah Fox Children's Convalescent Hospital, a hospital based in Silvertown, Western Cape. The hospital provides healthcare services to "communities which are severely impoverished and provides palliative, respite and sub-acute care, with the majority of the patients they serve having HIV/AIDS, TB and cancer" (Duncan 2016:66).

Although Sarah Fox Hospital deals with health and medical related cases, in recent years abandoned and poor children have been housed at the hospital. The GOG's involvement with the hospital began in July 2008 when the hospital was on the verge of closing due to financial constraints. By 2009, the GOG began providing food regularly and upgrading the home for the children. By the end of 2009, the GOG had painted various parts of the building, fixed broken windows, began a feeding scheme, installed carpets, replaced mattresses and provided towels, bed sheets and blankets. By July 2011, the GOG was still providing "furniture, equipment, toiletries, toys, baby food and linen to the hospital every month" (Mposo & Flemmit 2011) while the Department of Health paid the salaries of workers and staff. In July 2011, the Gift of the Givers collaborated with Operation Warm Hearts, an organisation which helps the needy communities in Western Cape to donate blankets, clothing and food parcels to Sarah Fox Children's Convalescent Hospital. Linked to the healthcare and medical services is the organisation's counselling services offered to underprivileged communities through support groups, life coaching, free telephone and face to face counselling and educational programmes. Such facilities fall under the organisation's Careline Counselling Services whose aim is to provide an open, confidential and sincere service to impoverished people who face different challenges of life.

The GOG runs feeding schemes and hunger alleviation initiatives in many parts of South Africa where many children and adults are starving, malnourished and destitute. Nutritional challenges are part of the daily life of many South Africans who lack access to adequate food. The GOG has developed two major feeding schemes in Western Cape and Gauteng provinces. The feeding scheme in Gauteng began in March 2008 in Berea, Gauteng and has since grown to over seven feeding points. In Gauteng, the GOG provides feeding schemes to the disadvantaged in locations such as "Leandra Early Childhood Development Centre, Reamogetswe Centre for the Disabled" (Gift of the Givers Foundation 2018) and Zenzeleni Children's Village which cater for the poor and disadvantaged.

Similarly, the feeding scheme in the Western Cape has feeding centres in places such as Gugulethu, Cloetesdal and Rondebosch. The feeding schemes provide bread, soup, stew and rolls to vulnerable children, the disabled, refugees and those living in rural areas. Apart from feeding schemes, the GOG runs the Food Parcel Project that was initiated in 2002 to focus on helping poverty-stricken areas. Through the Food Parcel Project, the GOG delivers food parcels to various parts of the country, thereby responding to the hunger crisis and starvation. The organisation's Food Parcel Project is the largest in South Africa and feeds children, the unemployed, the homeless and the needy. For example, in 2003 the organisation prepared more than two hundred thousand food parcels to feed thousands of people in the Eastern Cape and KwaZulu Natal provinces. In 2003, the Gift of the Givers had been made the sole provider in Eastern Cape and KwaZulu Natal provinces by the National Treasury. Furthermore, in 2004 the GOG developed Sibusiso Ready Food Supplement, which has become a renowned nutritional supplement for the malnourished. For Maharaj (2012:3), the Sibusiso Ready Food Supplement is:

a soya based high-energy protein food supplement ... The aim was to develop a nutritional supplement to meet the dietary challenges of people in disaster situations where there is limited access to clean, safe water, refrigeration and poor hygiene and sanitation practices. Sibusiso is indicated for weight loss, muscle wasting, low energy levels, nutritional challenges, weakness, and decreased appetite.

The GOG distributes the nutritional supplement to places where people face dietary and nutritional challenges, especially in cases were children are malnourished, underweight and suffer from debilitating diseases such as tuberculosis. For example, in December 2013 the GOG distributed "120 Sibusiso Ready Food at Teresanne Hall" in Sydenham and "300 Sibusiso Ready Food at Fairview Road" (Gift of the Givers Foundation 2013) in Verulam, KwaZulu Natal. To contribute to the alleviation of poverty in South Africa, the GOG has also been engaged in distributing agricultural inputs such as fertilisers, maize seeds, and tools to the unemployed, the elderly and women in rural areas and townships in South Africa. In January 2018, the GOG delivered fertiliser and maize seed to several needy and unemployed families in KwaJama, Kwa-Zulu Natal. In February 2018 a team from the Gift of the Givers provided seed and fertiliser to over 100 families in KwaJama having planted maize for them. Furthermore, housing development has been part of the GOG's operations through projects such as the Khayelitsha Housing Village and Alexandra Housing Village in 2013. In 2011, the organisation provided shelter to the people when a devastating Tornado in Duduza, Johannesburg left about more than 140 families homeless. The Gift of the Givers provided temporary shelter, material for the construction of permanent houses, clothing, blankets and clean water to the victims of a tornado at Duduza. The Gift of the Givers spent about R2 Million in this aid project. Through its water provision project, the GOG has responded to various water crises in South Africa, especially in Western Cape following the recent drought in the province by either constructing boreholes or distributing water. In 2015, the organisation provided water to over four thousand families along the South Coast in KwaZulu Natal province which had clean water shortages. The Gift of the Givers distributes water to thousands of underprivileged individuals in South Africa each year.

The water project continues to help people who lack access to clean water and areas that are affected by drought such as Western Cape. The organisation continues to distribute water to many underprivileged areas through bottled water, taps, boreholes and water tanks in areas affected by drought or that lack access to clean water.

The GOG also runs the educational support project through which it establishes open source computer laboratories, enhances educational infrastructure and furniture, distributes stationery and provides trophies to learners. The GOG also supports sports and cultural programmes in schools, entrepreneurship skills and life-skills workshops, provides uniforms, distributes blankets to learners and supports early childhood development centres for vulnerable children. The organisation continues to benefit thousands of underprivileged children across the country who lack access to quality education, learning material and educational facilities and a learner-friendly educational environment. The GOG also provides support to institutions that serve underprivileged and impoverished families and individuals. The support is provided to institutions that serve the needs of the elderly, orphans, mentally or physically challenged and abused children and women. Between 2008 and 2018, the GOG provided support to institutions such as Victory Outreach Rehabilitation Home, Sunrise Special Care Centre, Adelaide Tambo School for the Physically Challenged and Athlone School for the Blind.

The GOG has over the years developed collaboration with the government, especially through departments that are concerned with civil service and socio-economic development. The organisation also collaborates with local municipal councils and provincial government officials throughout the country in several humanitarian projects and disaster relief efforts. The Gift of the Givers has worked with the government in various humanitarian projects in the country. On several occasions, government officials have acknowledged the work of the GOG through letters, awards and material support. In 2003, the National Treasury through the Minister of Social Development granted the organisation the status of preferred provider for Eastern Cape and KwaZulu Natal provinces. According to Khan, Gabralla and Ebrahim (2013:733), the GOG was the "only organisation in the history of South Africa to receive sixty million rand from government to roll out 204 000 emergency food parcels" in the two provinces.

Although the National Treasury had granted the food parcels programme of the other nine provinces to seven companies on tender, the GOG was granted the two provinces without tender. The grant of R60 million which the government granted to the organisation for food parcels indicates the support of the government. Government officials often attend various distribution and building-opening events of the houses built by the GOG. In 2013, former President Jacob Zuma together with representatives from the Ministry of Social Development attended the official opening of the houses in Khayelitsha constructed by the GOG. Before the houses were built, the GOG team had discussions with the Cape Town City Mayor Ms Patricia De Lille and other officials from the city management concerning the organisation's plans to construct houses in Khayelitsha. On 25 January 2013, Dr Imtiaz Sooliman and other team members met with the Cape Town City Manager Mr Achmat Ebrahim and Ms Patricia De Lille, City's Mayor to discuss the building of new houses for the homeless victims of a devastating fire in Khayelitsha. Similarly, in March 2016 Senzeni Zokwana Minister of Agriculture, Forestry and Fisheries had discussions with members of the GOG regarding the Drought Relief Campaign.

Moreover, due to its work with refugees and its involvement in incidents of Xenophobia, the GOG has collaborated with the Minister of Home Affairs. Due to its various projects, the organisation has also collaborated with officials from the Departments of Defence and Military; Water Affairs; Social Development; Basic Education; Women, Children and People with Disabilities, Justice; Environmental Affairs and the Department of Agriculture, Forestry and Fisheries. The GOG has also collaborated with provincial government members throughout South Africa who have held discussions with the organisation, supported its programmes and attended GOG's distributions. Apart from cases where government officials attend distributions and official openings of humanitarian projects organised by the GOG or support the organisation financially, formal collaborations with the government have been minimal. For example, in July 2018 the Ekurhuleni Disaster and Emergency Services (DEMS) from City of Ekurhuleni Metropolitan Municipality in Gauteng signed a Memorandum of Understanding with GOG's officials to conduct awareness campaigns and collaborate in disaster relief cases.

The awareness programmes have been centred on educating the community on how to respond to disasters in the metropolitan. According to Sibeko (2018), Themba Gadebe Ekurhuleni metropolitan spokesperson stressed that the metropolitan and the GOG have "already worked together during disasters that happened in the metro previously. The two parties will now officially share expertise in disaster relief and response". The GOG partners with local municipalities in responding to natural disasters, fires and the transportation of rescue teams and the distribution of blankets, food parcels, wheelchairs and so on in many parts of South Africa. The GOG has also collaborated with the government in cases where funding is needed or when help is needed to deliver disaster relief to certain areas. According to Onwuegbuchulam (2016:184), Ayesha Sooliman of the GOG in an interview on 5 February 2015 remarked:

> If government comes through to be of assistance, well and good we work with them but otherwise we do what we can …
> If there is a kind of partnership, the role we would expect from the government is to help with funding. Delivering aid requires money; we have to buy the goods and deliver to the people that need. So, their role to provide finance will be appreciated.

Apart from the material support from the government, the GOG receives donations from several Muslim and non-Muslim individuals, projects, companies and organisations. For example, in 2017 the GOG received financial support from Msunduzi Rates Forum and Benoni Spurs, bottled water from Bedfordview Musalla, stationery from Bongani Rainmaker Logistics and blankets from South African Home Loans in Umhlanga. During the Covid-19 pandemic between 2020 and mid-2022, the GOG intervened mainly by providing food, water and medical support both within and outside South Africa. The organisation's website states that:

At the beginning of the COVID-19 pandemic, Gift of the Givers introduced medical intervention in a controlled manner, with the initial focus on health-care professionals at state institutions... The Gift of the Givers team remain committed to providing masks, coveralls, hazmat suits, re-usable and disposable surgical gowns, scrub suits, latex gloves, head covers, shoe covers, goggles, visors and thermal scans, as well enhancing the medical capacity of state institutions with the distribution of portable ultrasound machines, pulse oximeters, laryngoscopes and medicines for general use to support facilities.....With an aim to fight the spread of COVID-19, Gift of the Givers has in place a number of water projects which remain ongoing to give millions of South Africans access to running water... Due to severe water shortages and challenges in obtaining a regular and reliable supply of water, Gift of the Givers has included in its water projects, the distribution of bottled water; delivery of clean water for drinking and hygiene via our three water tankers; and the drilling and equipping of boreholes. Our water tankers deliver 600 000 litres of water per week in the Eastern Cape. In addition, we have drilled 420 fully-functional boreholes in the past two years, providing clean drinking water daily to a number of identified hospitals and many thousands of people... Providing food and access to basic supply necessities was an area of major concern during the country's hard lockdown. The assumption was that there would be a breakdown of primary services regarding the delivery of food and basic necessities to vulnerable communities throughout the country, most particularly those residing in rural areas...Gift of the Givers provided rations to more than 100 feeding centres and has delivered 320 000 food parcels to hungry families across South Africa. In addition, the organisation has played a critical role in ensuring the delivery of fodder, valued at millions of Rand, in order to save the lives of animals and, as a consequence, the livelihoods of needy farmers and their workforces. We envisage a much greater intervention in these areas into the future (Gift of the Givers 2022).

The GOG also collaborates with government tertiary institutions and other institutes of learning in its humanitarian work and the alleviation of poverty in poor and needy communities across

South Africa. In KwaZulu Natal, the GOG has formed partnership with the University of KwaZulu Natal's Faculty of Agriculture in Pietermaritzburg.

The partnership is centred on providing bursaries, scholarships, enhancing the research output on food security and production in impoverished areas and improving knowledge in agriculture. Moreover, apart from the many awards that Dr Sooliman has received as the founder and chairperson, the GOG has itself received several awards as an organisation in recognition of its humanitarian work. For example, 81 per cent of the awards the organisation has received have been from within South Africa, whereas only 19 per cent are from the international community. Key government officials both in South Africa and abroad have awarded some of the awards to Dr Sooliman.

The Minara Chamber of Commerce

The Minara Chamber of Commerce was formed in May 2000 as a need arose for an organisation that would promote unity and harmony in the business sector by unifying independent businesses within the Muslim business community. Before the formation of the organisation, Muslim entrepreneurs and businesses had been deliberating the importance of establishing a formal organisation that would assist them in representing their needs both to the government and within the business community. Since its establishment, Minara "has since grown tremendously and now serves as a platform to represent and assist South African businesses, entrepreneurs and professionals" (Minara Chamber of Commerce 2018). Minara has become an important forum within the Muslim community which helps its affiliates to establish and expand business networks by mediating for trade delegations with the government and other stakeholders. Minara focusses "on uplifting and promoting individual, family-owned and independent Muslim businesses with a vision and mission to bring them from the margins into the frontline of the mainstream economy" (KwaZulu Natal Business Sense News 2018) and promoting harmonious business transactions.

Based on the Code of Conduct and Ethics which are rooted in an Islamic ethos, Minara through its objectives and workings attempts to provide guidance and formal representation regarding business within and beyond the Muslim community. Although Minara is primarily an Islamic organisation, its membership is open to both Muslim and non-Muslim business professionals, entrepreneurs and businesses. Based on its collaboration with other stakeholders, Minara provides a primary platform for businesses based on the following services:

> (1) Creating Business Networking Opportunities; (2) Hosting of Inbound and Outbound Trade Missions; (3) Promotion of Youth & Women Entrepreneurship; (4) Providing and facilitating access to information and business best practice; (5) Dissemination of information via the Minara Chamber of Commerce website, the Minara Newsletter and mainstream and community media; (6) Establishment of a databank and resource centre; (7) Training seminars, workshops and mentorship programs; (8) Advocacy, lobbying and networking in various forums at the national, provincial and local levels in the Governmental and Economic spheres; and (9) Initiating research and development" (Minara Chamber of Commerce 2018).

Through such comprehensive and broad services, Minara fosters business initiatives and guiding principles for businesses within South Africa and internationally. The same idea is reflected in the vision of Minara that emphasises the centrality of establishing "a dynamic and vibrant business community which is guided by an Islamic tenet and which makes a meaningful contribution to the socio-economic development of the Muslim community and South Africa as a whole" (Minara Chamber of Commerce 2018).

Since its establishment, Minara has been involved in various initiatives, projects and issues concerning social, economic, political and educational aspects of the South African society generally. Such a broad outlook has enabled Minara to acquire political influence in the public sphere, mainly based on its engagement with government officials and other governmental and non-governmental business-oriented organisations. Minara has been interacting with the government on several occasions over round table discussions, panel discussions and gala dinners on matters concerning business initiatives or projects and community development. The organisation has interacted with the Trade and Investment KwaZulu Natal and Department of Economic Development and Environmental Affairs regarding redundant bureaucratic barriers for businesses.

When Jacob Zuma was elected president in 2009, Minara issued a statement expressing its confidence in his election and the new cabinet that he appointed. Minara noted that "the choice of the cabinet appointees reflects the President's commitment to service delivery and implementation of policy" and that "the incoming Minister of Trade & Investment, Minister of Finance and the Minister of Planning appointees are well chosen and will increase business and investor confidence" (Minara Chamber of Commerce 2009). Nevertheless, Minara cautioned that the expansion of ministries by former President Jacob Zuma should not lead to huge spending in bureaucracy but increase government delivery in South Africa. Minara also expressed hope for economic growth and more collaboration between government and businesses. In April 2009, Minara hosted a Gala Dinner during which the organisation gave recognition awards to forty influential Muslim individuals who have positively contributed to the development of society in South Africa in various ways. While acknowledging the presence of former ANC President Jacob Zuma, at the event and the centrality of the awards, Ebrahim Patel Minara president affirmed:

> The Muslim community has contributed tremendously to the development of South Africa. We are an integral and important part of this rainbow nation and we must continue in our efforts. This evening was to highlight the importance of the Muslim Community and to celebrate its success ... We are especially honoured that Mr Zuma was able to attend the event and that he presented some of the recipients with their awards. This was the ideal opportunity to showcase the Muslim contribution in building our nation (Minara Chamber of Commerce 2016).

During the event, Minara also presented the Leadership Award to a Member of the Executive Council for Economic Affairs and Development, Dr Zweli Mkhize in recognition of his leadership. Minara has also been involved in the social economic development initiatives especially by "teaming up with other organisations to raise funds and facilitate empowering the un-bankable and needy communities to create small businesses to generate continuous revenue" (Minara Chamber of Commerce 2009). Apart from the social economic development and empowerment programmes, Minara is engaged in the Education Fund through which it provides financial support to underprivileged children in the educational sector. Regarding the Education Fund, the Minara Chamber of Commerce's website affirms:

> Minara considers that education to our young and old is at the forefront to human empowerment and long-term sustainability of individuals and has therefore set up an education fund to support its members' contributions towards sponsoring bursaries for disadvantaged children's and youth's primary, secondary and tertiary education (Minara Chamber of Commerce 2018).

Minara has also been having panel discussions with government officials especially in Durban, KwaZulu Natal concerning local business issues such as basic service delivery with municipal and provincial leaders. In March 2016, Minara held a Round Table Discussion with KwaZulu Natal's ANC chairperson Sihle Zikalala under the theme "Transformation of the Economy in the Face of Global Economic Challenges" in/at Sherwood, Durban. In October 2013, Minara hosted The Provincial Round Table Discussion with the Department of Economic Development at Country Club in Durban based on the need to respond to the socio-economic challenges especially the shrinking economy. The Round Table involved relevant provincial government ministers, and departments and prominent business leaders. In a letter addressed to the Department of Economic Development, regarding the event, Solly Suleman president of Minara noted that his organisation "is now stepping up to the challenge of addressing the greater economic challenges of our country by creating a working partnership of leading business leaders and government" (Suleman 2013:1). The aim of the event was to create economic platforms that would foster employment opportunities, devise strategies for economic development, address the challenges of poverty and inequality and discuss the direction of the National Development Plan. Suleman (2013:1) noted:

> The Minara Chamber is committed to its vision of a prosperous and vibrant economy that will benefit all the people of this land. A partnership of a committed government and our leading business minds can unleash a growth path that will not only benefit all its people but will be the engine house of economic activity and prosperity in Africa.

In 2014, Minara organised the '20 Year Democracy Dinner' concerning elections awareness, which was attended by the Durban Mayor, the KwaZulu Natal representative Member of the Executive Council of Finance and the then Minister of Communications Yunus Carrim who attended as guest speaker. Despite the divergent opinions within the Muslim community in South Africa on the centrality of exercising the voting within the current political context, '20 Year Democracy Dinner' discussion focused on why the voting privilege and right fosters support for democracy and the type of government that is needed. In the same year, Minara held a congratulations dinner for the KwaZulu Natal Provincial Government, and hosted Pravin Gordhan, Minister of Finance.

In 2015, Minara held the "First Graduates / Entrepreneur Networking Dinner, Keynote Speaker Minister Lindiwe Zulu, MEC Mike Mabuyakhulu and Fatima Vawda" and offered a "budget speech analysis presentation" in partnership with other stakeholders (Minara Chamber of Commerce 2018). Moreover, Minara has been promoting business initiatives and projects within the broader South African community through awards, the main one being the Minara Chamber of Commerce's Annual Business Recognition Awards. In the 2016 Minara Chamber of Commerce's Annual Business Recognition Awards, the organisation awarded the best 'business achiever of the year', the 'businessperson of the year', the 'businesswoman of the year', the 'young entrepreneur of the year' and the 'community builder of the year.' The awards were given in recognition of the significant roles which the recipients play in their businesses and respective fields of profession in their communities within the South African society generally. Regarding the event, Minara president Ebrahim Patel said:

The impressive line-up of nominees makes for a very close contest among the contenders and the quality of candidates augurs well for this year's edition and helps Minara to set the bar higher for future events. The awards have become a hallmark of our contribution to inspiring high achievers, community workers and business people to strive for service excellence while adhering to the basic tenets of integrity, selfless service and contribution socially, economically and politically to the broader environment of our unique non-racial, non-sexist, multicultural and multi-religious society. Trade, commerce, business and social cohesion thrives in a free, transparent and democratic society such as ours and we believe these awards serve to highlight professional people, community personalities and bridge builders and has created a benchmark where business, community and government can interact towards strengthening our collective resolve to build a stronger economy, create jobs, eliminate poverty and promote the basic tenets of an open and a vibrant enterprise for all our communities to get ahead amidst the myriad of social challenges (KwaZulu-Natal Top Business Portfolio 2016).

In 2018, the organisation hosted the National Health Insurance Panel discussion with Dr Anban Pillay Deputy Director General of Department of Health. Minara is part of the Kwa Zulu Natal Business Chambers Council (KBCC) and was one of the host Chambers for two years to run with the Entrepreneur Competition supported by the Department of Economic Development and Environmental Affairs. This allowed twenty-five Entrepreneurs to undergo Training and thereafter participate/compete for a grand prize in the Provincial rounds for cash prizes. In October 2022, the Minara Chamber of Commerce held the Minara Business Recognition Awards. According to its website:

> The Awards evening now in its 11th year after a two-year set back with Covid restrictions was initiated that despite the busy business operations and everyday activities in the community it is important to acknowledge the contributors, successes, failures, challenges that businesses, business leaders, professionals and community leaders contribute towards building our country. Many leading Industry leaders, Stalwarts and community leaders have been awarded and

recognised on this platform over the years for their success and contributions...Categories for nominations are: Business of the Year, Businessperson of the Year, Businesswoman of the Year, Young Entrepreneur of the Year, Professional Achiever of the Year, Community Builder of the Year (Minara Chamber of Commerce 2022).

The Islamic Medical Association of South Africa

In the 1970s, some Muslim healthcare professionals came up with the idea of creating an umbrella healthcare and medical body for Muslim doctors (Amod 1996:22-23). As a result, the Muslim community started recognising the need to create an organisation that would assist Muslim healthcare professionals in dealing with ethical dilemmas and applying the Islamic teachings in their medical practices. This was because existing medical-oriented organisations such as the Christian Medical Fellowship of South Africa (established in 1950), the Medical Association of South Africa (formed in 1927) and the South African Medical and Dental Council (founded in 1928) were unable to cater adequately for these needs. While the Christian Medical Fellowship of South Africa had a Christian ethos and the Medical Association of South Africa had a secularistic outlook, the South African Medical and Dental Council had been formed as a legislative and governing body for all medical practitioners in South Africa.

In September 1973, a meeting of Muslim dentists, doctors and medical students was organised to discuss the possibility of creating a medical association that would be concerned with the needs of Muslim medical practitioners seriously. By 1974, the core committee had already proposed the name Islamic Medical and Dental Association of South Africa for the organisation and drafted the first constitution. Through further consultations and discussions by the core committee, members of the MYM such as Abu Bakr Mahomed and other Muslim stakeholders, the name Islamic Medical and Dental Association of South Africa was changed to *Lajnatul Atibba* (The Doctors' Committee) which was adopted as the appropriate name for the new organisation (Amod 1998:13). When the meeting of all Muslim medical practitioners and students was called for the official launch of the *Lajnatul Atibba* on 7 July 1974, there was substantial opposition from some members who attended the meeting while others did not attend the meeting at all. Only 30 people decided to attend the meeting which most Muslim doctors boycotted. During the meeting, which was chaired by Dr GM Hoosen, the majority of doctors opposed the idea of the creation of a Muslim medical association, because it would be in conflict with the Medical Association of South Africa, that was merely an 'ethnic' medical council and that it would bring divisions within the Muslim community in South Africa, especially among Indian Muslims.

Because the majority of those who attended the meeting opposed the idea of forming a national Islamic medical body, the new organisation evolved as a wing for Muslim doctors under the auspices of the MYM with Dr GM Hoosen as president, "Dr MAK Omar as secretary and Dr YH Mahomedy as treasurer" (Amod 1998:14). Having attended the Annual Convention of the Islamic Muslim Association of North America in 1977, Dr M Khan, a prominent Muslim doctor, raised the need to transform the *Lajnatul Atibba* into the Islamic Medical Association (IMA) of South Africa. Through a series of meetings and extensive discussions, the name Islamic Medical Association (IMA) of South Africa was finally adopted in September 1979 and ratified in March 1981 during the organisation's first Convention. During the meeting of the IMA South Africa on 8th July 1980 which marked the establishment of the organisation, the following aims and objective were adopted:

> (1) To promote a better understanding and appreciation of Islam and of medicine within the framework of Islam; (2) To constantly remind and educate the Muslim health care professionals of the Islamic values, morality, etiquette and ethics and to apply these in the health care sector; (3) To promote professional and non-professional contact among Muslim health care professionals at all levels through activities such as meetings, dinners, seminars, guest speakers and conventions; (4) To seek affiliation to medical institutions through professional co-operation; (5) To co-operate with other organisations on matters of mutual interest; (6) To orientate health care education with Islamic values and outlook in the application to patient care; (7) To promote research and publications in the field of Islamic Medical

History, Prophetic Medicine, Islamic Medical Ethics and Medicine in general from the Islamic viewpoint; (8) To be a 'mercy unto mankind' in the true example of our Prophet (s.a.w.s) by providing necessary assistance within our scope and capability and wherever needed in the form of clinics, relief work and rehabilitation; (9) To co-ordinate the relevant group and individual activities of Muslim health care professionals; (10) To have a central information bureau as a service to the members regarding employment opportunities, exchange programmes, scholarship and graduate and undergraduate training opportunities; and (11) To establish libraries for the use of the members and others who may wish to use them (Amod 1998:21-22).

Apart from medical care and health related issues, the meeting decided to be involved in public issues affecting South Africans, especially the social, economic and political injustices that were being perpetrated by the apartheid government. The organisation also decided to take a stand on matters concerning the Islamic Medical Ethics and other general issues through the Action Committee that was created as a contact forum for issues that needed a public response from the organisation. The IMA South Africa held its first convention in March 1981 which was attended by several Muslim doctors, paramedical personnel and many other Muslim healthcare practitioners throughout South Africa. During the convention, the Constitution was adopted, and a National Executive consisting of the President and Vice President, Secretary and Vice Secretary, Treasurer was elected. Dr Goolam Hoosen as the newly elected President issued a statement at the end of the convention which appeared in the *Natal Mercury* newspaper, reaffirming the aims and objectives of the organisation:

> An IMA was formed to satisfy the needs of Muslim doctors and para-medical personnel which could not be catered for by other existing organisations in South Africa. One of the main aims was to promote a better understanding and appreciation of Islam and of medicine within the framework of Islam. The organisation will constantly remind and educate the Muslim health care professionals of the Islamic values, etiquette and ethics. It would also promote research and publications in the field of Islamic Medical History, Prophetic Medicine, Islamic

Medical Ethics and Medicine in general from an Islamic viewpoint. Clinics, relief work and rehabilitation would also be provided" (Natal Mercury 1981; Amod 1998:29).

In 2018, IMA South Africa's website stated that the organisation was established as a body of Muslim healthcare professionals "for the sole purpose of practising medicine within the rules of the shari'a and providing healthcare to the underprovided and needy in South Africa" (Islamic Medical Association of South Africa 2018). Since its establishment, the membership of IMA South Africa has grown, and its structures and projects have evolved. As of 2018, IMA South Africa had five major branches based in Johannesburg, Klerksdorp, Durban, Cape Town and several sub-branches under each branch running various medical related local and national projects. The 2016/2017 National Executive Committee was composed of Solly Suleman (President), Ebrahim GM Hoosen GM Hoosen (Vice President), Mahomed Imraan Khan (Secretary), Mahomed Raiman (Assistant Secretary), Mahomed Ebrahim Mayet (Treasurer) and Ebrahim Khan (Assistant Treasurer) (*E-BIMA Newsletter* 2016:8). The IMA South Africa is among the organisations affiliated to the Federation of Islamic Medical Associations in South Africa. In 2013, the South African Medical and Pharmaceutical Industry Association (2013:29) gave a general description of the IMA South Africa:

> IMA, a non-governmental organisation, was officially launched in 1980 with the core mission of promoting and furthering a better understanding and appreciation of Islam and the Medicine within the framework of Islam. The association imparts relevant information, research and educational programmes relating to Islamic study circles, seminars, meetings, conferences etc. It offers humanitarian services such as relief operations, clinics, rehabilitation centres and hospitals to those in need".

Apart from dealing with healthcare and medical issues within the Muslim community, IMA South Africa has been participating in social, political and economic issues that concern South Africans. When Steve Biko, the South African anti-apartheid activist and medical student from the University of Natal Medical School died on 12th September 1977 in detention, IMA South Africa's Action

Committee took a stand on the case by drafting a policy resolution against the case that was published in the bulletin of the IMA. IMA South Africa has also been historically involved in relief work services primarily in the form of health and medical care aid and services to underprivileged communities throughout the country, especially to rural areas. When the floods in 1987 damaged property and left many people homeless in KwaZulu Natal Province, IMA South Africa partnered with the Islamic Relief Agency in providing medical supplies, clothing, food and blankets to affected families. In the late 1980s, the IMA South Africa provided relief services in the form of medical supplies to various parts of the country which were underprivileged and those displaced by political unrests during the apartheid era. The IMA South Africa has also historically provided medical and relief services to street people especially in Durban and Cape Town. For example, Farouk Amod (1998:38) asserts:

> The IMA has provided medical and relief service for the so-called 'street people' of Durban since 1989. In 1990, the IMA Durban Branch also ran a mobile clinic for six months on a once-a-month basis in Central Durban, providing medical assistance to the inner-city homeless community. The Western Cape Branch was also involved in assisting the 'street children' in Cape Town during the years, from 1991 to 1994.

The IMA South Africa has also historically provided relief work internationally to affected countries such as Somalia, Mozambique and Afghanistan. The major ways, which have been used by IMA South Africa to provide medical facilities to underprivileged communities, have been through primary healthcare clinics that provide comprehensive health care services in various parts of the country. The aim of establishing clinics was to both promote the healthcare system with an Islamic ethos and provide medical assistance to the underprivileged citizens in South Africa. The mission statement of IMA Clinics states that the Islamic Medical Association of South Africa "is committed to provide comprehensive, holistic, health care through its clinics programme to all needy, disadvantaged persons" and that "members of the organisation are committed to take health care to the people and dispense more than just medicines" (Amod 1998:38).

Apart from medical and healthcare services, some of the IMA South Africa's clinics have been providing vocational and educational programmes, training of community health workers, feeding schemes and health education on issues such as nutrition, hygiene, nutrition and substance abuse. In 1993, the IMA South Africa in Western Cape found a Home Care Nursing Programme aimed at educating community members generally on how to care for the sick and disabled. After the first workshop that was held in November 1993 was successful, several such workshops organised by the Home Care Nursing Programme have been held in various parts of the Western Cape. The workshops are often centred on imparting knowledge to community members about bathing the sick, bed making, caring for stroke and unconscious patients and basic physiotherapy. Although the medical and healthcare services, educational programmes and workshops offered by the organisation are sometimes free when offered to underprivileged communities, IMA South Africa's clinics often require patients and recipients to pay a small amount of money. In some cases, "the fee is not compulsory as those who cannot afford this levy are treated free of charge and in some cases the fee is reduced to accommodate the patients" (Amod 1998:98-99).

In 1996, the IMA South Africa partnered with the *Jamiatul Ulama* (Council of Muslim Theologians) and the Islamic Council of South Africa to launch the Muslim AIDS Programme (MAP) for both Muslims and non-Muslims. According to Logan Cochrane and Suraiya Nawab (2016:257), the Muslim AIDS Programme focuses on social problems such as "HIV/AIDS, tuberculosis (TB) and poverty, as well as crime" which the "individuals, families and the South African government struggle to address". The Muslim AIDS Programme has evolved into an NGO and has been collaborating with provincial Departments of Correctional Services, the departments of Health and other governmental departments that concern social development. The IMA South Africa interacts with the government through departments such as the Department of Health especially when providing medical care to the underprivileged communities in South Africa. In November 2007, the IMA South Africa collaborated with the Iqraa Trust South Africa in setting up and launching a Community Renal Dialysis Centre at Shifa Hospital in Durban, KwaZulu-Natal. The major aim of the centre was "to provide much needed relief for renal dialysis patients who cannot access treatment from state facilities and also cannot afford private treatment" by providing free "access to quality healthcare, education and skills training" (Iqraa Trust South Africa 2017).

At the IMA South Africa's Convention held from 25th to 27th April 2009 in Gauteng province under the theme Matters of the Heart, Barbara Hogan Ex-Minister of Health said: "I must congratulate the IMA for nurturing a culture of professional morality amongst its members. You seek to give expression to the Islamic faith ... through your collective work as an organization" (Islamic Medical Association of South Africa 2018). Between April and July 2017, IMA South Africa collaborated with the Gauteng Department of Health on a free-of-charge health initiative that doctors and volunteers administered for the benefit of impoverished patients suffering from temporary blindness and other cataract problems. The initiative was implemented and funded by Islamic Relief South Africa with the help of sponsorship from private and corporate donors. IMA South Africa has also done cataract programmes with St Aidans Hospital, a government hospital in Berea, Durban in which the organisation supplied the consumables for cataract procedures. Moreover, IMA South Africa has been either donating funds to cater for the dialysis, surgery and other medical expenses for underprivileged individuals. For example, in August 2017, the IMA South Africa, in partnership with Ahmed Al Kadi Private Hospital, Netcare St Augustine Hospital and other stakeholders catered for the surgery and dialysis costs for an underprivileged resident in Durban, KwaZulu Natal. Between 2020 and 2022, the IMA South Africa provided guidance to both Muslims and non-Muslims with relevant and current information concerning Covid-19. In February 2021, the IMA South Africa produced a statement encouraging people to consider taking Covid-19 vaccines:

> Vaccines are among the most effective and permanent way of inducing artificial immunity. The benefit of vaccination is at a population level. Enough people need to be immunised to reduce the opportunities for the disease to spread. The virus will not have enough eligible hosts to spread the infection and eventually be eliminated... After careful consideration of the

role of the vaccine, mechanism of action and its potential impact, we are of the view that the benefits of the vaccination outweigh its risks and potential harm. The use of vaccines is an extremely cost-effective intervention and potentially prevents severe disease. The administration of the vaccine makes good economic sense in that it has the potential to reduce the adverse economic costs due to illness on society and will allow us to return over a period of time to our normal activities including our religious observances and being able to travel for Umrah and Hajj. As Muslims, it is our fundamental belief that life and death, illness and good health are all from the Almighty and no intervention can change destiny. However, as mortal beings it is our obligation to pursue all Sharia'h acceptable avenues that reduce our risk to adverse circumstances (Islamic Medical Association of South Africa 2022).

Major Ways of Political Participation

The previous sections explored the political involvement of different Muslim organisations in South Africa. The sections also emphasised that some Muslim organisations primarily focused on the needs and issues affecting Muslims in South Africa. The other organisations have been actors in politics through their contribution to issues of nation building, democracy and political transformation. Muslim organisations have been politically involved in three ways: that is, overt political involvement, political radicalism, and through social welfare activities. Apart from these three ways, individual Muslims have also been involved in politics in several other ways, and some of them continue to hold key positions in the structures of government and its political parties. The political involvement of Muslim organisations in the democratic South Africa has been based on the flexible relations between religion and the state generally.

Major ways of political participation

Overt political involvement

The Muslim organisations explored in the preceding sections have not used the same approach in their involvement in political issues. The major political role has been played by anti-apartheid Muslim organisations, such as the MJC and Muslim political parties. The second section showed that during apartheid, Muslim organisations such as the Call of Islam, Qibla, MYM and MSA participated in the political sphere and secured some influence. Such political engagement continued in the post-apartheid era through the formation of various Muslim political parties and other organisations. In South Africa pre-1994, several Muslim organisations employed various methods and strategies such as protest campaigns, publications, mass mobilisation and supporting religious and non-religious liberation movements in the liberation struggle. Such involvement in politics enabled some Muslim organisations to secure political influence in society.

Secular liberation movements recognised Muslim organisations as fundamental political actors in South Africa. For example, in the 1980s some Muslim organisations affiliated themselves to the UDF which had formed a non-racial coalition against the Tricameral Parliament and other apartheid racial-based policies. Such political involvement demonstrates that Muslims made a positive contribution to the demise of apartheid and the dawn of the new democracy. In his speech at an Intercultural Eid Celebration on 30 January 1998 in Johannesburg, President Nelson Mandela stressed:

> Our country can proudly claim Muslims as brothers and sisters, compatriots, freedom fighters and leaders, revered by our nation. They have written their names on the roll of honour with blood, sweat and tears. During the apartheid years Muslims rose to the call to unite in struggle against oppression. Here in this area of Johannesburg we witnessed resistance to the Group Areas Act which will live in the annals of history. Victory in our struggle, with the support of the international community, has won for all South Africans the right to govern themselves. It has also brought a constitution that guarantees the equality of all religions and gives them full protection" (South African History Online 2019).

Although some Muslim organisations such as the Call of Islam, Qibla and MYM which had political influence in the public sphere during apartheid became inactive in the post-apartheid era, there are several organisations that have continued to be active in politics and secure political roles in different ways. For example, the MJC which was formed during apartheid continues to occasionally engage with the government on social, political and economic issues. The fact that the MJC engages in discussions with political leaders on divergent issues that affect South Africans and often encourages Muslims to participate in the democratisation process by actively taking part in voting during elections shows its involvement in politics. For example, at a time when the IUC and Qibla proposed an election boycott in the 1996 local government elections, the MJC and Call of Islam along with other Muslim organisations encouraged Muslims and non-Muslims to actively participate in the elections.

Part of the reason for the ongoing political involvement of the MJC is that it has employed an inclusive and nationalistic approach in its political and religious discourse. The organisation has been able to "link the position of Islam and Muslims with a racially-neutral and geographical interpretation of the discourse" (Matthee 2008) in its approach. This means that the MJC occasionally stresses the impossibility of achieving an exclusively 'Muslim identity' in a diverse and globalised society. Muslims find themselves living with neighbours of diverse cultural, linguistic, ethnic and religious backgrounds. Even Muslims themselves are from divergent origins as shown in the first and second sections.

Like the MJC and other Muslim organisations, some Muslim political parties have remained active in politics. They represent a principled position by Muslims in South Africa to be directly involved in South African politics. The the Islamic Party, Africa Muslim Party and *Al-Jama-ah* Political Party were partly founded by Muslims to give a voice to Muslims in the new political dispensation while representing the interests of Muslims in the public sphere. Although the three political parties have often claimed to represent the interests of all South Africans regardless of religion or race, their objectives and goals shows otherwise. These political parties, especially *Al-Jama-ah* through various politically motivated activities, clearly demonstrate the clear political involvement of Muslims in South Africa by engaging in political issues, being elected into positions at local levels and the ongoing intention of forming a government. This, especially, applies to *Al-Jama-ah* although it is not the case for other smaller Muslim political parties.

The formation of Muslim political parties, their campaigns and several political activities indicates their commitment to the democratic values and political transformation of the country. This is because their existence does not only indicate the involvement of Muslims in politics but also that the centrality of political parties in any multiparty democratic state is sometimes rooted in the fact that they are formed to promote and strengthen democracy. In South

Africa, Muslim and non-Muslim opposition political parties act as alternatives to the ruling ANC government, they foster and strengthen parliamentary debates and hold the government accountable for failure to implement policies and constitutional values. Opposition political parties also aggregate the political interests of citizens and represent them in parliament, collaborate and instil political awareness; and finally, they ensure electoral transparency by working with the Electoral Commission of South Africa during elections. Thus, South African Muslim parties with their Muslim leaders are vital to the political context as they promote democracy and represent the participation of Muslims in politics.

Although Muslim political parties have generally performed poorly during elections due to various reasons; their very formation, existence and ability to win some seats at the local and national level indicate that they are political actors and agents of democracy. This is because they represent the attempt by some Muslims to participate in the democratic system. Although representing a minority group, Muslim political parties seek to make an impact on the larger society. This is explicit in the case of *Al-Jama-ah* which has contested provincial and national elections, and the Islamic Party which sought to make some political influence at a provincial level in the Western Cape. Clearly, the democratic context allows for any group, regardless of its background to form a political party, based on the values and principles enshrined in the Constitution. The formation of religious parties is a positive element in any open and democratic society and points to the political engagement of some Muslims in the country.

Political radicalism

PAGAD is an example of a Muslim-linked organisation which employed political radicalism. From its early stages PAGAD employed political radicalism through its revolutionary and militant strategies to change the political and social welfare spheres in South Africa, especially within the Western Cape. PAGAD's political radicalism was triggered by the escalation of drugs, gangs and crime in the neighbourhoods which destabilised the safety of the community. The formation of PAGAD's political radicalism was an attempt to bring the necessary change to the terrorized community due to the inability of the government and community protection initiatives to curb the challenges and bring about safety, peace and social stability to the community. One might question whether PAGAD's campaign of violence, alleged assassinations and intimidation directed at gang leaders, drug merchants and in some cases on law enforcement personnel meant to bring about social and political change. The methods or strategies of protest, its effect on society and relations with the police and government, indicate that the political radicalism which the organisation employed brought both positive and negative change to society.

The organisation employed both pacifist and violent or illegal strategies as a way of directly dealing with the problem of drugs, gangs and crime. The approach of PAGAD and its impact on society shows a different way in which some Muslims have been participating in politics in the democratic South Africa; that is, causing essential revolutionary societal change. In a democratic context, the state has the obligation to protect and safeguard the safety of its citizens, a vacuum that PAGAD filled: "the positive duties imposed by the right to life mean, at the very least, that the state is under a constitutional obligation to protect its citizens from life-threatening attacks" (Chappell, Chesterman & Hill 2009:228). While the repression of PAGAD by the State might seem justifiable based on some of the illegal and violent strategies employed, the organisation was a direct challenge to the police and government who were not solving the problem. PAGAD was convinced that if the state could not act accordingly, to curb the problem, then the people had the power and right to defend themselves and ensure their safety and that of the community.

However, the escalation of drugs and gangsterism on the Cape Flats explains why PAGAD understood the struggle against crime and drugs as a major objective. This was based on PAGAD's willingness to "challenge the legitimacy of the political and legal dispensation created through democratic process" to the extent of perceiving itself as "above the law and the constitution" (Müller P 2000:70). By acting against the problem through various strategies especially in Cape Town, PAGAD's political radicalism was aimed at assisting the state in ensuring the safety and security of its citizens. The organisation's failure can be attributed to its attempt to present itself as an alternative agency of law enforcement. At the same time, the growth of the organisation between 1996 and 2000 can be attributed to the inability of the government to solve the problem of crime perpetuated by drugs and gangs in the Western Cape.

Its supporters and leaders point to crime as the main reason why the group was formed. Throughout its existence, various leaders of the organisation have asserted that they have the power as concerned citizens to intervene if the government is incapable. To some pro-PAGAD members and leaders, the failure of the local law enforcement commissions and the police to curb the problem is one of the justifications for PAGAD's radical strategies. Such a sentiment was emphasised by Cassiem Parker a PAGAD leader when he affirmed that "communities are forced to take a stand for crime when the police fail to deliver …The police are doing nothing about it, so we are saying that if the police are not doing something then we will" (Hassan 2011:108). One might question the extent to which PAGAD had the legal basis for maintaining or safeguarding the safety of the citizens in a democratic state.

Maintaining the safety of citizens falls under the custodianship of the state through law enforcement commissions and personnel who legally draw their proper power and functions from the State. For example, both the Constitution (section 205) and the South African Police Service Act of 1995 grant police officers the mandate to investigate and fight against crime, enforce the law and preserve public order and safety. Because police officers are empowered by the law of South Africa and fall under the direction of the Minister of Police, they do their work as law enforcers on the behalf of the State. While PAGAD claimed that its relevance had been due to the state's inability to combat crime, drugs and gangs, it has historically lacked the legal standing to interfere with the work of the police in law enforcement. The prevention, combating and investigation of crime fall under the jurisdiction of the Ministry of Police and not PAGAD. The reality is that members of PAGAD are ordinary citizens who do not have the legal right of taking the law into their own hands in their fight against crime, drugs and gangs.

The South African laws does not recognise PAGAD as a law enforcement agency since the organisation is not a legal creation, but a socially and religiously engineered one. As an organisation consisting of ordinary citizens, PAGAD does not have any legal basis to interfere with the running of the State. In Western Cape, the form of interference exhibited by PAGAD presents a challenge by creating unjustifiable influence over the fight against crime, drugs and gangs. Because the safety of the community is not something that falls within PAGAD's purview, the organisation can engage with the fight against crime, drugs and gangs through other means. For example, the drug rehabilitation and anti-drug awareness programmes which PAGAD managed can be considered as the positive influence which the organisation secured in the Western Cape. This is because any citizen can employ such methods to ensure the safety of the community without necessarily interfering with the work of police officers and other law enforcement agencies which are empowered by the State. Since matters relating to the safety and security of the citizens are entrusted to police officers, PAGAD can abstain from interfering with the governance of the country through unlawful, militant and violent ways. The failure on the part of PAGAD is based on its claim of control using violent strategies resulting in several killings and bombings in the Western Cape. This discredit the efforts of PAGAD to use any means possible in achieving its objectives.

Social welfare and political activism

Apart from overt political involvement, some Muslim organisations have focused on partnering with government on social, economic and political issues. The three FBOs; namely GOG, IMA and Minara and their public engagement explored in the fifth section indicated how they have been involved in social, economic and political transformation of South African society. The organisations participate in South Africa's public sphere in two ways: firstly, through social welfare initiatives and programs by the means of relief response and humanitarian initiatives, and secondly, through political activism. The two ways can be considered as strategies used by the FBOs to influence society since political influence also involves cases where religious organisations act on their own initiative for the common good of society, thereby contributing directly or indirectly to the political process.

Regarding political activism, the GOG, IMA and Minara have engaged in various discussions with the government on social, political and economic issues with the aim of instilling positive societal change. For example, IMA and Minara have historically hosted round table and panel discussions with different government officials on divergent issues such as voting, basic service delivery, and other social, economic and political challenges affecting the country. Through political activism, IMA and Minara have secured influence in society, especially by engaging with municipal and provincial leaders in KwaZulu-Natal.

Through relief and humanitarian initiatives, the organisations provide employment opportunities, initiate sustainable poverty alleviation schemes, bridge the economic divide and engage with the government on several issues. The various projects geared towards poverty alleviation and empowerment run by these organisations clearly demonstrate their public engagement. The discussion on the GOG for example, showed how some Muslim organisations have been practically involved in the public sphere in South Africa.

The partnership between the government and FBOs such as the GOG indicate that both actors have the same goal – economic development and the alleviation of poverty. In his empirical study of the FBOs in KwaZulu Natal, Onwuegbuchulam (2016:175) found that there exists no "friction between the state and other social forces competing for control in certain arenas of society" and that "the government does not see itself as competing with FBOs in the task of poverty alleviation and development". The government perceives FBOs as valuable agents for social and economic change, bringing development to the lives of thousands of poor people across the country. From that perspective, the success of the GOG does not indicate the government's inability to effectively address the challenges of poverty and unemployment on the one hand and the FBOs, on the other hand, representing economic growth and development. The government and the Muslim welfare organisations have points of interaction; that is, they all aim at contributing to the betterment of society, especially uplifting the socio-economic standards of South Africans.

In post-apartheid, the South African government has been attempting to device various strategies and programmes for economic development, job creation and poverty alleviation. In this context, the invaluable role of GOG in the economic development and disaster relief of the country shows that Muslims are agents of poverty alleviation in society. The proper structures and projects of the organisation help the government in its efforts and plan to eliminate poverty and foster economic growth in the country. Creating measures for economic development and job creation and implementation is the function of the state in any democratic context. The poverty alleviation initiatives, disaster relief response and other socio-economic activities done by FBOs such as the GOG and Minara indicate the involvement of the organisations in addressing the challenges faced by the citizens.

The severity of the poverty situation in South Africa shows that this is an issue which should be addressed by the government. Thus, the GOG has adopted a welfare-type role due to the inability of local government "to satisfy basic social and infrastructure needs, resulting in widespread frustration as well as a decline in confidence levels where the government's ability to deliver is concerned" (Day 2010:20). Poor service delivery and the escalating poverty levels force people to place high expectations on the Muslim FBOs to provide humanitarian aid, disaster relief and foster poverty alleviation programmes. Generally, some FBOs find themselves doing the work of the government in economic development due to the inability of the state to deal with the problem. Because FBOs find themselves in marginalised areas providing for the poor and needy, they have developed networks. Through its humanitarian activities and projects, the GOG can be considered as an effective agent in the alleviation of poverty and service delivery. The operations and activities of the GOG portray it as having influence in society through its relief initiatives, humanitarian work and joint outreach programs with the government.

Individual political involvement

Apart from the involvement of Muslim organisations in the political and public sphere, the preceding sections have indicated the important political engagement of numerous individual Muslims both before and after 1994 in South Africa. This presents another aspect of the political participation of Muslims in South Africa. For example, Vahed's book *Muslim Portraits: The Anti-Apartheid Struggle* contains various stories and narratives regarding the influence and role played by prominent Muslim leaders during apartheid, especially in advocating for non-racial politics. By exploring the political efforts of several prominent Muslims, Vahed illustrates the political participation of individual Muslims and the organisations they represented during apartheid. For example, Goolam Vahed discusses the active political participation of Imam Mohamed 'Moulvi' Cachalia (1908 – 2003) who was a prominent South African political activist and leader. Cachalia was part of both ANC and TIC's leadership and he also played a central role in both the 1946 Indian Passive Resistance Campaign and the 1952 Defiance Campaign.

Cachalia is one of the Muslim political activists who played central roles both as individuals and through the organisations which they belonged to during apartheid. The political activism of individual Muslims continued post-1994, and many have joined established political parties, especially the ANC. In the democratic South Africa, some Muslim individuals remain actively involved in politics and hold several leadership positions in local and national government. For example, Abdulkader Tayob (2011:21) states that in 2007, "18 out of 490 members of parliament from both houses (3.7%); 2 out of 26 ministers (7.6%); 2 out of 22 deputy ministers (9%); 15 out of 210 Cape Town city councillors (7%); 4 out of 173 councillors in Johannesburg (2.3%)" were Muslim.

Muslim individuals have historically maintained a significant representation in politics with considerable political influence. For example, three Muslims held key ministerial positions: Enver Surty, former Deputy Minister of Basic Education; Fatima Chohan, former Deputy Minister of Home Affairs, and Naledi Mandisa Pandor, who has been Minister of both the Ministry of Higher Education and the

Ministry of International Relations and Cooperation. Similarly, several Muslims belonging to different political parties are members of the National Assembly of South Africa. Ebrahim Rasool is one of the key political figures among Muslims who has secured political influence in South Africa as an individual. During apartheid, Rasool was associated with anti-apartheid Islamic organisations such as MSA, MYM and Call of Islam, and he also played a major role in the UDF. From 1994 to 1997, he became the Western Cape's Executive Council (MEC) for Health and Social Services provincial member, before he was elected Western Cape's ANC chairperson in 1999.

From 2004 to 2008, Rasool was premier of the Western Cape, and having resigned from the premiership position, he became a special advisor to Kgalema Motlanthe, the then Minister in the Presidency. Rasool maintained his advisory appointment even after Motlanthe was made the interim South African president in 2008. In 2010 under the presidency of Jacob Zuma, Rasool became South Africa's ambassador to the United States. Despite the political participation of individuals such as Ebrahim Rasool and Imam Mohamed 'Moulvi' Cachalia, one may question the extent to which such individuals represent the political involvement of the Muslim community in South Africa. The political involvement of most Muslim political activists both before and after 1994 shows that they are influenced by their Islamic faith. Most Muslim political activists have themselves testified to that fact, though this, cannot be generalised. For example, Imam Mohamed 'Moulvi' Cachalia himself affirmed:

> My political outlook was influenced by the teachings of the Islamic religion. We believe in the equality of man. The Islamic religion imposes upon me as a teacher and a theologian duty in regard to the carrying out of the fundamental tenets of Islam. Equality, being one, tolerance, justice and so on should be meted out to all (Vahed 2012).

The fact that Muslim individuals were moved by their faith to fight against apartheid and that they continue to be actively involved both as political activists and governmental officials affirms the place of Islam in politics. Abdulkader Tayob (1998:6-7) argues that Muslim individuals with both high and low political profiles at different levels of government, "particularly those holding ANC seats, believe that they represent the values of liberation, freedom and democracy which are values integral to Islam". Although Muslim individuals are primarily answerable to their political parties, some of them have the desire to conform to certain Islamic religious standards and stand as Muslim political representatives in the broader society. Some Muslim political leaders within established parties such as DA, ANC and EFF have employed Islamic ethos and value when justifying the values of democracy, advocating for social, economic and political transformation and other national building initiatives in their political rhetoric. Some Muslims who work within non-Islamic political parties, do not allow their faith to be compromised but bring the Islamic outlook to non-Muslim political parties such as ANC. At the same time, they cannot challenge their party position on issues that contradict Islamic values by abstaining from voting rather than necessarily voting against. As such, some Muslims have opted to support and vote for Muslims who are part of the mainstream political parties rather than typical Islamic parties such as *Al-Jama-ah* Political Party. The centrality of working within the established non-Islamic political parties was emphasised by ANC member Gassan Solomon at a Muslim seminar prior to the 2009 elections. Muslims who hold key positions within different non-Muslim political parties have political influence within the broader South African society though they represent their party and not the Muslim community. This indicates that Muslims are involved in South African politics not only through established political organisations but also at different levels of the government.

Conclusion

It is apparent that though a minority religion, Islam has maintained political influence in South Africa. The early extensive political engagement by Muslims in South Africa was generally a response to severe racial-based policies and laws after the establishment of the apartheid government in 1948. Before 1948, Muslims had been part of broader resistance organisations which were primarily concentrated in certain regions and at times attached to racial and ethnic identity. These organisations demonstrate the early involvement of South African Muslims in politics both as individuals and as a community before the formation of Islamic organisations. Between 1948 and 1994, Muslim organisations such as MYM, Qibla Mass Movement, the Call of Islam and the MSA played an important political role through numerous strategies and approaches such as protest campaigns, mass mobilisations, distributing anti-apartheid publications and by supporting liberation movements and other resistance initiatives. This then enabled them to be actors in the anti-apartheid political struggle. Although the main goal was to fight for justice and liberation for all South Africans, some of these organisations sought to advocate Islamic values with a focus on the needs and challenges facing Muslims in the country. The clear strategies and methods of political protest by Muslim organisations during apartheid indicate that they secured political influence, thereby gaining recognition from liberation movements, the apartheid government and other religions in the country.

Apart from Islamic organisations, various Muslims who were political activists as individuals as well as leaders and members of liberations movements, interreligious organisations and other anti-apartheid activist organisations had some political influence. There were also prominent Muslim political actors such as Faried Ahmed Adams, Rashid Ahmed Mahmood Salojee, Hoosen Haffejee, Fatima

Meer, Aziz Goolam Pahad, Abdul Kader Asmal, Rick Turner, Cassim Amra, Ebrahim 'Cass' Saloojee, Saloojee and Mohammed Abdulhai Ismail. Such individuals and the organisations they represented secured significant political influence during apartheid in the country. This indicates that political involvement of Muslims before 1994 was part of the whole anti-apartheid movement.

Apart from Islamic organisations, there were also various religious and non-religious organisations that resisted the apartheid laws and policies such as the South African Council of Churches and Southern African Catholic Bishops' Conference. However, the fact that different Islamic organisations were founded based on divergent goals and objectives meant that they would not have the same political influence. For example, while the Call of Islam embraced an open and more direct approach in its political involvement, the MYM and MJC remained conservative and emphasised Islamic ideology and Muslim interests, thereby affecting the two organisations' political influence. Nonetheless, the fact that organisations such as MYM and MJC were formed to primarily address the needs of Muslims explains their marginal political involvement. Unlike solely politically oriented movements such as the ANC, Muslim organisations had religious obligations to fulfil and deal with, apart from political ones, which was an additional component motivated by the political upheavals. From this perspective, the influence of Islamic organisations in politics during apartheid is worthy of recognition though Islam was and continues to be a minority religion in the country.

After the first democratic elections in 1994 and the promulgation of the new Constitution in 1996, various democratic changes and elements inspired the active participation of religion in South African politics. Several religious related constitutional rights and an emphasis on religious freedom became the basis for state-religion relations, thereby motivating greater and open political influence of religious organisations in the country. The different ways employed by Islamic organisations to participate in broader issues indicate that the post-apartheid period continues to witness active participation and contribution of religion in society. Such a context which portrays South Africa as an open and democratic state is the basis for the political involvement and influence of Islamic organisations in the new South Africa. While Islamic organisations and individuals pre-1994 had a common political enemy to fight against – the apartheid regime – the political engagement of such organisations has taken different forms in the democratic South Africa. The formation and growth of Islamic political parties was inspired by the flexibility of the state-religion relations post-1994, although some of these parties such as the Islamic Party were formed during the period of political transition between 1990 and 1994. Virtually all Islamic parties; namely, the Islamic Party, the Africa Moral Party, *Al-Jama-ah* Political Party and SUN demonstrate the aspirations of some Muslims to secure political influence in the country. While they have different objectives, goals and aims, all Islamic political parties have attempted to project Islamic values and principles on to the public sphere. Their campaign manifestos and political rhetoric have emphasised Islamic ideologies and an attempt to present Muslim interests. Nevertheless, some of these parties especially *Al-Jama-ah* Political Party have often claimed to represent and cater for the needs of all South Africans, regardless of religion. Although the statistics show that these parties perform poorly during both national and local elections throughout the country, the fact that they have continued to acquire votes and that they have historically won a few seats at local levels indicate that they continue to receive some support. The MJC is one of the major Islamic organisations that continues to be influential since its formation in 1945 in the Western Cape. Apart from the MJC's direct anti-apartheid initiatives and programs pre-1994, in the democratic South Africa the MJC has continued to occasionally engage with the government on various social, political, moral and economic issues. The activities and programmes of PAGAD demonstrate the desire on the part of some Muslims to take practical action in the process of fostering change and transformation, thereby contributing to the political and social landscapes of society. Having been formed with the aim of practically dealing with the challenge of gangsterism, drug-violence and crime in Western Cape, PAGAD secured a mixture of positive and negative social and political influence. The public involvement of Muslim FBOs; namely the GOG, the IMA and Minara is also has been remarkable. The three FOBs are examples of various Islamic organisations that actively engage with the government on divergent issues affecting the country by addressing such problems practically. The FOBs have often partnered with the government through discussions, empowerment initiatives and programs, and humanitarian activities relating to the provision of basic needs and other medical and business opportunities. While the three FBOs have not primarily engaged with purely political issues, they have often partnered with the South African government on the social, economic and political challenges facing the country through humanitarian and relief services and have held various discussions with government officials.

The political involvement of Muslim individuals both before and after 1994 presents another aspect of the influence of Islam in South African politics. Individuals such as Imam Mohamed 'Moulvi' Cachalia and Ebrahim Rasool are mere examples of many Muslims who have secured a lasting political influence in the broader South African politics. Most Muslims who are involved in politics as individuals are influenced by their faith, and as such, they represent an important aspect, regarding the political influence of Islam in South Africa. However, despite the political influence maintained by Islam in South Africa through Islamic organisations and individuals, the emphasis on Muslim interests has not been absent. Historically, some Islamic organisations that have been involved in politics have emphasised the need to secure the Islamic identity by focusing on Muslim interests in the country.

Glossary of Arabic Terms

Halaqat: This referred to the weekly study circles and orientation camps which were organised by the Muslim Youth Movement during the apartheid era.

Kufr: Disbelief in Allah and the denial of Truth as prescribed by the Islamic faith. Therefore, *kufr* politics means politics for non-believers.

Haram: Any form of behaviour, action or speech which is contrary to the teachings of the Quran and Islam generally.

Maulana: A form of address for learned Muslim scholars. The word also appears as *malaa*, meaning a guardian.

Quran: The Holy Book for Muslims and the major source of Islamic Jurisprudence. Muslims, especially Sunnis perceive the Quran as a self-commentary, complete divine law and word of Allah thereby making it a fundamental source containing general principles regulating belief and practice.

Sunnah: This can be translated to mean 'tradition', and is another important source of Islamic belief and practice. It contains teachings and practices of the Prophet, primarily contained in the books of *hadith* which provide details of the habits and sayings of the Prophet and the circumstances of Quranic revelations.

Sunni: The largest branch of Islam, followed by over 80 percent of the world's Muslims. The word Sunni means 'traditionalists' or those who follow the acts, words and deeds of prophet Mohammed.

Hadith: The authentic habits, sayings and silent approvals of the Prophet and the circumstances of Quranic revelations. The *hadīth* are authentic reports, sayings and actions of prophet Muhammad as transmitted through chains of reliable narrators.

Tauheed (Tawḥīd): The belief in the oneness of Allah, which is the essence and primary pillar of the Islamic faith. The tawḥīd requires that one profess with total submission to the One Supreme God who is the absolute Sustainer and Creator of the universe. Surah Al-Ikhlas [112] explicitly upholds the indivisible oneness of Allah: 'Say, "He is Allah, The Only One. Allah, The Everlasting Sovereign. He has not begotten and has not been begotten, and to Him, none could be co-equal'.

Eid al-Fitr: A Muslim holiday celebration that emphasises on giving a special charity known as *Sadaqat al-Fitr* (translated as "Charity of Breaking the Fast") to the poor. It marks the end of fasting for Ramadan.

Ulama: From the root *'ilm* meaning 'knowledge', this refers to a group of Muslim scholars trained in Islamic religious sciences and doctrines with the authority to interpret Islamic law.

Sheikh: This has been traditionally used as a form of address for elderly male members of a tribe, clan, village or royal family in Arabian countries. In the most general sense, the word is sometimes taken to mean Mr, mister or honourable by some Arabic speakers. In Islam, the word Sheikh is sometimes used to refer to a Muslim religious scholar. For Sufi Muslims for example, a Sheikh is a learned Muslin scholar authorized to teach and guide other Muslims.

Masjid (Mosque): Any place where prayers are performed. In the Islamic tradition, mosques are often covered buildings.

Madaris: Any type of educational institution (at all levels) with some kind of Islamic content. Generally, a distinction is made between, *madaaris al hukmi* (secular schools), and *madaaris al Islamiyyah* (Islamic schools).

GLOSSARY OF ARABIC TERMS

Bibliography

AFQLAYAN, F. S. 2004. *Culture and Customs of South Africa.* London: Greenwood Press.

AFRICA, D. 2007. 'Countering Ideological Support for Terrorism: A South African Case Study' in Aldis, A & Herd, P G (eds). *The Ideological War on Terror: Worldwide Strategies for Counter-Terrorism.* London: Routledge.

AFRICAN NATIONAL CONGRESS, 2009. Speech by ANC President Jacob Zuma at the Muslim Sultan Bahu Fete. [Online webpage], *Official Website of The African National Congress.*
Available from <http://www.anc.org.za/content/speech-anc-president-jacob-zuma-muslim-sultan-bahu-fete>.

AL-JAMA-AH, 2009. *Al-Jama-ah Manifesto 2009.* [Online webpage]. Available from <http://aljama.co.za/wpcontent/uploads/2009/03/media_pack_-al_-jama_-manifesto_-2009_-version_-1.pdf>.

_____2019. *Vote Al Jama-ah.* [Online webpage]. Available from <http://www.aljama.co.za/2019/05/07/vote-al-jama-ah/>.

_____2019. *Al-Jama- ah Manifesto.* [Online webpage]. Available from <http://www.aljama.co.za/2019/03/10/al-jama-ah-manifesto/>.

_____2019. *About.* [Online webpage].
Available from <https://www.aljama.co.za/about-us>.

_____2017. *Al-Jama-Ah Taking the Lead on Recognition of Religious Marriages and Sewage Free Informal Settlements and Real Public Participation.* [Online webpage]. Available from <http://www.aljama.co.za/>.

_____2022. *About Us.* [Online webpage]. Available from <https://www.aljama.co.za/about-us/>.

AMOD, F. 1996. *Formation of the Islamic Medical Association of South Africa - The Early Years.* Durban. Islamic Medical Association of South Africa.

_____1999. *Islamic Medical Association of South Africa: Activities and Projects.* Durban: University of Durban-Westville.

AMRA, M 2001. *The Arrival of Islam in Southern Africa.* Durban: Impress Printers.

BAKER, A. 2009. *Exploring the Foundations of an Islamic Identity in a Global Context: A Study of the Nature and Origins of Cape Muslim Identity.* Durban: University of Kwazulu-Natal.

BANGSTAD, S. & FATAAR, A. 2010. Ambiguous Accommodation: Cape Muslims and Post-Apartheid Politics. *Journal of Southern African Studies* (36)4, 817-831.

BANGSTAD, S. 2005. Hydra's Heads: PAGAD and Responses to the PAGAD Phenomenon in a Cape Muslim Community. *Journal of Southern African Studies* (31)1, 187-208.

BAMFORD, H. 2005. Pagad Is Back ... To Work 'Within the Law'. [Online Article], *Independent Online*. Available from <https://www.iol.co.za/news/south-africa/pagad-is-back-to-work-within-the-law-250797>. [Accessed 9 April 2018].

BERKOWITZ, P. 2019. *Al Jama-ah Shows How Small Parties Can Win Seats: Al Jama-ah Benefited from Communal and Cultural Networks.* [Online webpage]. Available from <https://www.businesslive.co.za/bd/national/2019-06-06-news-analysis-al-jama-ah-shows-how-small-parties-can-win-seats/>.

BHANA, S. 1997. *Gandhi's Legacy: The National Indian Congress, 1894 – 1994.* Pietermaritzburg: University of Natal Press.

BOTHA, A. 1999. *People against Gangsterism and Drugs (PAGAD): A study of Structures, Operations and Initial Government Reactions.* Johannesburg: University of Johannesburg.

BORER, A. T. 1998. *Challenging the State: Churches as Political Actors in South Africa, 1980 – 1994. Notre* Dame: University of Notre Dame Press.

CALLINICOS, A. 1996. South Africa after Apartheid. *International Socialism Archive,* [Online Article]. Available from <https://www.marxists.org/history/etol/writers/callinicos/19 96/xx/safrica.htm>.

BIBLIOGRAPHY

CHAPPELL, L., CHESTERMAN, J. & HILL, L. 2009. *The Politics of Human Rights in Australia.* New York: Cambridge University Press.

CHHABRA, H. S. 1999. *South African Foreign Policy: Principles, Options, Dilemmas.* New Delhi: Africa Publication.

DAILY SUN, 2017. *Cape Town Suburb Like A 'War Zone'.* [Online article]. Available from <https://www.dailysun.co.za/News/National/cape-town-suburb-like-a-war-zone-20170926>.

DAY, V. J. 2010. *The Role of Faith-Based Organisations in Poverty Alleviation in South Africa: Challenging Putnam's Conception.* Howard: University of KwaZulu-Natal.

DARIES, M. 2018. MJC (SA) Urges Muslims to Register to Vote This Weekend. [Online webpage], *Muslim Judicial Council.* Available from <http://mjc.org.za/2018/03/09/mjc-sa-urges-muslims-to-register-to-vote-this-weekend/>.

DESAI, A. 2004. *The Cape of Good Dope? A Post-Apartheid Story of Gangs and Vigilantes.* Durban: Centre for Civil Society School of Development Studies.

DESAI, A. & VAHED, G. 2013. Non-Governmental Organisations and Xenophobia in South Africa: A Case study of the Gift of the Givers (GOTG). *Alternation* (7), 241-266.

DIXON, B. & JOHNS, L. M. 2001. 'Gangs, Pagad & the State: Vigilantism and Revenge Violence in the Western Cape' in *Violence and Transition Series (2).* Johannesburg: Centre for the Study of Violence and Reconciliation.

DU TOIT, N. F. B. 2014, Gangsterism on the Cape Flats: A Challenge to 'Engage the Powers'. *HTS Teologiese Studies/Theological Studies* (70)3, 1-7.

EBRAHIM, S. 2019. 'Al Jama-ah Party: We'll Tackle Inequality with Islam And Ubuntu.' [Online webpage], *Daily Vox – Citizen.* Available from <https://www.thedailyvox.co.za/al-jama-ah-party-tackle-inequality-islam-ubuntu-shaazia-ebrahim/>.

EDITORIAL, 1983. 'Goal, Objectives and Programme of MSA' in *Al-Mizaan* (2)2, 8.

EDITORIAL, 1998. Violating the Sacred. *Boorhaanol Islam* (33)1, 2-3.

EDITORIAL, 2016. 'Election of new NEC at the IMASA AGM 2016', *E-BIMA Newsletter*, June Issue, 8.

ELECTORAL INSTITUTE FOR SUSTAINABLE DEMOCRACY IN AFRICA, 2019. *South Africa: 2019 National Assembly Election Results.* [Online webpage]. Available from <https://www.eisa.org.za/wep/sou2019results.htm>.

ELECTION RESOURCES ON THE INTERNET, 1994. April 26-29, 1994 General Election Results - Western Cape: Provincial Legislature. [Online webpage], *Republic of South Africa General Election Results Lookup.* Available from <http://electionresources.org/za/provinces.php?election=1994&province=WC>.

ELECTORAL COMMISSION OF SOUTH AFRICA, 2009. *IEC Election Report 2009.* [Online webpage]. Available from <http://www.elections.org.za/content/>.

_____2016. *Results Summary - All Ballots.* [Online webpage]. Available from <http://www.elections.org.za/content/LGEPublicReports/.../Detailed%20Results/National.pdf>.

ERASMUS, C. 1996. Islamic Vigilantes. *Maclean's,* 109 (37), 24.

ENCA, 2019. *Muslim SANDF Major Considers Constitutional Challenge Over Headscarf.* [Online article]. Available from <https://www.enca.com/news/muslim-sandf-major-considers-constitutional-challenge-over-headscarf>.

ESACK, F. 1988. Three Islamic Strands in the South African Struggle for Justice. *Third World Quarterly* (10)2, 473-498.

_____1997. *Quran, Liberation and Pluralism: An Islamic Perspective of Interreligious Solidarity Against Oppression.* Oxford: Oneworld Publications.

_____1989. 'But Moosa Went to Fir-aun! A Compilation of Questions and Answers about the Role of Muslims in the South African Struggle for Liberation.' *Call of Islam Publication.* Cape Town: Clyson Printers.

ETHERIDGE, J. 2019. *SANDF Headscarf Case: Muslim Major May Get Interim Relief as Policy Talks Continue.* [Online article]. Available from <https://www.news24.com/SouthAfrica/News/sandf-headscarf-case-muslim-members-may-get-interim-relief-as-policy-talks-continue-20190718>.

FUNKE, N. S. 2004. *The Ideology of Islamic Fundamentalist Groups in Algeria, Sudan and South Africa: A Political Analysis.* Pretoria: University of Pretoria.

GERBER, J. 2018. 'The Bo-Kaap's Battle to Keep its Heritage.' [Online article], *News24.* Available from <https://www.news24.com/SouthAfrica/News/the-bo-kaaps-battle-to-keep-its-heritage-20181125>.

BIBLIOGRAPHY

GIFT OF THE GIVERS, 2022. *Covid-19 Intervention - South Africa*. [Online webpage]. Available from <https://giftofthegivers.org/disaster-response/covid-19-intervention-south-africa/8513/>.

GÜNTHER, U. & NIEHAUS, I. 2004. 'Islam, Politics, and Gender during the Struggle in South Africa' in Chidester, D, Tayob, A & Weisse, W (eds). *Religion, Politics, and Identity in a Changing South Africa*. Berlin: Waxmann.

GÜNTHER, U. 2004. The Memory of Imam Haron in Consolidating Muslim Resistance in the Apartheid Struggle. *Journal for the Study of Religion* (17)1, p. 117-150.

GOTTSCHALK, K. 2005. *Vigilantism vs. the State. A Case of the Rise and fall of PAGAD, 1996-2003*. Pretoria: Institute for Security Studies.

HAGHNAVAZ, J. 2014. Spread of Islam in Africa. *American International Journal of Research in Humanities, Arts and Social Sciences* (14)368, 124-128.

HARON, M. 2017. *Qibla Mass Movement and its Leadership: Engaging with the Quran in an African Setting. 10th International Conference on Quranic Researches Qum, Iran*. [Online article]. Available from <https://www.academia.edu/31722804/Qibla_Mass_Movement_and_its_Leadership_Engaging_with_the_Quran_in_an_African_Setting>.

HASSAN, R. 2011. *Identity Construction in Post-Apartheid South Africa: The Case of the Muslim Community*. Edinburgh: The University of Edinburgh.

HISKETT, M. 1994. *The Course of Islam in Africa*. Edinburg: Edinburg University Press.

HORRELL, M 1963. The Group Areas Act. *The Black Sash*, [Online Journal]. Available from <http://www.disa.ukzn.ac.za/webpages/DC/>.

IQRAA TRUST SOUTH AFRICA, 2017. *Iqraa Trust Partnerships*. [Online webpage]. Available from <https://www.iqraatrust.org/index.php/activities-projects/ongoing-projects/43-projects/iqraa-trust-projects/156-medical-project-islamic-medical-association-and-iqraa-trust-community-renal-dialysis-centre->.

ISLAMIC MEDICAL ASSOCIATION OF SOUTH AFRICA, 2018. *About*. [Online webpage]. Available from <http://ima-sa.co.za/about/>.

ISLAMIC MEDICAL ASSOCIATION OF SOUTH AFRICA, 2022. *Position Statement of the Islamic Medical Association of South Africa [IMASA] – Covid-19 Vaccines*. [Online webpage]. Available from <https://ima-

sa.co.za/position-statement-of-the-islamic-medical-association-of-south-africa-imasa-covid-19-vaccines/>

JACOBS, A. 2014. *Punching Above Its Weight: The Story of the Call of Islam.* Bloomington: AuthorHouse Publishing.

JEENAH, N. 1996. 'Pagad, Aluta Continua' in Galant, R & Gamieldien, R (eds). *Drugs, Gangs, People's Power: Exploring the PAGAD Phenomenon.* Cape Town: Claremont Main Road Masjid.

JEPPIE, S. 1991. Amandla and Allahu Akbar Muslims and Resistance in South Africa 1970 – 1987. *Journal for the Study of Religion* (4)1, 3-19.

KANE-BERMAN, J. 1993. *Political Violence in South Africa.* Johannesburg: The South African Institute of Race Relations.

KOTZE, N. 2013. 'A Community in Trouble? The Impact of Gentrification on the Bo-Kaap, Cape Town.' *Urbani Izziv* (24)2, 124-132.

KUMAR, A. 2017. *Coolies of the Empire. Indentured Indians in the Sugar Colonies, 1830 – 1920.* Cambridge: Cambridge University Press.

KWAZULU NATAL BUSINESS SENSE NEWS, 2018. *Minara Chamber - Recognition Awards 2018.* [Online webpage]. Available from <http://www.kznchamber.co.za/News/mobile/index.php/;focus=HETZA_cm4all_com_widgets_News_757729&path=?m=d&a=20180712124143-3250&cp=1>.

LEHMANN, U. 2006. *The Impact of the Iranian Revolution on Muslim Organizations in South Africa during the Struggle against Apartheid.* Journal for the Study of Religion (19)1, 23-39.

LAMBRECHTS, D. 2013. *The Impact of Organised Crime on State Social Control: Organised Criminal Groups and Local Governance on the Cape Flats, Cape Town, South Africa.* Stellenbosch: Stellenbosch University. [Unpublished PhD Thesis].

LUBBE, G. J. A. 1989. *The Muslim Judicial Council – A Descriptive and Analytical Investigation.* Pretoria: University of South Africa.

NADVI, L. 2008. *South African Muslims and Political Engagement in a Post-Apartheid Context with particular reference to Durban.* [Online webpage]. Available from <http://www.kznhass-history.net/files/seminars/Nadvi2008.pdf>.

BIBLIOGRAPHY

_____ 2009. *Political Islam in the 21st Century: An Analysis of the Contestation between "Militant" and "Progressive" Islam, with particular emphasis on forms of Political Expression amongst Muslims in post-apartheid South Africa.* Available from <https://researchspace.ukzn.ac.za/handle/10413/889>.

NDLOVU, S. M. 2006. 'The Soweto Uprising' in South African Democracy Education Trust (ed). *The Road to Democracy in South Africa (Volume 2),* 317-368. Pretoria: UNISA Press.

NKRUMAH, G. G. 1989. Islam: A Self-assertive Political factor in Contemporary South Africa. *Journal of the Institute of Muslim Minority Affairs* (10)2, 520-526.

MAHINDA, E. M. 1993. *History of Muslims in South Africa: A Chronology.* Durban: Arabic Study Circle.

MANJRA, S. 1996. 'Battle Plans in the Pagad Struggle: Political Fascism vs Democracy' in Galant, R & Gamieldien, R (eds). *Drugs, Gangs, People's Power: Exploring the Pagad Phenomenon.* Cape Town: Claremont Main Road Masjid.

MATTHEE, H 2008. *Muslim Identities and Political Strategies: A Case Study of Muslims in the Greater Cape Town Area of South Africa, 1994-2000.* Kassel: Kassel University Press.

MEIRING, J P G 2005. Truth and Reconciliation in South Africa: The Role of the Faith Communities. *Verbum et Ecclesia* 26(1), 146-173.

MINARA Chamber of Commerce, 2009. *Minara Hosts Successful Gala Dinner.* [Online webpage]. Available from <http://www.minara.org.za/index.php/183-minara-hosts-succesfull-gala-dinner>.

MINARA Chamber of Commerce, 2022. *Minara Business Recognition Awards.* [Online webpage]. Available from <https://www.minara.org.za/index.php/homepage/minara-business-recognition-awards>.

MONAGHAN, R 2004. 'One Merchant, One Bullet': The Rise and Fall of PAGAD. *Law Enforcement* (12)1, 1-19.

MORTON, S 2014. *Imtiaz Sooliman and the Gift of the Givers: A Mercy to All.* Johanesburg: Bookstorm Publishing.

MUJLISUL ULAMA OF SOUTH AFRICA, 1994. *Muslim Participation in Kufr Politics.* [Online webpage]. Available from <http://www.asicsa.co.za/images/muslim_participation_in_kufr_politics_pdf.pdf>.

MULLOO, A. 2004. *Voices of the Indian Diaspora.* Delhi: Motilal Banarsidass Publishers.

MÜLLER, H. P. 2000. The Invention of Religion: Aspects of the South African Case. *Social Dynamics* (26), 56-75.

MUSLIM STUDENTS' ASSOCIATION, 2022. *About.* [Online webpage]. Available from <http://www.msa.org.za/about.as>.

MUTELO, I. 2021. The Nature of Relations Between Religion and State: The Case of South Africa. *Journal of Contemporary African Philosophy* (2), 14-28.

MUTELO, I. 2017. *The Influence of Christian Values in Post-1996 South Africa: A Philosophical Perspective.* Pietermaritzburg: University of KwaZulu Natal [MA Dissertation].

OKOYE, J. C. 2019. *Al Jama-ah Puts Student, 20, Second on Candidates List.* [Online webpage]. Available from <https://citizen.co.za/news/south-africa/elections/2127234/al-jama-ah-puts-student-20-second-on-candidates-list/>.

ONWUEGBUCHULAM, S. P. C. 2016. *Where Faith is a Healer? Assessing Faith-Based Organisations Strategies and their Partnership with Government Towards Poverty Alleviation: Case Study of Pacsa and Gift of the Givers in Kwazulu Natal (South Africa).* Pietermaritzburg: University of KwaZulu-Natal.

PANDY, R. 1994. *A Critical look at the role of the Muslim Judicial Council in the Struggle for Liberation in South Africa from 1960 to 1994.* Cape Town: University of Cape Town.

PALOMBO, M 2014. The Emergence of Islamic Liberation Theology in South Africa. *Journal of Religion in Africa* (44), 28-61.

PARLIAMENTARY MONITORING GROUP, 2011. *Party Leader Al-Jama-Ah Submission.* [Online webpage]. Available from <pmg.org.za/files/docs/110803aljamah_0.doc>.

RAFUDEEN, A. 2013. The Orion Cold Storage Saga: Debating Halaal in South Africa. *Alternation Special Edition (*11), 134 – 162.

RASOOL, E. 2004. 'Religion and Politics in South Africa' in Tayob, A, Weisse, W & Chidester, D (eds). *Religion, Politics, and Identity in a Changing South Africa.* New York: Waxmann Publishing.

BIBLIOGRAPHY

RITCHIE, K. 2017. Gift of the Givers celebrates 25 Years of Giving to Mankind. [Online article], *Independent Online*. Available from <https://www.iol.co.za/weekend-argus/gift-of-the-givers-celebrates-25-years-of-giving-to-mankind-10720913>.

SALIH, M. A. R. 2009. 'Islamic Political Parties in Secular South Africa' in Salih, M A R (ed). *Interpreting Islamic Political Parties*. London: Palgrave Macmillan.

SCHÄRF, W. & VALE, C. 1996. The Firm - Organised Crime comes of Age during the Transition to Democracy. *Social Dynamics* (22)2, 30-36.

SERFONTEIN, J.P.H. 1982. *Apartheid Change and the NG Kerk*. Emmarentia: Taurus Publications.

SHELL, R. C. 2000. 'Islam in Southern Africa, 1652-1998' in Levtzion, N & Pouwels, R (eds). *The History of Islam in Africa*. Ohio: Ohio University Press.

SHIMONI, G. 2003. *Community and Conscience: The Jews in Apartheid South Africa*. London: University Press of New England.

SINGH, R. & VAWDA, S. 1988. What's in a Name? Some Reflections on The Natal Indian Congress. *Transformation* (6), 1–21.

SWAN, M. 1987. 'Ideology in Organised Indian Politics, 1891 – 1948' in Marks, S & Trapido, S (eds). *The Politics of Race, Class and Nationalism in Twentieth Century South Africa*. London: Routledge.

SOLOMON, H 1987. 'I will Return' in *South*. Cape Town, 9 April – 15 April.

SOUTH AFRICAN HISTORY ONLINE, 2011. *South African Indian Congress (SAIC)*. [Online article]. Available from <http://www.sahistory.org.za/organisations/south-african-indian-congress-saic>.

_____2011. *People Against Gangsterism and Drugs*. [Online article]. Available from <http://www.sahistory.org.za/organisations/people-against-gangst erism-and-drugs>.

SOUTH AFRICAN PRESS ASSOCIATION, 2006. Muslim warden reinstated after uniform appeal. [Online webpage], *Independent Online*. Available from <https://www.iol.co.za/news/ south-africa/muslim-warden-reinstated-after-uniform-appeal-289069>.

SOUTH AFRICAN PROMO MAGAZINE, 2009. *Africa Muslim Party AMP*. [Online webpage]. Available from <https://www.sapromo.com/african-muslim-party-amp/3029>.

SULEMAN, S. 2013. *Provincial Round Table (Letter to the Department of Economic Development)*. Durban: Minara Chamber of Commerce. [Unpublished Letter].

STATISTICS SOUTH AFRICA, 2015. *General Household Survey 2015 – Report*. [Online webpage]. Available from <https://www.statssa.gov.za/publications/P0318/P03182015.pdf>.

SOUTH AFRICAN MEDICAL AND PHARMACEUTICAL INDUSTRY ASSOCIATION, 2017. *South African Medical and Pharmaceutical Industry Business Law Handbook: Healthcare Regulations and Management (Volume 2)*. Washington: International Business Publications.

STETS, E. J. & BURKE, J. P. 2000. 'Identity Theory and Social Identity Theory'. *Social Psychology Quarterly* (63)3, 224-237.

STRATON, A. 2014. Africa Muslim Party – AMP. [Online webpage], *Mype News*. Available from <http://mype.co.z a/new/africa-muslim-party-amp/34053/2014/02>.

TAYOB, I. A. 1995. *Islamic Resurgence in South Africa: The Muslim Youth Movement*. Cape Town: UCT Press.

TERBLANCHE, D. 2015. *Socio-Historical Development Of Ḥalāl Certification in South Africa: A Study of The Halaal Trust of the Muslim Judicial Council (MJCHT)*. Howard: University of KwaZulu Natal. [Unpublished PhD Thesis].

WILLIAMS, G. & HACKLAND, B. 1988. *The Dictionary of Contemporary Politics of Southern Africa*. Abington: Routledge.

WOLPE, H. 1990. *Race, Class and the Apartheid State*. Trenton: Africa World Press.

Contents

Foreword 7

Acknowledgements..9

List of abbreviations 11

Introduction 13

Phases of Immigration and Muslim Identities 19
    Phases of Islamic Immigration into South Africa 20
    Muslim Identities in South Africa 24

Political Involvement of Muslims During Apartheid..................29
    The Apartheid Racial-Based Policies and Laws 29
    Muslim Participation through Broader Movements: Indian Congresses .. 36
    Muslim Organisations and the Apartheid System 43
    Islamic Identity and the Anti-Apartheid Political Struggle......... 67

Muslim Political Parties...71
    Background to the Emergence of Islamic Political Parties......... 71
    The Islamic Party 76
    The Africa Muslim Party... 80
    Al-Jama-ah Political Party... 87
    Support for Islamic political parties 105
    Identity and Islamic Political Parties... 110

Muslim Judicial Council of South Africa 115
    Establishment of the Muslim Judicial Council SA 115
    Muslim Judicial Council during Apartheid 117
    Muslim Judicial Council's Public Engagement Post-1994....... 127
    Islamic Identity and the MJC 134

The People Against Gangsterism and Drugs (PAGAD) in Western Cape 137
    Background to the Emergence of PAGAD 137

    PAGAD's Phases and Methods of Protest 142
    PAGAD, State and Impact in the Western Cape 158

Muslim FBOs and their Public Engagement 167
    Muslim Faith-Based Organisations in South Africa 167
    The Gift of the Givers 168
    The Minara Chamber of Commerce 188
    The Islamic Medical Association of South Africa 194

Major Ways of Political Participation 203
    Major ways of political participation 203

Conclusion 215

Glossary of Arabic Terms 219

Bibliography 223

DOMUNI-PRESS
publishing house of DOMUNI University

« Le livre grandit avec le lecteur »
"The book grows with the reader."

The University

Domuni University was founded in 1999 by French Dominicans. It offers Bachelor, Master and Doctorate degrees by distance learning, as well as "à la carte" (stand-alone) courses and certificates in philosophy, theology, religious sciences, and social sciences (including both state and canonical diplomas). It welcomes several thousand students on its teaching platform, which operates in five languages: French, English, Spanish, Italian, and Arabic. The platform is accompanied by more than three hundred professors and tutors. Anchored in the Order of Preachers, Domuni University benefits from its centuries-old tradition of study and research. Innovative in many ways, Domuni consists of an international network that offers courses to students worldwide.

To find out more about Domuni:
www.domuni.eu

The Publishing House

Domuni-Press disseminates research and publishes works in the academic fields of interest of Domuni University: theology, philosophy, spirituality, history, religions, law and social sciences. Domuni-Press is part of a lively research community located at the heart of the Dominican network. Domuni-Press aims to bring readers closer to their texts by making it possible, via the help of today's digital technology, to have immediate access to them, while ensuring a quality paperback edition. Each work is published in both forms. The key word is simplicity. The subjects are approached with a clear editorial line: academic quality, accessible to all, with the aim of spreading the richness of Christian thought. Six collections are available: theology, philosophy, spirituality, Bible, history, law and social sciences. Domuni-Press has its own online bookshop: www.domunipress.fr. Its books are also available on its main distance selling website: Amazon, Fnac.com, and in more than 900 bookshops and sales outlets around the world.

To find out more about the publishing house:
www.domunipress.fr

EXTRACT FROM THE CATALOGUE

Jean-François ARNOUX,
  Et le désert refleurira.

Sabine GINALHAC,
  Désir d'enfant. L'éclairage inattendu des récits bibliques.

Pierrette FUZAT,
  Un nom au bout de la nuit. Le combat de Jacob.

Patrice SABATER,
  La terre en Palestine/Israël.

Marie MONNET,
  Emmanuel Levinas. La relation à l'autre.

Apollinaire KIVYAMUNDA,
  Maurice Zundel, une biographie spirituelle.

Juliette BORDES,
  Viens Colombe. Saint Jean de la Croix.

Joseph MARTY,
  Christianisme et Cinéma.

Michel VAN AERDE,
  Le père retrouvé

Monique-Lise COHEN, Marie-Thérèse DESOUCHE,
  Emmanuel Levinas et la pensée de l'infini.

Claire REGGIO,
  Le christianisme des premiers siècles.

Ameer JAJE,
  Diaconesses. Les femmes dans l'Église syriaque.

Jean-Paul COUJOU (sous la direction de),
  L'État et le pouvoir.

Françoise DUBOST,
  L'Évangile des animaux.

Markus JOST,
  La Bible à l'école d'Ignace de Loyola et de Menno Simons.

Paul TAVARDON, ocso,
  Trappistes en terre sainte. Des moines au cœur de la géopolitique. Latroun, 1890-1946 (T.1).

Paul TAVARDON, ocso,
  Trappistes en terre sainte. Des moines au cœur de la géopolitique. Latroun, 1946-1991 (T.2).

Marie MONNET (sous la direction de),
  La source théologique du droit.

Nilson Léal DE SA,
  La vie fraternelle.

Apollinaire KIVYAMUNDA,
  Maurice Zundel. La relation à Dieu.

Lara LOYE,
  Fraternités.

Bernadette ESCAFFRE,
  Vocations. Quand Dieu appelle.

Raphaël HAAS,
  Pleine conscience. Bouddhisme et christianisme en dialogue.

Augustin WILIWOLI,
  Axel Honneth. Lutter pour la reconnaissance.

Louis FROUART,
  Pascal. Cœur, Corps, Esprit.

Emmanuel BOISSIEU,
  Platon. Une manière de vivre.

Emmanuel BOISSIEU,
  Kant. Une philosophie de la liberté.

Marie MONNET,
  Dieu migrant.

Thérèse HEBBELINCK,
  L'Église catholique et les juifs (T.1 et T.2).

Béatrice PAPASOGLOU,
Qu'est-ce que l'homme ?

Augustin WILIWOLI SIBILONI op,
Ce que les philosophes disent du vivre-ensemble.

François MENAGER,
Yves Bonnefoy, poète et philosophe.

Nicole AWAIS,
L'art d'enseigner le fait religieux.

Thérèse M. ANDREVON,
Une théologie à la frontière (T.1 et T2).

Michel VAN AERDE,
Venez vous reposer. Antidotes spirituels au burn-out.

Agnès GODEFROY,
Bien vieillir, dans les pas d'Abraham.

Olivier BELLEIL,
Résolution des conflits dans l'Église primitive.

Anton MILH op & Stephan VAN ERP,
Identité et visibilité. Conflits de générations chez les Dominicains.

Denis LABOURE,
Astrologie et religion au Moyen Age.

Jorel FRANÇOIS,
Voltaire, philosophe de la religion.

Augustin WILIWOLI SIBILONI op,
La reconnaissance. Réparer les blessures.

Jean Baptiste ZEKE,
Loi naturelle et post-humanisme.

Emmanuel BOISSIEU,
Paul Ricœur. Un inconditionnel de l'amour.

Ameer JAJE,
Le chiisme. Clés historiques et théologiques.

Jean-René PEGGARY,
    L'aube d'une pensée américaine. L'individu chez H. D. Thoreau.

Jean-François ARNOUX,
    Comme un feu dévorant. Flammèches d'une lecture incarnée de la Bible.

Olivier BELLEIL,
    L'autre dans l'islam coranique.

Sœur Agnès DE LA CROIX,
    Miroir juif des évangiles.

Jean-Michel COSSE,
    Au centre de l'âme.

Jean-Paul BALDAZZA,
    Antoine. Un saint d'Orient et d'Occident.

Ameer JAJE,
    Marie dans l'islam.

Olivier PERRU,
    Le corps malade.

Jesmond MICALLEF,
    Trinitarian Ontology.

Abel TOE,
    Pauvreté et développement au Burkina-Faso.

Jude Thaddeus MBI AKEM,
    Le développement en Afrique.

Claude LICHTERT,
    Lire la Bible ensemble.

Jorel FRANÇOIS,
    Voltaire, philosophe contre le fanatisme.

Bruno CALLEBAUT,
    Les Évangiles. Leurs origines, leurs exégèses.

Claude LICHTERT,
    La parole pour sortir de soi. Dieu et les humains aujourd'hui : parcours biblique.

Heriberto CABRERA REYES,
 Effondrement, apocalypse ou renaissance ? Théologie en temps de crise.

Patrick MONJOU,
 Comment prêcher à la fin du Moyen Âge ? (T. 1 et T. 2).

Robert PLÉTY,
 À la découverte du Rabbi de Nazareth (T. 1).

Robert PLÉTY,
 À la rencontre du Rabbi de Nazareth (T. 2).

Jules KATSURANA,
 Guide pour la Prévention de la violence sexiste.

Jacques FOURNIER,
 La Trinité, mystère d'amour.

Louis D'HÉROUVILLE,
 Marie-Madeleine, femme pascale.

Olivier PERRU,
 Martin-Stanislas Gillet (1875-1951). La peur de l'effort intellectuel.

Paul-Marcel LEMAIRE,
 Vivre l'Évangile.

John Jack LYNCH,
 Judith, Sarah and Esther. Jewish heroines.

Paul NYAGA,
 Moral Consistency with Lonergan's Thought.

François FAURE,
 Emmanuel Mounier : La personne est son engagement (T. 1).

François FAURE,
 Emmanuel Mounier : Montrer, sans démontrer (T. 2).

Olivier-Thomas VENARD, Gregory TATUM,
 Conversations sur Paul. « Supportez-vous les uns les autres ».

www.ingramcontent.com/pod-product-compliance
Lightning Source LLC
Chambersburg PA
CBHW060348250426
43667CB00051B/2589